Do you have troubl

Does NO sound like a mean or selfish word to you?

Do you have trouble dumping a date who treats you badly?

When you and your partner disagree, do you have trouble standing up for yourself?

Do you choke on your NOs because you fear abandonment?

Do your parents make intrusive requests that you give in to?

Do you hesitate to comment on employees' poor work performance?

Are you afraid to question policies or defy directives that you think are wrong?

Are you worried about not being generous enough to causes or your community?

Are you reluctant to confront men who harass you on the street, bus, or train?

Do you have trouble questioning treatments that your doctors recommend you get?

When you are caring for someone who is ill, do you get overwhelmed because you can't cut back on other responsibilities?

Has a dying relative made an inappropriate request that you felt you could not refuse?

Are there some people to whom you've never been able to say NO?

If you answer YES to three or more of these questions about saying NO, then you may need this book to find out how to set healthy boundaries and still preserve the relationships that matter to you.

Praise for
My Answer Is NO . . . If That's Okay with You

"NO . . . So it's only two letters, but that tiny word can make the difference between a small raise and the corner office. The dirty little secret is that when it comes to the workplace you don't have to do everything that is asked of you in order to succeed. In fact, setting realistic expectations for yourself and for the people around you is often the key to professional happiness. *My Answer Is NO* teaches all of us how to set boundaries and reclaim our self-respect by employing that tiny yet potentially life-changing word."

—Caitlin Friedman, co-author
The Girl's Guide to Kicking Your Career into Gear and
The Girl's Guide to Being a Boss (Without Being a Bitch)

"This book is like having a great therapist at your side—smart and compassionate with on-the-spot advice on how to set limits in all aspects of your life. Give this book to your daughters as they negotiate their way through school, friendships, and first jobs."

—Rosalind Wiseman, author of *Queen Bees and Wannabes* and
Queenbee Moms and Kingpin Dads

"Sound advice and fascinating insights on why we have trouble setting limits as women. Dr. Gartrell shows us that even the most accomplished women in a countless variety of careers are challenged by saying NO, and that they, like the rest of us, can learn to do it with conviction and joy."

—Patti Breitman, co-author of
How To Say No without Feeling Guilty

"Gartrell's new book gives women important, practical tools for saying NO gracefully and without guilt. Gartrell covers the basics (parents, dates and mates, friends and work) before moving on to more tricky, emotionally treacherous territory like assault and harassment, doctors and psychologists, and the dying. Including excellent tools and work management advice for women in the military, the advice here will help anyone with a problem saying NO, man or woman."

—*Publishers Weekly*

"She provides case studies of more than 100 accomplished women from diverse backgrounds to demonstrate how they have learned to be assertive in difficult situations and recommends ways of saying NO that allow women to be considerate without jeopardizing their well-being. Practical assistance for a prevalent problem; recommended for all libraries."

—Deborah Bigelow, *Library Journal*

". . . Gartrell emphasizes that being kind and empathetic isn't bad. But women need to establish stronger guilt-deflecting boundaries for their own well-being and sanity. Her book presents specific scenarios and suggests language for women to use when they feel bullied at home, at work, in doctors' offices, and in public."

—Deirdre Donahue, *USA TODAY*

"The book is packed with examples of compromising situations as well as anecdotes from high-profile women who share how they've learned to say NO directly and compassionately."

—Julia McKinnell, *MACLEANS*

When people ask for time, it's always for time to say NO.

Edith Wharton, 1928

MY ANSWER IS NO—

If That's Okay with You

How women can say NO with confidence

Nanette Gartrell, M.D.

Free Press
New York London Toronto Sydney

*f*P

Free Press
A Division of Simon & Schuster, Inc.
1230 Avenue of the Americas
New York, NY 10020

Copyright © 2008 by Nanette Gartrell, MD

All rights reserved, including the right to reproduce this book or portions thereof in any form whatsoever. For information address Free Press Subsidiary Rights Department, 1230 Avenue of the Americas, New York, NY 10020

First Free Press trade paperback edition January 2009

FREE PRESS and colophon are trademarks of Simon & Schuster, Inc.

For information about special discounts for bulk purchases, please contact Simon & Schuster Special Sales at 1-800-456-6798 or business@simonandschuster.com

Designed by Nancy Singer Olaguera, ISPN Publishing Services.

Manufactured in the United States of America

10   9   8   7   6   5   4   3   2   1

Library of Congress Cataloging-in-Publication Data
Control Number: 2007015291

ISBN-13: 978-1-4165-4693-1

ISBN-13: 978-1-4165-4695-5 (pbk)

For Dee, whose compassion and generosity know no limits.

author note

This book is based on interviews with those portrayed. In some instances, names and identifying details have been changed. I have used only first names for pseudonyms. All other interviewees are identified by their full name and occupation.

contents

chapter one
women's ways of NOing (introduction)   1

chapter two
there's NO place like home for the holidays
(saying NO to parents)   7

chapter three
getting to NO you (saying NO to dates
and mates)   29

chapter four
NOthing personal (saying NO to friends)   53

chapter five
opportunity . . . NOts (when saying NO
at work doesn't work for you)   80

chapter six
no-nonsense NOs (saying NO at work)   98

chapter seven
saying NO when the president calls   127
(saying NO in public service)

chapter eight
NOblesse oblige (saying NO in the community)   149

chapter nine
NOt on your life! (saying NO to assault and
harassment)   175

chapter ten
Doctor, NO (saying NO to your shrink or doctor)   196

chapter eleven
NOble intentions (saying NO as a caregiver)   214

chapter twelve
heavens NO! (saying NO to the dead and dying)   238

a final note   251

acknowledgments   253

index   255

chapter one

women's ways of NOing

(introduction)

NO is a very simple word. One syllable. Two letters. A complete sentence. NO is one of the shortest words in the English language, yet one of the most difficult for women to say. We hear "NO!" in our heads while our mouths are saying "YES," "Sure," "I'd be glad to," "Of course I will," or "I wouldn't miss it for the world!" It's often easier to agree than to *just say NO*.

Saying NO for women can be a genuine struggle because of our deeply rooted need for connection. To be considerate without jeopardizing our well-being or livelihood, and assertive without losing the relationships we value—these are two of life's most compelling challenges. Sometimes, out of a desire to be helpful or charitable, we choose to say YES even when it's difficult. At other times, we discover that we're too concerned about being liked, loved, or respected to be able to say NO. If we muster the courage to speak up, we tend to be cautious: "my answer is NO . . . if that's okay with you."

This book grew out of my realization that women's reluctance to say NO comes from traits that we should value—empathy, sensitivity, thoughtfulness, and compassion—rather than suppress, as we are often advised to do when saying NO. These traits are necessary elements of human connection and preservation. When I think back over my own life, I find that the paths I took to NO, however circuitous, often helped me grow. Like most women, I have sometimes held on too long to relationships that I knew I'd be better off without. But I would never trade a guillotine-style NO for what I learned through my unwillingness to let go.

The idea for this book emerged one morning when I was having breakfast with TV journalist and surgeon Nancy Snyderman, who told me about a former employee who had repeatedly asked for special favors. "First she asked for time off to get a haircut," Nancy said. "Then she needed to run errands." Even though the employee took advantage of Nancy's generosity, Nancy tried to accommodate these requests. Why? The employee was a single mom, and Nancy empathized with her situation.

I could certainly relate. I'd been despairing over a research collaboration that had gone sour. A colleague who'd volunteered to help with a major project had missed deadlines and dropped the ball on numerous occasions, always with a mile-long list of excuses—health problems, dying relatives, car accidents, and the like. I couldn't think of a way to get tough without feeling like a completely insensitive jerk.

As a surgeon, Nancy is accustomed to making decisions with authority and conviction. Assertiveness is mandatory in life-and-death situations. My psychiatric specialty involves teaching patients about boundaries and limits. Role-playing how to say NO is a routine part of my clinical work. So, after thirty years in practice, I should be able to say NO when I need to, right?

Wrong. When I'm not with patients, I'm often reluctant to use the NO word because—well, frankly—I don't like to disappoint people. Is this a serious shortcoming? Many assertiveness training books say it is.

I disagree.

For most women the prospect of being less sensitive to the needs of others isn't appealing, even though attending to others' needs can result in personal sacrifice or hardship. We'd rather weigh the pros and cons of helping out, and struggle to find the best way to take care of ourselves as well as the many others who are dependent on us. That's how women's brains are wired: we have an aptitude for compassion and connection.

Why, then, do we get down on ourselves for not being more assertive? How can we avoid criticizing ourselves when we are bombarded with the message that there's something terribly wrong with the way we say NO? "Listen to your own needs," we're told. "Put yourself first." "Stop being a people pleaser." "Quit worrying about everyone else." This is advice that Daddy Warbucks parodies in *Annie*—"You don't have to be nice to people on the way up if you don't plan to come back down."

But do we really need more self-centered people on this planet? Most women would never trade compassion for insensitivity. If women as a group became substantially less concerned about the general well-being of everyone around us, the consequences for children, the infirm, the disadvantaged, and the elderly would be disastrous! After all, where would we be without empathy? Or the generosity of spirit that sustains the planet and nurtures the soul?

Our strength as women is grounded in the ability to reach out and lend a helping hand. We consider the thoughts and feelings of others as we conduct our own lives. We can be firm when we need to be, though usually, we prefer to be kind. Saying NO can feel alienating, distancing, and harsh. It clashes with our belief in being generous. Very often it involves a loss. And dealing with loss is a recurrent challenge for most women.

Each of us is familiar with the experience of being told "NO." Throughout our lives we are denied things we want. We feel frustrated, sad, hurt, angry—even heartbroken—when we are refused. Sometimes the compassionate NOs are easier to swallow than the thoughtless NOs, or the brush-off NOs, or the how-dare-you-ask NOs, but in many cases, the experience of NO carries disappointment with it.

So when it's our turn to do the nay-saying, we are attuned to the feelings of the person asking, and we empathize with the pain of being turned down. Saying NO involves putting our own desires and needs above the wishes or expectations of others, which isn't always an easy thing to do. Some people become spiteful or rude when we don't give them what they want. Since being liked and appreciated is important to women, we're always on the lookout for the moment to say NO that has the least risk of incurring wrath or loss—modeling our own NOs after those we find most helpful and considerate.

Even so, guilt-free NOs are hard to come by. In a life-or-death situation—to protect a child, for instance—"NO!" is instinctive. When operating from a clear sense of purpose or principle, setting a limit is easy. In other cases, however, saying NO involves sorting out your priorities, narrowing your focus, or sticking to a specific goal. Developing a set of ready-made responses gives you an edge on saying NO when you need to. Yet try as you might, there's no getting around the fact that your choices may deprive others of what they want. And it's always more difficult to set limits when you are conscious of others' hardships.

Just this morning Terry, a photographer, told me a story that illustrates this point. Several times a week, Terry drives to a senior housing complex to take Lulu, the beloved dog of an elderly man whose health is failing, out for a walk. Recently, Terry invited the gentleman to lunch. As he politely pushed the food around his plate, every now and then nibbling on a tiny morsel, the gentleman explained that he wasn't expected to live much longer and that he had no one to care for Lulu—would Terry be willing to take the dog after he dies? Terry was in quandary about what to do. She couldn't keep the dog, but she didn't want to break the poor man's heart. I suggested that she offer to keep Lulu until she found a loving home for her. This solution worked for Terry. She told the gentleman that he could rest assured that Lulu would be well cared for.

One caution: when we lend a helping hand, let's not call that "co-dependency"! Caregiving is often devalued, trivialized, and pathologized by calling it "co- dependency." Kindness is NOT the same as being a doormat. There is a world of difference between being an enabler to an addict or an abusive partner, and being a considerate, compassionate individual.

In the chapters that follow I present the challenges we women have to face when saying NO to family, lovers, friends, employers, colleagues, subordinates, strangers, healthcare professionals, and even to people on their deathbeds. I examine why it's difficult to say NO, and I explain how the desire to connect and the fear of loss figure into our reluctance to set limits. I show how our goals, needs, values and life experiences influence our willingness to let go, and suggest creative ways to handle situations in which we feel stuck. I recommend ways to say NO that diminish the discomfort of disappointing others and give pointers on how to turn a knee-jerk YES into a consideration, and a consideration into a choice. And I explain how learning to deliver a knockout NO—if you're assaulted—may not only save your life, but empower you in other areas as well.

Along with examples from my own life, I have incorporated interviews with a diverse group of more than one hundred talented women whose stories capture the complexity of our efforts to set limits in a world that values simple assertiveness and cocksure NOs. These women reveal what saying NO means to them, and how the goal of maintaining connections with people who matter to them influences their ability to set limits. They describe how they learned to say NO, and how they struggle to be compassionate even as they enforce boundaries. Many of the stories are inspiring, some are funny, some sad, some deeply disturbing. All will help you understand better how and when you can say NO.

The women I interviewed share one important characteristic: each is very accomplished in her field. They differ in age, education, socioeconomic class, racial/ethnic background, and sexual orientation. Some are identified by their real names, others by a pseudonym. As this book will demonstrate, being powerful, savvy, or talented has little bearing on a woman's ability to say NO. Police chiefs, politicians, military officers, martial artists, judges, and CEOs all contend with the same issues. And having boundaries in one arena—such as work—may be unrelated to the ability to set limits with lovers, family, or friends.

Dip into this book anywhere you like. Pick a topic that's timely for you. Step into the shoes of other women as they describe their limit-setting dilemmas and achievements. Each chapter contains information that I hope will be relevant whenever you are struggling to say NO. At some point this book will speak to you, and you'll discover that you're not alone.

After reading this book, you will have a better understanding of your own reluctance to say NO. You will also learn how to say NO without losing the connections that you care about the most. I encourage you to value empathy but to use it selectively, taking pride when you choose to be generous. Above all, I hope that you will appreciate how a NO to one thing is often a YES to something else, as you enjoy the freedom that saying NO can bring.

chapter two

there's NO place like home for the holidays

(saying NO to parents)

*My parents lived in New York and I lived on the West Coast.
Once I had children, they wanted me to come for holidays.
It was very hard for me to say NO. They never celebrated
Christmas when I was growing up because we were Jewish, but they never celebrated Chanukah or Thanksgiving
either. They didn't celebrate holidays. All of a sudden the
holidays became this big deal. Occasionally I said NO, and
stuck to my guns, but I didn't want to hurt them. It was
often easier just to go.*

**Bettina Aptheker, professor of
women's studies, U.C. Santa Cruz**

There's no request more likely to stress us out than one from
Mom or Dad. Talk about guilt when we refuse! Healthy parents encourage us to be independent, but they're still sad when
we leave. Dysfunctional parents can be so disparaging that we
accommodate them to ward off their criticisms, since, after some
twenty years of trying to please and impress them, we don't want
to lose any hard-won ground we may have gained.

Even before birth, the female brain develops an aptitude for connection, communication, and responsiveness. During the first three months of life, we become attuned to every nuance of our parents' moods. From the get-go, we learn that it doesn't pay to say NO to Mom or Dad. They rewarded us as children for compliance and punished us for defiance, and if we were lucky enough to have healthy parents, we probably figured out how to make them happy. Those of us who weren't dealt such a favorable hand spend a lifetime looking for the love and approval that every child seeks—ever hopeful that our emotionally troubled parents will one day appreciate who we are.

Yet even when we're no longer concerned about bringing home an impressive report card or winning a school election or excelling as a student athlete we may have trouble distinguishing between what our parents *want* and what they *need*. Ambiguous communications that began shaping our behavior as children often cloud our perceptions about how much choice we have as adults when a parent asks for something. For children, "I *need* you to finish your dinner" is interchangeable with "I *want* you to finish your dinner" or "I'd *like* you to finish your dinner" or "You're not leaving the table until you finish your dinner." So when we are adults and our parents say, "We'd *like* you to come for Thanksgiving," we hear "like . . . need . . . want . . . you'd better or else!" And before we know it, we're making airline reservations.

Just today I had such an experience with my seventy-seven-year-old mother in which I wanted to say NO, but instead I did what she asked. I have explained to her that it's very difficult for me to handle problems that are not urgent while I'm seeing patients. This morning she left a message asking me to call back as soon as possible. Mom cannot live alone without assistance, and she wanted me to counsel her new helper, who is taking an antidepressant medication, about her dosage. Of course it would have been professionally inappropriate for me to offer advice when I have never met the helper and know nothing of her medical history. Even a phone call to discuss the best way to approach her doctor would consume more time than I had available.

Did I defer that conversation to a less hectic moment? Of course not. I called back immediately, hoping to make a favorable impression on the new helper. I rationalized that Mom's reputation as a "good" employer hinged on my responsiveness.

There are many occasions as adults when our priorities or choices don't jibe with our parents' wishes. Most parents would like to see and talk to their adult children more than the children are able or willing to do. To say NO to whatever they ask us to do takes a huge effort. First, we've got to figure out what we stand to lose. Next, we have to overcome primitive fears of abandonment or punishment. Then we have to remind ourselves that disappointing them doesn't make us bad. And finally, we must convince ourselves that the connection won't be severed if we set a limit. That's a tall order with parents we love—and taller still with parents we don't.

dutiful daughters

Even healthy parents sometimes manipulate, threaten, or withdraw when you don't do what they ask. Those tendencies are magnified tenfold with dysfunctional parents who have serious emotional problems stemming from their own history of being rejected and abused, the legacy of which they pass along to you. They can be excessively harsh when you disappoint them, because they count on you to provide the love they never had. They have poor boundaries and frequently sabotage your efforts to be independent. Often inflexible, self-centered, and thoughtless, dysfunctional parents expect you to take care of them, which means you're often frustrated with them, and they are angry and unhappy with you.

Despite your familiarity with these dynamics, you are reluctant to write off your parents. Why? Because, even though they are rarely there for you, they have trained you to feel anxious about abandoning them. Deeply etched in your psyche is the fear of losing what little love they have to offer. You still look to them for approval, even when you're not dependent on them for anything else. There's always a chance they will grow up and get therapy, or sober up and make amends, right?

Setting limits with psychologically impaired parents is a lifelong struggle. They have a talent for chiseling away at your resistance and circumventing your limits. All too often you feel trapped into saying YES, though you've promised yourself that you would say NO.

The topic of saying NO tapped a deep well of pain for the women I interviewed who have difficult parents. Most shared their stories anonymously, because they are still trying valiantly to be kind and considerate.

Rosalind, a stockbroker, grew up in a family where alcohol ruled and the children obeyed. Even when she became an adult, it was "Dad's way . . . or else!"

My father was a very functional alcoholic from New Orleans. Alcohol was a big problem in our family. It was the elephant in the room all the time. My mother was always furious at him. I was the go-between and the peacemaker. I would run to Dad and make him laugh and run to Mother and make her laugh and patch everything up.

My father was a bear of a man. Whatever he asked, whether it was late at night, "Run to the drug store and get me something, go downstairs and get me this"—there just was no saying NO. Even as I was older and married, he would say, "Why don't you come over, we'll go to dinner tonight." Well, maybe we had other plans, but we'd drop them and go.

Regardless of your age, if your parents are psychologically troubled they're probably still telling you what to do. They maneuver, bully, criticize, and punish to control your behavior. They expect you to take care of them—to be there when they need you, to talk with them when they feel lonely or down, to live nearby or visit often. Despite your frustration, you feel sorry for them, and you dread the consequences of saying NO.

LOCKED IN

My mother is f——ing crazy! When I was a kid, none of the doors in our house had locks on them. There was no private space. Whatever I was doing—studying, even peeing—Mom interrupted. If I complained, she'd say, "Your family is more important than your homework." Imagine that! Most parents would be thrilled to have a kid who wanted to do her homework.

When I went to college, I had to call home twice a week. Big drama if I missed a call. Sobbing, worrying that I was dead, calling the campus police to track me down—totally embarrassing. I hated talking to her, but boy did I pay for it if I missed a call.

When my father left her for his secretary—oh my god! Mom took a total nosedive. She'd call me sobbing, saying she was going to kill herself. She begged me to transfer to a college near home so I could live with her. I practically got an ulcer over saying NO to that. When I went home that spring break, we were driving on the freeway and Mom started speeding up, saying she was going to smash the car into a cement wall. I had to grab the wheel, pull the car over, change places with her, and drive her to her shrink.

Last year Mom was diagnosed with breast cancer. Her doctors say she's going to be fine, but she hasn't let up on me about moving back home. Every conversation starts with "since I'm not going to be around for long, I hope you're thinking about looking for a job here." She's going to live forever and torture me until the end of time. I just know it.

MJ, editorial assistant

WHY SHE'S CONFLICTED ABOUT SAYING NO:
She's even more impossible when I say NO. I feel like it's my responsibility to deal with her even though I hate it.

ONE WAY TO SAY NO:
(To moving back home) "Mom, I was very lucky to get this job, and I don't want to give it up. But I will be home for your birthday. Let's talk about some things we might do while I'm there that both of us will enjoy."

• • •

At some point you reach the end of your rope, and you decide that you're not going to take it any more. As you prepare to say NO, what steps can you take to boost your confidence?

KILLING ME SOFTLY

My dad died when we were really little. My mom moved me and my little brothers and sister to the United States and cleaned rich people's houses to support our family. My two brothers dropped out of school. Both of them do drugs. My sister got pregnant when she was fifteen, and my mom's raising her kids now. My mom's not that old, but she's had a hard life.

It's killing my mom to deal with all the stress of their lives, and killing me to deal with the stress of hers. My mom has a lot of medical problems that only get worse when my brothers get into trouble. She's always giving them money—bailing them out of one crisis or another. I wish I could move to another city to get away from it all.

Maria, film editor

WHY SHE DOESN'T SAY NO:
I worry about my mom's health. I'm afraid she'd die if I stop taking care of her.

ONE WAY TO SAY NO:
"Mom, it stresses me out when you talk about my brothers. Please tell me about you."

Step 1. Figure out what you're most afraid of losing.

Will your parents refuse to speak with you? Will they act out in some disastrous way? Will their hurtful remarks make you doubt the path you have taken? Will your siblings be angry at you for being honest?

Reviewing your worries helps you decide whether you can handle the NO on your own or if you need support. Check it out with somebody you trust. Ask this person if she or he thinks you have what it takes to manage your parents' reactions without professional guidance. If you decide to seek counseling, make sure you select an experienced professional who is both sympathetic and pragmatic.

Step 2. Remind yourself why you deserve to be treated respectfully and lovingly.
Make a list of at least five reasons, such as: "I am a considerate, respectful, helpful, responsible, and supportive daughter."

Step 3. Ask yourself how your life could be improved if you set limits on your parents' unacceptable behavior.
Might you experience less verbal abuse? More respect? Might you feel stronger, healthier, happier? Could you conceivably find things to appreciate about your parents if they clean up their act?

Step 4. Tell yourself that your goal in setting limits with your parents is not to lose anything you value but to gain self-respect, self-confidence, and self-esteem.

Now you are ready to work on your NOs.

Begin by establishing boundaries. Some women are unable to set limits when they live near dysfunctional parents, so they move farther away. Distance does create an automatic boundary, since you aren't immediately available for crises. Even if you live nearby, caller ID, voicemail, or an answering machine will allow you to communicate only when you're prepared. With parents who pressure you to talk more than you'd like, consider establishing a prearranged schedule: select a specific time each week that is convenient for all parties. If they ignore the plan and call more frequently, as long as the request isn't urgent, try waiting until the designated time to call back.

Develop a list of standardized responses to things your parents say that distress you. Post it by your phone until you have it memorized. For instance, when your mom or dad complains about something that upsets you, you might say, "This is too painful for me to talk about. Let's talk about something else." If your mom or dad counters with, "But you're the only one who understands," you can suggest speaking with a professional: "I feel like I'm at a loss to help. I think you need input from a professional who knows how to handle situations like this." Be prepared to be repeat yourself as much as you need to.

If parents continuously complain but reject your help, act as unresourceful as they are. You've undoubtedly given it your best shot for years, suggesting, "Try this . . . Try that . . . How about this option . . . What about . . . ," but nothing has worked. Strangely enough, you'll feel less distressed if you stop offering solutions that they invariably ignore. Try a new tactic: throw up your hands and say: "I haven't a clue . . . You got me . . . That sounds really difficult . . . Whew, I wish I had an answer."

All-purpose responses include: "I am sorry that you feel that way." "Yes." "Uh huh." "Um." "I hear you are frustrated." Often you don't even need to elaborate if you just stay with these standard replies. Listen, but don't agree or volunteer anything, including your own feelings. If pushed, and you can't quite get to NO, try "I don't think so." Again, be prepared to repeat yourself.

If your parents drink or use drugs, seek the support of Al-Anon or similar twelve-step recovery programs. Parents who abuse substances have unpredictable behavior and poor boundaries. Since they may not recall offending you if you wait to confront them, you need to set limits on the spot. Until they are clean and sober, don't expect them to learn from past mistakes.

Make it clear that you will not tolerate abuse of any kind. Convey the message at an uncharged time. "For the record, I will not speak with you if you've been drinking." "Yelling is off limits." "I will hang up if you say mean things to me." "If you throw things, I will leave the room until you have cooled off." Explain that you expect an apology for the offensive behavior before you will resume the conversation. Be polite. Be firm. Be consistent.

A general rule when saying NO to difficult parents: set your sights low. Limit yourself to one or two goals each time you visit or speak with them. Congratulate yourself when you stick to your script; don't berate yourself if you are sandbagged. Your parents know how to push your buttons—not surprising, when you consider that they installed them. Don't expect to stymie their efforts at manipulation without making a consistent effort.

Keep in mind that unhealthy parents always want more from you than you can provide, and they are often dissatisfied with your best efforts. But with firm limits, they can learn to treat you more respectfully. Reward them for the behavior that you appreciate, and call them on it when they behave inappropriately. Your goal is not to change them into the parents you've always wanted, but to prevent them from further injuring you.

Speaking of injury, let's take a closer look at parents who suffer from narcissistic personality disorder or borderline personality disorder—two psychiatric conditions that are associated with particularly punitive behavior toward anyone who attempts to set limits.

saying NO to narcissists

With narcissistic parents, it's all about them, rarely about you. Narcissistic parents are self-absorbed, self-important, and generally oblivious to other people's feelings or needs. They expect to be the center of attention, and they can be cruel if they don't get what they want. They're always right, so when you disagree, watch out: they punch below the belt. When you say NO they retaliate, because their needs always come first.

Narcissism is a lifelong pattern of behavior that is relatively immutable and affects more men than women. Although this personality disorder derives from a combination of factors, narcissism is strongly associated with having been neglected or abused as a child. Very often, as adults, narcissists create emotionally abusive environments for their spouses and children. Narcissists become enraged when confronted about their inappropriate behavior. You can sometimes stop their abuse by calling them on it, but you have to stand your ground.

REMOTE CONTROL

I come from a big Irish Catholic family and we all go to my parents' home for Thanksgiving. It's the one family holiday we do each year. I think we show up mainly because we feel sorry for my mom. Our dad is a belligerent, self-centered jerk. He never listens; he has no interest in anyone but himself. He belittles everything that matters to my mom.

Here's a story that will show you what a creep he is. Last Thanksgiving, after dinner, we were all sitting in the living room watching *Jeopardy*. We'd been watching for about twenty minutes when Dad walked in, picked up the remote, and changed the channel to the news. There were, like, fifteen of us watching *Jeopardy* and they have three other TVs, and he decides he needs to watch the news on the TV we're using. So we all got up and moved to another room to watch the end of the show.

Shannon, hospital administrator

WHY SHE'S RELUCTANT TO SET LIMITS:
You don't know the half of it. He is vicious if you cross him. "This is my house and my TV and I paid for it and I'll watch whatever damned program I want to watch." If he really lets loose, then he starts on everything that's wrong with us—and he's very sadistic. When he's not going after us, he lets Mom have it.

Here's what I recommend when setting limits with narcissistic parents who, as a rule, have limited self-awareness and no desire to change:

Step 1. Enlist the support of your siblings.

Prior to a family gathering, talk with your siblings about confronting your parent when he or she is out of bounds. Agree on who will speak first, and who will be the backup person.

Shannon's father (in "Remote Control") was used to getting his way, but Shannon decided to challenge him the next time he was out of line. She spoke privately with her siblings, and they agreed to support her when she set limits.

Step 2. State your complaint clearly and forcefully.
Shannon's opportunity to set a limit with her dad happened sooner than expected. Her mother had surgery. Shannon and her siblings were sitting around their mother's hospital bed watching her favorite TV show when their father impatiently grabbed the remote and began channel surfing. Shannon got up, walked over to him, looked him straight in the eye and said, "Dad, mom is watching a program. Don't change the channel without asking." Two siblings echoed her request.

Step 3. When you say NO, be prepared for nastiness.
Shannon's dad threw the remote on the bed and walked out.

Step 4. Don't back down. Narcissists despise wimps.
Shannon and her brother followed their dad into the waiting room. He ignored them. They took turns explaining why it was unacceptable to switch channels without consulting the other family members. Shannon's dad picked up a magazine and pretended to read while they were talking. Eventually, he returned to their mother's hospital room acting as though nothing had happened.

Step 5. Acknowledge considerate behavior.
Shannon's dad sat through another TV program without commandeering the remote. Later, when she was alone with him, Shannon thanked him for letting her mother choose the program.

An adult child's instinctive response to narcissistic parents is to defer to their wishes to avoid their wrath, but narcissists will walk all over you and anyone you care about if you don't set limits. Suffering in silence is bad for your mental health. Saying NO to injurious behaviors that damage your self-esteem or undermine your self-confidence or hurt your loved ones is a far better choice.

borderlines without boundaries

Parents who suffer from borderline personality disorder (BPD) have poor boundaries and are terrified of losing connections. Their relationships are characterized by instability, fears of abandonment, suicide attempts, and inappropriate anger. Parents with BPD experience chronic feelings of emptiness, depression, anxiety, and despair, no matter how talented or successful they are. They project their own self-hatred onto others, becoming violently enraged when they feel criticized, judged, or disappointed.

Like narcissists, most people with BPD were abandoned, neglected, or mistreated as children. The abuse, in conjunction with other factors such as genetics, personality, and upbringing, leads to emotional and behavioral patterns that are relatively fixed over time. Unlike narcissism, BPD affects more women than men.

To borderline parents, limits feel the same as rejection. If you say NO, they make you pay for it. When they do, it's not pretty and it's not nice. For your own well-being, you must learn to protect yourself when their behavior gets out of hand.

If you suspect that your parent has BPD, and you are trying to set limits, you may wish to seek professional help. Borderlines are desperately unhappy people whose mood changes can be entirely unpredictable. They can be verbally or physically abusive when they feel criticized. Very often, they engage in serious self-destructive behavior when you try to distance yourself. They want you to take care of them, and they will punish you for saying NO.

Knowledgeable psychotherapists who are familiar with these dynamics can help you understand your borderline parent and teach you the value of consistent communications, as well as how

HOLIDAY MADNESS

I feel too guilty to avoid my mother at the holidays, even though she pretty much tortures me while I'm there. When I went home for Rosh Hashanah, the first words out of her mouth were, "You look fat in that dress. Have you gained weight?" I said I weigh the same as I always do, and I reminded her that she had given me the dress.

Mom then asked how long I was staying. I said I'd be there for four days, and then I needed to get back to work. Well, that was the kiss of death. Mom went into a major pout that lasted for my whole visit. She mentioned my departure at least ten times a day. She was very nasty about my work being more important than she is.

She turned everything into drama. She went to take a bath, and all of a sudden I heard her screaming at the top of her lungs in the bathroom. I ran to the door and she yelled at me, "Did you turn the hot water heater up? I burned myself in the bathtub. The water is too hot!" Of course she blamed me—though I had nothing to do with the water heater, or turning on the tap, or checking the temperature before she got in.

The coup de grace came my last night. She "accidentally" burned her hand while making dinner. I took her to the emergency room. She had third degree burns. Of course I couldn't leave when I was supposed to because she needed me to drive her to the clinic to have her dressings changed.

Ellen, attorney

WHY SHE IS AFRAID TO SET LIMITS:
Look at what I'm up against—she's suicidal whenever I leave. I'm the only one in the family who even speaks to her.

ONE WAY TO SAY NO:
(To criticism the moment Ellen walks in) "Mom, I'm going for a walk. When I return, let's start over and greet each other in a positive way."

to avoid triggering your parent's fears of abandonment. Therapists can also work with you to develop strategies for setting effective limits. And when a borderline parent blows through your boundaries, therapists can help you regroup and rebuild.

saying NO to healthy parents

Psychologically healthy parents try not to make unreasonable demands. Most of the time, they are respectful, considerate, generous, affectionate, open-minded, flexible, and thoughtful. They probably have useful advice about the people you date, the way you raise their grandchildren, or the work you do, but they don't share unless asked. Healthy parents affirm your unique interests and try to be supportive when you adopt a perspective or lifestyle that is wildly out of sync with the rest of the family. They believe in you, encourage you, and tell you not to be afraid of failure.

What's not to love about these folks? Since they ask so little of you, you show up on most special occasions. And when you can't, you're sorry and they understand. That's another characteristic of good parenting—the ability to get over disappointments, to let them go.

Healthy parents are also able to tolerate periods of greater and lesser connection with their adult children. When you were growing up, their limits were clear but not harmful. They tried to explain why they were saying NO. They also worked to ensure a relatively smooth transition from your complete dependency to your taking responsibility for your own choices. Very often, you share a respectful appreciation of one another's strengths and imperfections, and you admire their efforts to understand your decisions and values, especially those that differ from theirs.

So what happens when your priorities conflict with your parents' in a more dramatic way—say, they think your future spouse isn't good enough for you, or they are lifelong Democrats and you work for a Republican politician, or you come from a very religious family and you choose not to have your children baptized? Because they care about you, your parents will probably share their concerns and hope you will reconsider. If you don't or won't, this may be your first really big NO.

Sound the trumpets! Roll out the guilt! It's terribly distressing to refuse parents who've been so supportive. You don't want to hurt them, nor do you want to part ways. Since you respect them, you wonder if you're making a mistake. You worry that they might not forgive you, or that your relationship will be forever damaged.

In the following stories, we hear from four women who struggled to say NO at an important juncture when they and their parents didn't agree.

Seeking an education and a meaningful career, **U.S. Air Force Colonel Patricia Rose** broke with her family tradition by going away to college.

I come from a large Catholic family in New England—Portuguese and Irish—it's very ethnic where I come from. We were very poor. I was the fourth of six kids so by the time I came around, my parents had run out of aunts and uncles—blood relatives—to be my godparents. So they asked a young seventeen-year-old woman who sometimes babysat for us if she wanted to be my godmother. She was going to U Mass to get a degree in early childhood education. I was a little experiment for her in child development.

My godmother was always telling me, "You're going to college some day," but really nobody in my family had gone away to college. To leave home to go to college is very insulting in my family. It's like, "Your home's not good enough for you anymore?" I literally had to go behind my parents' backs to apply for scholarships and loans. I got accepted to college without their knowledge or permission. Basically I told my father one day, "I'm going to college," and he said, "NO, you're not."

I refused to back down. He didn't talk to me for two months, he was so angry. But eventually he got over it.

Vivian Stephenson, who recently retired from the position of **chief operating officer** at **Williams-Sonoma**, grew up in Havana, Cuba. Against her family's wishes, she moved to the United States after the revolution.

A long time ago when I was leaving Cuba after a year of Castro being in power, there was a fair amount of pressure from my family to stay. That was a very difficult NO.

First of all, I had a clear vision that I needed to leave. I didn't want to continue to live in a country where my freedom was going to be impaired in so many ways. It was about not being able to say what you were thinking, not being able to express yourself freely in public, not being able to vote. So it was freedom along those lines and it was clear as a bell to me that I didn't want to live in a country that had those limitations.

Even though they knew it was the right decision, my family didn't want me to leave. It was kind of an evolutionary conversation, but still a resounding "NO, I'm leaving. My freedom is too important."

Bettina Aptheker, women's studies professor, University of California at Santa Cruz, was raised as a red-diaper baby. As an adult, she dreaded telling her parents that she was leaving the Communist Party.

My parents were communists. I was raised in the fifties at the height of the McCarthy period when there was terrific persecution. My father was blacklisted and there was a lot of anxiety and fear in my family. I grew up hearing him screaming from nightmares.

Probably the most difficult thing I ever did emotionally and personally was leaving the Communist Party, which I had been a member of for nineteen years. I had to tell my parents, and that was the hardest thing I've ever had to say NO to. I had made up my

mind and there was nothing that was going to change it. It was my
life. I felt like I would die if I didn't.

Episcopal priest Jennifer Hughes's decision to accept a faculty
position in Massachusetts meant moving three thousand miles
away from her parents who are very attached to her young son.

Recently my husband and I made professional choices to move to
the East Coast. That meant saying NO to what my family wanted
me to do. I love my family very much, and it was an extremely dif-
ficult choice because it means that my son will not be as close to his
grandparents as they and we would like.

My mom, who is a well-known anthropologist and academic,
tried to talk me into staying, and even though I completely under-
stand her rationale, it was extremely difficult to say NO. But this
was an opportunity that felt right to me—it was both substantive
and compelling. I did what I had to do.

The process of saying NO was complicated for these four
women, because in each case, the lifestyle they chose involved a
geographic, philosophic, political, or emotional separation from
beloved parents. Yet the hallmark of a healthy family is the ability to adapt to changing circumstances.

For other women with loving parents, getting to NO involved
thoughtful soul searching about what they stood to lose and an
examination of their reluctance to set limits.

Real estate developer Carol Kerley's parents had fantasized about
her wedding ceremony ever since she was a small child. She was
already engaged to a man when her life took an unexpected turn
and she fell in love with a woman. If she called off the wedding,
Carol worried that her parents might disown her—a prospect
she found intolerable.

I was engaged to a man who was in Vietnam when I fell in love with Linda. I came from a very conservative Christian background that was very homophobic. I had three brothers and I was the only girl, and my parents had this big dream of having a big wedding for me. There I was—planning my wedding—getting tapes from my fiancé with gunfire in the background, terrified he was going to die.

When he got back from Vietnam, I saw no way out. I went through with the wedding, and spent my honeymoon calling Linda every free minute, sobbing hysterically. I stayed with him almost two years. I just couldn't let my family down or disappoint him after all he'd been through.

The angst of saying NO to healthy parents derives from the deep-seated desire to please them and the fear of losing their love. Refusing them is painful at any stage, but if you've made it all the way to adulthood without a major disagreement, you may be unprepared for the intensity of your distress when you don't see eye to eye. Very often the most upsetting choices involve some sort of separation. It's challenging to assert your needs when faced with the prospect of disconnection.

How do you work up the nerve to say NO to healthy parents? Start with the following four steps:

Step 1. Figure out what you're most afraid of losing.
Do you worry that your parents will stop loving you? Will they no longer respect you or feel proud of you? Will they distance themselves from you? Will they stop being supportive?

Check in with a trusted friend or family member to decide if your fears are realistic and if you can handle the potential loss without professional help.

Step 2. Ask yourself what decision you would make if disappointing your parents weren't part of the equation.
Then, rate how important this choice is to you on a scale of 10 =

essential to 0 = worthless. If the score is 6 or higher, it's time to speak up.

Step 3. Consider what you and your parents may learn when your wishes are not compatible.

For instance, you may learn that you can still respect one another even though you disagree. Or find that you can maintain the emotional closeness that has been a hallmark of your relationship. Or discover that a successful resolution to this conflict makes it easier to assert your preferences in the future.

Step 4. Tell yourself that your goal in setting limits with your parents is not to lose anything you value but to follow a path that is important to you.

PRE-ADOPTION BLUES

When Liam and I finally got the news that we could go to Thailand to pick up our baby, we were ecstatic. They sent us a photo and we immediately fell in love with her. I took the health report to the pediatrician we'd picked out. The doctor was concerned about the baby's head size. I called my mom, who had some of her pediatric neurologist colleagues look at the report. They said the same thing. Mom tried to talk us out of adopting that baby. She thought we should wait for another child: "What if the baby ends up retarded or severely dyslexic or mentally ill?"

I've never done anything Mom had huge objections to, but we wanted this little girl. We'd waited so long already.

Sarah, musician

WHY SHE'S AFRAID TO SAY NO TO HER MOM:
I've always relied on Mom whenever I've had a hard time. I'm afraid she won't be there if I need her.

The best strategy for coping with your anxiety is to talk with your parents about your wishes and concerns, to hear each other out. Disclosing your worst fears gives your parents a chance to reassure you, and listening to theirs offers you the opportunity to reassure them. Each of you will experience growing pains as you explore the unfamiliar territory of a disagreement that doesn't have an easy solution.

In *"Pre-Adoption Blues,"* Sarah felt conflicted about adopting a baby whose head was smaller than average, because her mother strongly objected. Sarah mustered up the courage to say she was less worried about the baby's brain size than her mother's withdrawal. Her mother was initially surprised that Sarah had found her so controlling. Sarah's mom met with a rabbi to talk about why she felt so strongly that Sarah should pass on this child. At the rabbi's suggestion, Sarah's mom began volunteering at a school for developmentally challenged children to learn more about their special

---

A HOME OF OUR OWN

I was born when my birthmom was a teenager. She gave me up for adoption. I tracked her down when I was in college, and we've gotten to know each other since then. She's sort of like a big sister/parent to me. My adoptive parents totally respect my relationship with her.

I got married last year, and my husband, who's also a writer and who mostly works at home, doesn't like having a lot of people around. When my birthmom visits, she sometimes stays for two weeks. My husband wants me to tell her she can't come so often and she can only stay a week. I feel torn trying to please both of them.

Judy, journalist

WHY SHE'S AFRAID TO SAY NO TO HER BIRTHMOM:
I don't want to lose her a second time

needs and talents. By the time Sarah returned from Thailand with the baby, her mom was fully on board as a grandparent. The baby is now two years old and so talkative they call her "chatty Cathy."

In *"A Home of Our Own,"* Judy reconnected with her birthmother after a twenty-year separation. Understandably she is reluctant to say NO to her birthmother's request for frequent visits, but when she examined her own feelings about the visits, Judy realized that it seemed unfair to spend more time with her birthmother than her adoptive parents. She has decided to explain to all parents—birth, adoptive, in-laws—that she and her husband would like to divide their time equally among all of them. If Judy's birthmother is as willing to share Judy as her adoptive parents have been, Judy may become less anxious about losing her birthmother a second time.

Sometimes your parents don't care nearly as much as you think they do about an event you've been dreading. For instance, there are many ways to celebrate birthdays and anniversaries,

---

PARTY POOPER

My parents' thirtieth wedding anniversary is coming up this year. In their community, it's a tradition for the kids to throw a gigantic party when their parents celebrate big anniversaries. Those parties are hugely expensive. My sisters and I can't really afford it. My parents are already talking about the people they want to invite. I love them so much and I don't want to make them feel bad. If we needed things they couldn't afford when we were kids, they always found a way.

Olympia, teacher

WHY SHE'S RELUCTANT TO SAY NO TO HER PARENTS:
Their whole community will think we're good-for-nothing daughters, so my parents will feel hurt and embarrassed in front of everyone.

and most loving parents can understand budgetary constraints. Before committing to a plan, try to speak with each parent separately to get an accurate read on his or her preferences. Then, get everyone together in the same room or on the same conference call to plan the celebration.

In *"PARTY POOPER,"* Olympia wanted to celebrate her parents' anniversary in a way that would make them happy, even though she couldn't afford it. When she spoke with each parent individually about the party, her mother claimed that it was something her father wanted, and he insisted that it was her mother's doing. During a trip home for Easter, Olympia and her sisters emphasized their appreciation for the parents' lifelong generosity, and said they wanted to celebrate the anniversary in a way that worked for everyone. The parents settled on a small dinner party for their thirtieth, and a family trip to Greece for their thirty-fifth. Everyone agreed that five years gave them plenty of time to save up.

For most of us, saying NO to our parents is quite stressful. We never entirely outgrow the feeling of discomfort at the prospect of disappointing or losing them. Whether our parents are healthy or emotionally troubled, we want their love and approval. We worry about the conflict that might ensue if we don't comply with their wishes. Exploring our fears about setting limits in these first relationships—with parents—lays the groundwork for understanding our reluctance to say NO in subsequent relationships—with friends, lovers, and co-workers—as I discuss in the following chapters.

chapter three

getting to NO you
(saying NO to dates and mates)

*I had a very difficult marriage to somebody I loved enor-
mously and he loved me. I was totally traumatized, ended
up suicidal over it, yet I went back to him twelve times,
which is just unbelievable considering that was a totally
destructive situation. And still every time he calls and
wants something, it's like, "Oh, sure, darling." And I sit
there thinking, "Do you remember what this man did to
you?" I mean, it's a nice quality to be nice but it isn't hon-
oring the terrible pain he caused me.*
Danielle Steel, author

Are you afraid to be alone? Are you holding onto a disastrous
relationship to avoid being single? Are you pessimistic about
your prospects for a better relationship with someone new? All
too often we cling to partners who don't share our values or
our interests, who are neither loving nor respectful, or who are
downright hostile and abusive, because we can't bear the thought
of letting go or starting over. Sometimes the more appallingly
we're treated, the more we clutch at the fantasy that an adoring
soul mate is trapped inside the body of our tormentor, waiting
to be freed.

Nothing is more heart-wrenching than closing the door on a relationship that was supposed to last a lifetime. Giving the final heave-ho to an intimate partner is always difficult. Many women have experienced a breakup that we imagined we couldn't survive. Rejection sucks, but disconnecting feels worse. Some of us will do anything to avoid issuing the final NO.

What exactly is so frightening to women about letting go? How do we account for our reluctance to say NO even when we're treated badly? Why is the loss of a lover so painful?

It's really very simple: we thrive on connection. When we've got it, we feel happy, alive, energetic, generous, and high; without it, we often feel lost, lonely, empty, frightened, and remote. Having the ability to sustain intimate relationships feeds our self-esteem. Even if we enjoy living alone or being single, for many of us, terminating a relationship feels like wrenching out vital organs, leaving a giant, gaping hole. Unless we are absolutely certain we will be better off ditching Mr. or Ms. Unworthy, *letting go is hard to do.*

The excruciating pain of breaking up stems from the basic human hunger, since childhood, for a loving, protective parent. Women transfer the desire for love and security from our parents to our intimate partners, while our brains—built-in mission control centers—constantly monitor the level of closeness we're experiencing. The prospect of losing a partner sets off series of neurophysiologic reactions that make us feel anxious, fearful, and distressed. Sometimes a potential loss feels so catastrophic that we'll put up with almost anything, from benign neglect to physical abuse, to keep a connection alive.

Admitting that a relationship isn't working is the first step in setting limits. Sometimes there's a fine line between going with the flow when we don't get what we want, and censoring ourselves when we're unhappy because we're afraid of speaking up. If disconnection or rejection weren't at issue, we'd confront our partners, and either stay with them or bail depending on the outcome. But relationship dynamics are rarely that straightforward, and the fantasy that a curmudgeonly spouse will morph into a doting lover is ever so persistent. So we end up complaining to friends, relatives, and shrinks—who toughen our resolve to say NO even if we never utter the word.

For many women, this reluctance to speak up reflects a deeper cost-benefit analysis about what we stand to gain or lose by expressing our dissatisfaction. In the same way that we try to estimate the speed of an oncoming car before dashing across the street, we're continually weighing the pros and cons of saying NO as we balance the family's best interests with our own needs for self-esteem and self-preservation. Is it better to bring up a minor act of thoughtlessness or let it go? Is a partner's desire to accept a new position in another city selfish or considerate of the whole family? Is name calling or shoving a prelude to more dangerous forms of abuse by a spouse? If we divorce, can we count on an ex to keep his commitment to pay half of the kids' tuitions?

In the stories that follow, women who have no problem being tough as nails professionally discuss their reluctance to say NO to significant others (SOs). Because I wanted them to be candid about their experiences, I have changed certain identifying details to protect the privacy of those who requested it. Some women were embarrassed that their boundaries with SOs were so murky. Others were self-conscious about exposing their vulnerabilities. All in all, their stories illustrate the complexity of saying NO when there is a risk of disappointing, hurting, alienating, or losing an intimate partner.

dates

When you're eager to find a mate, the biggest obstacle to being candid in a dating situation is the fear of being dumped. It's difficult to set limits on obnoxious behavior when you worry that assertiveness might be a turnoff. The stigma of being single and the glorification of being coupled make it easy to minimize how badly you are being treated. You may try to conceal your dissatisfaction, hoping that your inconsiderate date will blossom into a compatible mate. Sadly, this is a fantasy—it NEVER happens. You're better off raising the bar to an appropriate height and refusing to settle for less. Forget the glass slipper: lace up your running shoes and split!

DOUBLE DIPPING

I've been dating this divorced guy who wants to know where I am every minute he's not with me. He's still seeing his ex-wife, and he wants to make sure I'm not out when he's with her. I probably shouldn't put up with this double standard.

Rashida, educator

WHY SHE DOESN'T SAY NO:
I really like him and I want it to work out. I don't want be a nag.

These are familiar refrains by now—he or she is "just not right for you" or "just not good for you" or "just not into you." You've heard them from girlfriends, guyfriends, parents, and shrinks. Yet it's difficult to give up until you're absolutely sure that:

1. You can survive the loss of Mr. or Ms. Wrong
2. You might find somebody better
3. You are better off being alone

If your friends won't hear another word about the relationship, your parents won't have anything to do with him or her, and you're still overanalyzing every nuance of your date's thoughtless behavior for signs of an impending commitment, what steps can you take to stop obsessing and get out of this rut?

Here's what I suggest:

Step 1. Figure out what you stand to lose.

Do you dread starting over? Will your family give you grief for another poor choice? Do you equate being single with being a failure? Do you imagine that your date will disclose your intimate secrets to others? Does it seem that anyone you're intimate with takes a piece of your heart when you break up?

Reviewing your worries helps you decide whether you can handle the NO on your own, or if you need support. If you decide to seek counseling, make sure you select an experienced professional who can understand your fears and provide practical advice to resolve them.

REVOLVING DOOR

We have nothing in common—we don't like the same films or books or anything. He likes sports, I like opera. That pretty much sums it up, doesn't it? We can't even have a decent conversation because we're just not on the same wavelength. Even though I've only been seeing him a few months, it *kills* me every time I say, "I think we should stop dating." He storms out, I end up calling him an hour later, and then he's back. And then I start to feel crazy all over again.

Lydia, actor

WHY SHE DOESN'T SAY NO:
My girlfriends who are single are so unbelievably miserable.

Step 2. Ask yourself how your self-esteem might be enhanced by calling it quits with Mr. or Ms. Wrong.

Would you feel happier without the inconsiderate treatment and daily disappointments? Would you have more self-confidence if you weren't constantly being criticized? Would you spend more time with friends and other people who appreciate you if you weren't trying to meet all of his or her demands?

Step 3. Tell yourself that you are worthy of a healthy, fulfilling, mutually respectful relationship.
Make a list of at least ten reasons why you deserve to be happy, such as: "I am smart, interesting, funny, generous, friendly . . ." If you can't get to ten, ask your friends why they like you. Write the reasons down, make two copies, and post one on your bathroom mirror and the other on your refrigerator. Review the list first thing in the morning, while you're preparing meals, and before you go to bed. Sing with Aretha: "R-E-S-P-E-C-T: find out what it means to me."

COITUS INTERRUPT US

An old boyfriend was visiting last month. One thing led to another, and I hadn't been seeing anyone for a couple of years, so I thought, what the heck? But then I thought he might change his mind if I got up to get a condom, so I didn't. Of course he didn't bring one—when do guys ever carry them?! Well, he gave me herpes, and on top of that I had to worry about being pregnant. I'm so angry at myself. All those teenage girls having unsafe sex—and I did the same thing. It's ridiculous.

Deb, district attorney

WHY SHE DIDN'T SAY NO:
I kept remembering when he used to tell me I was too controlling.

Step 4. Remind yourself that your goal in setting limits with an uncaring date is to recover your self-respect.
Recall a time when you felt really good. Remember how relaxing it was to wake up without immediately checking to see if Mr. or Ms. Wrong left a message on your phone or email. Experience the

pleasurable sensation of appreciating all that you have to offer, and knowing that you won't put up with less than you deserve.

Everyone deserves to be treated lovingly, considerately, and thoughtfully as a fully equal partner. Though it's nice to be valued for what you have accomplished, it's even more important to be loved for who you are. Even outside of Oz, you need to be appreciated for having a *heart* (compassion, generosity, nurturance), a *brain* (intelligence, wit, resourcefulness), and *courage* (flexibility, openness, integrity), along with your unique and individual qualities. Ideally, you will find someone else with these same attributes—an emotionally available, verbally and physically expressive mate who is willing to meet your level of commitment, who listens to your concerns, and who respects your limits.

EXCLUSIVE BONDING

I'm totally focused on her, and she is totally focused on her three-year-old son, Gabe. Whenever I ask her out, she brings Gabe along. She only calls me when she needs a babysitter. I like taking care of him, but I spend too much time hanging around hoping she'll invite me to spend the night. When she does, it's really great. But it doesn't happen very often.

Grace, nonprofit administrator

WHY SHE DOESN'T SAY NO:
I understand how important Gabe is to her, and it's kind of ridiculous to compete with him for her attention.

Women have varying degrees of tolerance for obnoxious behavior—depending on the kind of parenting we've had and the relationships to which we've been exposed. Many women really don't know what constitutes a healthy, loving partnership. If constructive, growth-enhancing interactions are unfamiliar to you, you need to learn how to recognize and encourage positive behavior, an important, painstaking process. In psychotherapy it involves a thoughtful comparison of current and past relationships and coaching about the qualities that contribute to mutual compatibility. Even with a good therapist, the prospect of letting go creates enormous separation anxiety for women who have never experienced anything better.

Perhaps someday soon, with the use of genetic mapping, specialized neuroimagery, and brain biochemistry, we will be able to explain the complex bio-psycho-social phenomena of falling in love, setting limits, and breaking up. Neuroscientists have already begun to explore how our brains relay signals in different emotional states—when we crave closeness, fear rejection, or grieve the loss of partners. Evidence is mounting that you can train certain regions of your brain to generate pleasurable sensations that override pain.

JUST NOT INTO ME?

I can't figure out what's holding him back, but I don't think he's gay. He's happy to come over when I invite some of my more interesting friends, but he cancels at the last minute when it's just me. Once he didn't show up at all, and another time he was two hours late. Last week he asked if I'd introduce him to a friend of mine who just won a Pulitzer. I hope I'm not connecting random dots and making a bigger deal of his feelings about me than I should.

Heather, environmental engineer

WHY SHE DOESN'T SAY NO:
I know he enjoys my sense of humor.

In the meantime, pay attention to disappointment. Rate your date on a ten-point scale, with 10 = prince or princess charming and 0 = scumbag. Make a note of the score each day, and keep a record of these scores for two months. Be sure to delete points for any hurtful, disinterested, disrespectful, or inconsiderate behavior. It's more important to focus on behavior than on what he or she proclaims to feel for you. At the end of two months, add up the scores, and divide by the number of days you recorded a score. For anything lower than a 7, open the trap door. A low score does not mean that you should try harder. It means you need to MOVE ON. You will not be loved in the way you deserve if you hang on when the feelings aren't mutual.

> *I decided years ago that if I ever married again, it would be to celebrate a great relationship, not to fix a bad one. A lot of people think, "Well this isn't working, if we get married it will." I've done that and that's a huge mistake.*
> **Danielle Steel**

mates

(saying NO in loving partnerships)

Even with a loving partner, it can be difficult to say NO. No one likes to disrupt a harmonious connection, and it's painful to disappoint a loved one. Sometimes we'd rather find a way to resolve our discomfort internally than voice our objections or insecurities out loud. At other times, acquiescing to our mate might seem preferable to being honest, particularly when we're trying to avoid injuring him or her.

Although everyone conceals feelings at one time or another—even in a healthy relationship—sharing your disagreements in a loving way can bring you closer. Just initiating a conversation could increase your sense of connection. Besides, one characteristic of a healthy relationship is the ability to hear each other out when there are differences.

If your relationship was founded on a commitment to hon-

DANCIN' MAN

I had polio as a child and I can't dance because of the pain. I've been married for twenty-three years, and my husband never mentioned dancing—I guess because he didn't want me to feel bad. Recently at a wedding a junior faculty member asked him to dance. I was stunned watching them. He was quite good and seemed to be having so much fun. She asked later that evening if he might be interested in joining a dance class she teaches. He wanted to know how I'd feel. She's very flirtatious, and that makes me uncomfortable.

Adriana, librarian

WHY SHE DOESN'T SAY NO:
I don't want to stand in the way of his enjoyment.

ONE WAY TO START A CONVERSATION:
"Sweetheart, if you'd like to take a dance class, you should. But it seemed like your colleague was coming on to you. I think we should talk about that."

esty, yet you're anxious about setting a limit, how do you work up the nerve to say NO?

Start with the following steps:

Step 1. Figure out what you're most afraid of losing.
Are you worried that your significant other will be angry? Hurt? Feel unsupported? Unappreciated? Unloved? Become distant?

Again, check in with a trusted friend or family member to decide if you can handle your concern without professional help.

Step 2. Consider the consequences of continuing to conceal your dissatisfaction.
Has the issue created a wedge between the two of you? Is your

unhappiness seeping into other interactions or conversations? Does your significant other, sensing that something isn't right, feel distressed about his or her inability to put a finger on the source of your sadness?

Step 3. Rate how important it is to you to be honest with your significant other about areas of disagreement.
On a scale of 10 = honesty is essential, to 0 = honesty doesn't matter here, if your score is 6 or higher, it's time to speak up.

Step 4. Remember that your goal in stepping up to the challenge of setting limits with your significant other is to enhance your sense of connection, and to deepen your commitment.
You are opening new channels of communication, not losing

SCARY SOLUTION

In the first seven years we were together, I didn't pay much attention to her med school loans. We have a commitment to handle all our educational debt as a joint responsibility, even though we can't legally marry in our state. But lately, the loan payments have really been weighing her down. She asked how I'd feel if she joined the reserves to get rid of the debt. I told her I'd respect her decision, but the military? That scares me to death, with the war in Iraq and all. What if she gets sent to war?

Geri, chiropractor

WHY SHE DOESN'T SAY NO:
I know she wants to get started on having kids and she doesn't want to do that when we have so much debt.

ONE WAY TO START A CONVERSATION:
"Let's try to come up with other alternatives. Maybe I could work longer hours. Or we could meet with a financial planner . . ."

anything you value about the relationship. To bolster your self-confidence, remind yourself of previous occasions when the two of you resolved conflicts in a mutually satisfactory manner.

In a healthy relationship, your partner will likely understand your concerns and appreciate your reluctance to disappoint him or her. If he or she is the reassuring type, expressing your insecurities might give you some peace of mind. Even if he or she is unhappy with your NO, communicating your opposition directly is better than conveying it in a roundabout way. And coming to a mutually satisfactory compromise or resolution enhances your feelings of connection.

FREQUENT FLYER

I knew when we married that my husband would spend a lot of time on the road. He plays in a band, and that's the nature of the business. But with so many groupies, I worry that he's having an affair whenever he doesn't call. He's been gone so much this year I feel like I hardly know him any more. I sometimes think about looking for somebody I could actually share a life with, but I have panic attacks and intermittent depression, which make it hard for me to deal with change and loss.

Jocyln, attorney

WHY SHE DOESN'T SAY NO:
I'm afraid of getting depressed if I leave him.

It can be much more challenging to set limits if you suffer from anxiety or depression. Even with antidepressant or antianxiety medication, you may feel deep distress at loss or change. Relationship difficulties on top of a mood disorder can be a double-edged sword—if you don't speak up and you're chronically unhappy, eventually you'll end up depressed; if you do set a limit that results in a loss, you may suffer a relapse.

As a psychiatrist, I recommend the following: if depression or anxiety is hindering your freedom of expression, think about seeing a mental health professional who can monitor your moods, prescribe medications if needed, and help you find your voice. It is important to push through your fears to a new safety zone where you define your own boundaries and limits.

DEAD-END JOB

My husband is depressed. He hates his job, and he talks about it nonstop. He's had a serious depression before, and even though he has a psychiatrist, when he asks if it's okay if he tells me about work, I worry that he'll feel like he has no outlet if I say NO. Then he'll get even more depressed—maybe even quit.

Katie, author

WHY SHE DOESN'T SAY NO:
I'm afraid he might kill himself.

ONE WAY TO START A CONVERSATION:
"I notice that you get really down in the dumps when you tell me what happened at work. Do you think you might feel better if we talk about other things when you're not there?"

---

damage control

If your relationship is in trouble, swallowing whatever is dished out to avoid dealing with issues of divorce, child custody, and financial support will hurt you in the long run. You stand a good chance of ending up full of self-loathing, if you aren't already. This is a tall price to pay especially when considering that many troubled relationships don't survive, regardless of the concessions made by one partner. Better to speak up and hold onto your pride than be left with a tattered psyche as well as a broken heart.

Saying NO or setting a limit may feel strange in the beginning. That's okay. It sometimes feels weird when you're unaccustomed to standing up for yourself, but it will get easier with practice.

COUCH POTATO

I work ninety hours a week, and he's sitting home doing nothing—except maybe exercising his fingers channel surfing. There's no dinner planned, no laundry done—nada. I know I have a problem with co-dependency. I had these totally crazy alcoholic parents and I became the adult in the family and I've been taking care of everyone since I was a kid.

Montana, software developer

WHY SHE DOESN'T SAY NO:
Good question! The abuse stuff, I guess. I have trouble saying NO to anything short of, like, *major* abuse.

So how do you get started? Here are my suggestions:

Step 1. Timing is crucial.

You'll want to say NO when you are prepared to deal with the consequences as well as you can. This isn't an excuse not to do the right thing, just a way to do it successfully—to have a plan—so you are not forced back into a bad situation after taking a stand.

Step 2. Financial self-sufficiency usually gives women a stronger voice.

My advice to women who take a leave of absence from earning an income is to make it a brief time-out. Plan to return to part-time or full-time income-generating work as soon as possible. It's wonderful to spend time with kids or to pursue other interests without having to worry about money, but self-esteem and assertiveness are, for most people, inexorably linked to bringing home a paycheck. If something isn't working in a relationship, you need to know that you could survive on your own if you had to. Your pay stub could be your ticket to saying NO and moving on.

STRANGE BEDFELLOWS

This is embarrassing. We've been together for nine years, and we live in separate apartments because he wants his own space. He's a recording engineer and he's up all night when he's working. I need sleep for my job. His apartment is a total disaster. About a month ago I woke up with bites all over my body. We'd heard scratching noises on the roof and behind the furniture for weeks. The place was infested with rats, and there were mites in the bed. I ended up in the emergency room with a severe allergic reaction.

Cecelia, executive

WHY SHE DOESN'T SAY NO:
He'd probably rather break up than clean up his act.

ONE WAY TO SAY NO:
"I'm afraid of having another allergic reaction. When we get together, let's spend the night at my apartment."

Step 3. Tell yourself you will be okay, even though the transition will be difficult.
You may be thinking:

Impossible! What about the kids? The mortgage? I don't want to give up this lifestyle. I'll never find anyone else I want to be with. There's nobody I'm interested in. I'm not as attractive or desirable

as I used to be. I'm too old or fat. If I lose my partner, that's it. I'll
never be happy again.

PHONE SEX

My husband told me last week that a huge bill to 900 numbers
was coming by mistake and I should just ignore it. I called the
phone company, and they played a tape of him. I was shocked.
When I confronted him, he said he'd go with me to therapy
but only if we don't discuss the calls. He thinks we should talk
about my weight instead.

Dawn, consultant

WHY SHE DOESN'T SAY NO:
He's brought up separating before. I don't want my kids to
grow up without a dad.

ONE WAY TO START A CONVERSATION:
(About therapy) "Let's try to find a therapist who can help us
feel safe enough to talk about the things that are stressful to
both of us."

Women have such a tough time with loss that we can't con-
ceive of training for it. Though most of us will lose a spouse to
divorce or death, we often pretend it won't happen or tell ourselves we couldn't survive if it did. A more realistic approach
is to remind ourselves that we are likely to be alone at various
times and to think about ways to make ourselves happy when
that occurs. Anticipating loss prepares us for the inevitable and
gives us a stronger voice when we're unhappy in a relationship.
Self-talk to prepare for a loss goes something like this:

I have so many things going for me. I'm a great mom, architect, friend,
daughter, sister. Many people love and appreciate me. If I had to be

alone, I would find a way to be happy like _____(fill in a name) who has been alone for years. She has an interesting and meaningful life. She raised her kids on her own and they turned out great. She had a fascinating career and did good work. She is my role model.

Just as we can grow to love our bodies when we tell ourselves how beautiful we are every day, with loss-preparation self-talk, we start to believe we can manage on our own, if it comes to that. And if we can imagine surviving the loss of a spouse, we can learn to say NO.

Step 4. When you are ready to draw a line, you need to spell it out.
This is the point where you may put on the brakes or stall for time.

SHUT OUT

We agreed that I'd quit my job to be a stay-at-home mom for the first five years. My husband was incredibly loving and supportive throughout the pregnancy, but he's been totally absent since the twins were born. Breast-feeding is a real turnoff for him, and he doesn't seem attracted to me any more. He's been inviting his new assistant home for dinner—this real babe—and they sit around for hours drinking martinis and watching baseball. Meanwhile, I'm upstairs feeding the twins and feeling like shit.

Jemma, political lobbyist

WHY SHE DOESN'T SAY NO:
I can't deal with divorce on top of everything else. And I can't get my job back.

ONE WAY TO START A CONVERSATION:
"I feel like we've grown apart since the babies were born. I'd like to get a sitter one night a week so we can go to dinner or a movie and have fun like we used to."

I can't do it this week/month because it's my brother-in-law's birthday, my friend's mother just had a stroke, it is Passover/Christmas/ Ramadan, we're leaving for a family trip . . . .

These and similar situations are perfectly understandable justifications for postponing the confrontation. Just be clear that you are choosing your partner's or family's welfare over your own—temporarily. You have put the NO on hold because something else is more important. This is a choice. You are in the driver's seat. You have made your decision. You have clarified what you need to do at this moment, and what you plan to do in the near future.

DYING MAN'S WISH

My husband was diagnosed with lung cancer two years ago. After he finished chemo, he told me he wanted an open relationship. How could I say NO? I haven't met anyone I'm interested in, but he has a girlfriend. He's doing fine health-wise—for now anyway— but I feel like I've lost him in a different way than I expected.

Pat, auto dealership owner

WHY SHE DOESN'T SAY NO:
I can't deal with divorce on top of his dying. That would be too awful for the kids.

Step 5. Make sure to note the date of your decision to say NO, and then check your progress at least once a month so you don't lose momentum.

Above all, don't beat yourself up if you take an occasional step sideways or backwards. Saying NO in relationships is rarely a linear process and may take longer than you anticipate.

saying NO after abuse

I had a very abusive childhood. My mother abandoned me when I was six. Having a history of abandonment as an adult and as a child, my fear is that if I'm not nice, or I don't do what someone wants, or I don't take a popular position, or I stand up for myself, then I'll be abandoned by my loved ones.

Because of the abuse, I don't have good meters. It's so familiar to me to be disregarded or badly treated that my red lights go on so much later than they should. That's why I have manual meters, because I don't have automatic meters. I used to try the crown of thorns on fourteen different ways to see if I could get more comfortable instead of throwing it in the garbage. Now I turn on the manual meters and go on a checklist of what exactly is happening here?

I know women who don't have money or careers and want to leave husbands, and they think that in my situation you wouldn't hesitate. It doesn't have to do with money or a job. It has to do with your internal stuff. I stayed in an abusive relationship because of my own fears even though I have money and a job.

I hate the fact that an abusive childhood is so much work forever. It is something I have to deal with almost every day. I'm so pissed it has taken me so much work and time, and has had such a major impact on my life, even now, despite years of therapy, hard work, introspection, and major effort to change it. The impact of an abusive child-hood is forever.

Danielle Steel

The path to NO can be particularly torturous for women who have been abused. Abuse or abandonment obliterates a child's ability to set boundaries. Women who grew up in dysfunctional families often have great difficulty saying NO as adults because of the fear that they or someone they love will be hurt if they don't acquiesce—whenever, wherever.

Entrepreneur Marilyn Jaeger explains how childhood sexual abuse influenced her ability to say NO to destructive adult relationships.

My ability to say NO to a man in a sexual situation was completely nil because of being abused by more than one family friend. For many, many years—up until adulthood—saying NO to a man who wanted to have sex with me was actually the most challenging of all because of the blurry lines between love and being needed and wanted, and the hunger for interaction. Growing up without any parental guidance or mentor in the home affected my relationships from a very early age, whether it was a first date and me not really being attracted to someone, not even having any intention of kissing him and before I know it, I'm in bed with him in the back of his van or wherever. Their intentions were not always good, but I misconstrued them as being wanted or loved.

Until I was about thirty, I felt like I was just a white trash slut—somebody who was only good enough to sleep with, but not good enough to be the girlfriend. This one guy I was dating for three or four months had me sneaking around so people wouldn't see we were together. It was such an awful feeling. I vowed to myself I would never let that happen again.

But it took a lot more work than starting my own business completely on my own to learn how to say NO. That change has to come from within. Because when you don't want sex and you don't say NO, it's so devaluing, and the more you devalue yourself, the more you start to believe it. It's a really nasty cycle.

One very successful treatment for the residual injuries from childhood trauma is called Eye Movement Desensitization and Reprocessing (EMDR). Developed in the late 1980s by a psychologist named Francine Shapiro, it involves alternating light, vibratory, or auditory stimulation to the right and left sides of the brain while a trained therapist guides you through a reenactment of the abuse. As therapy goes, EMDR is a relatively short-term process, depending on the frequency and the severity of the trauma. For example, a fear of snakes after stepping on a rattler might warrant a few treatments, whereas childhood sexual abuse by a close relative may require twenty or more sessions. In theory, the way EMDR works is to reprogram the brain so that thinking or talking about abuse no longer triggers a feeling of terror.

Rachel, a physician, was forced to care for abusive parents when she was a child. Here's how she found EMDR helpful in saying NO to an unhealthy relationship:

I was involved with a guy who grew up near Chernobyl—after the nuclear power plant explosion. Two of his aunts and many other relatives died of cancer. Petr had suffered so much, and—I can't believe I'm saying this—I still love him, even though I found out after supporting his family for years that he'd been lying to me—a lot. Petr got fired from two jobs because he lied about his education (to me, too). He cheated on me, and lied when I found out about it. He lied about money. He said he needed to send money to his parents for food, and I gave him thousands of dollars. But it turned out Petr was gambling.

Still, I couldn't leave him. Petr begged me not to go. I felt like it would be so cruel to abandon him since he had such a hard life. Sometimes it seemed like I would die—I mean literally—*if I broke up with him.*

I've had a lot of therapy, because my stepfather sexually abused me when I was ten. He threatened to kill my mother if I told anyone. So, it's no surprise that I have difficulty saying NO. I thought I had done all the work I could do on that issue, and in some ways, just come to terms with the possibility that the injury from that would never be completely healed.

But I realized I needed help figuring out what to do about Petr. This time, my therapist recommended EMDR. It seemed kind of new-agey to wear headphones and listen to these pulsating sounds as I talked with my eyes closed about my past and my fear of losing people. Tears poured out of my eyes—I wouldn't even call it crying, not like sobbing, it was more like flooding—when I talked about my childhood stuff. I have never cried that much before or since.

After about ten treatments, the terrible fear of saying NO, the feeling that I would throw up or die if did, was gone. I couldn't even make it happen. In retrospect, I realize I'd been living with an open wound, and after EMDR it felt like somebody had poured cold milk on it. When I thought about saying NO, instead of feeling like I was going to die, I felt nothing, like a blank. I could finally break up because it was the right thing to do. Period. It was amazing.

Rachel has no regrets about the years she spent in talk therapy, because it taught her what to look for in a healthy relationship. Petr came into her life when she was on the rebound from a breakup, with lower defenses than usual. The struggle to terminate that relationship took her to EMDR, which transformed her ability to say NO in a way that she never imagined possible. "I'm so grateful for all I learned when I was trying to let go of Petr, because now I'm better equipped to protect myself in all kinds of relationships," she said. "I know I'd still be miserably guilty if I'd kicked him out before I did EMDR, and anyway, he probably would have found a way back in."

EMDR can be an effective aid to women whose ability to say NO has been severely diminished by trauma. As with any kind of psychotherapy, it is important to work with a trained, licensed clinician.

I'll never take him (her) back!

Even when it's clear that it's unhealthy to continue a relationship, the actual process of separating is agonizing for many women.

Our stress hormones skyrocket, and our brains go into panic mode. We fixate on a relationship's good qualities and minimize the bad—and decide to try again, and again, and again, because disengaging is so painful.

But once we have completed the breakup and taken a bit of a breather, our ex-partners rarely look so appealing. We're surviving or thriving without them, and it's a relief to be free of the conflict. After a couple of years, even if we had the option, most of us would NEVER take them back!

Dr. Marny Hall, a **couples therapist** and **author**, describes how women rewrite the narratives of lost loves once we're no longer in the throes of disconnecting.

When I'm lecturing about relationships, I try to illustrate how distorted our perceptions become when we're trying to wrench ourselves away from a partner. I ask women in the audience to raise their hands if they've ever considered suicide when they were trying to leave a relationship—if they would have been willing to give anything—an arm or leg—to have it work out. Hundreds of hands shoot into the air.

Then I ask how many would actually take the person back if he or she showed up now. Not a single hand goes up. And how many believe now that losing that relationship was one of the best things that ever happened to them? Again, hundreds of hands in the air.

Very often in my work I hear "this is the love of my life" when couples are together, and "that was the most destructive, abusive relationship I've ever had" two years after they split.

When we're in the midst of a breakup, disentangling can seem so dreadful that many of us will do anything to avoid the final NO. But once we've recovered from the loss, former intimates rarely seem so special. And every time we let go of an unhealthy or unsuitable relationship, we learn how to take better care of ourselves in the future.

Our self-esteem and need for connection are on the line in intimate relationships. That makes setting limits with lovers especially challenging—and an important opportunity to examine your reluctance to say NO.

chapter four

NOthing personal

(saying NO to friends)

A friend of mine said that, ironically, she found it very use-ful to have cancer, so she could finally say NO when people asked her to do things she didn't want to do.

Dorothy Allison, author

Cats give me asthma. I almost died at Elizabeth Taylor's house once from asthma, but I was so excited to be there. I wasn't about to say anything—I was just sitting there dying.

Danielle Steel, author

Are you able to say NO if your best friend asks you to do some-thing you don't want to do? What if a pal asks you to lie for her? Or pressures you to break a confidence you've promised to keep? Or insists on talking when you're totally wiped out? Or asks for a favor that puts you in the uncomfortable position of indebting yourself to someone else?

Ask any woman to think of a time when she had trouble saying NO to a friend. Something springs to mind for most of us. I posed the question to my closest friends, giving them the additional assignment of specifying which situations stress their limit-setting capabilities the most. From their responses, along with the interviews I conducted for this book and the stories I've heard from women patients, I developed a list of ten scenarios where many of us get stuck:

1. Trying Times
When friends are suffering, we want to be helpful but sometimes find it difficult to buoy our own spirits, let alone theirs.

2. Stale Rituals
When an established pattern of visiting or gift giving or celebrating holidays with certain friends has become a chore, and we'd like to change it up.

3. "I . . . I . . . I . . . me . . . me . . . me"
When self-focused friends don't take a hint that it takes two to talk.

4. Quid Pro Quo, Quo, Quo
When we feel obligated to friends who help us through difficult times, yet can't figure out when we have repaid the debt.

5. Love Me, Love My Mate
When a dear friend hooks up with a creep, then expects us all to hang out.

6. Relentless Badgering
When friends pester us to get what they want.

7. Special Dispensation
When friends who have experienced a major hardship ask for a favor that feels awkward.

8. Broken Record
When we've listened to a friend talk about the same dreadful lover or unfulfilling job or fascinating child, for years.

9. Passive Aggressive
When friends are good on promises, bad on delivery, good on excuses, and bad on apologies, yet we're hooked—hoping they'll come through, knowing they won't, but afraid to call them on it.

10. No Reciprocity
When friends continually ask for more emotional support than they provide.

Thinking about this chapter, I considered my own ambivalence when friends want me to do something that feels uncomfortable. Because I'm a physician, friends occasionally ask me to write or renew prescriptions for them. I've been called on for all sorts of meds—Rogaine (for a boyfriend who was losing his hair), steroids (for a cat who was having an allergic reaction), stimulants (for a child with attention deficit disorder), Prozac (for a father who was becoming belligerent), and even a "lethal injection" (for a friend who didn't want to be without, "just in case").

It's unethical, unwise, and potentially illegal to prescribe medications to people who aren't your patients. When I authorize a medication as a prescribing doctor, I am obligated to be familiar with a patient's medical history, and I am responsible if anything adverse were to happen. And the penalties for misuse of a prescribing privilege are severe: one of my Harvard Medical School colleagues was apprehended by the Drug Enforcement Administration for casually writing scripts for colleagues and family members. This doc now has a felony on his record.

Of course in most cases, my friends are asking for a medication that has already been prescribed by another doctor. Invariably I refuse, because I only write scripts for patients I've thoroughly evaluated. But I always suggest strategies for getting refills when the prescribing physician is unavailable.

Some friends react to my refusal as if I'm being totally uptight, and they hang up in a huff. Though I could make things easier for those who are truly having a hard time by pulling out my prescription pad, I'd rather help out in some way that doesn't compromise my professional standards.

denying our nearest and dearest

Why is it so uncomfortable to say NO to friends? Basically, it boils down to this: we care about them and don't want to lose them. These are the people we turn to when we're in bad shape—heaven forbid we should bow out when they need us! After all, we're disappointed when they decline our invitations or can't talk as often as we'd like, so we imagine they feel the same if we don't accommodate them.

Besides, our closest friends know us well enough to recognize the ways we get out of difficult situations. Some friends have even helped us out of obligations to others. Since they can see straight through any excuses we offer, it's nerve-wracking to say NO when our pals want us to do things we'd rather avoid.

GIVE ME A BLURB

It's so frustrating when one of my writer friends calls at the last minute to get me to do a blurb for her books. Even if I value her work and I'm happy she's doing it, I rarely have time to drop everything to read the book and write the copy in a week. Basically, these friends want my name on their books. They say they're giving me more visibility with my name on their books, when it's really the other way around.

Jackie, writer

WHY SHE HAS TROUBLE SAYING NO:
If I say NO, I appear unsupportive of their writing or unhelpful as a friend.

ONE WAY TO SAY NO:
"I'm really sorry but I need more lead time. I can't do it justice on such short notice and I'm on deadline myself."

. . .

A self-described good-natured people pleaser, a **Spirit Rock Meditation Center co-founder, psychotherapist, and author Sylvia Boorstein** explains why she feels distressed when she has to say NO to her friends:

For anybody to make a request of me is never a conflict-free situation. It's never a neutral thing. Either I do it because I really want to, or sometimes because I can do it, sometimes because it's the right thing to do. If I can't, then I feel bad. I don't think that's true of a single man that I know.

My experience in life is I expect people will like me. I had a very cheerful, good-natured mother who was pleasant, kind, and mild-mannered. People liked her and they like me. So my expectation always is that people will like me. I'm not worried that they won't like me. And I'm not worried that I have to please them. I just like to please.

Even when she's maxed out, **TV host, supermodel, and author Emme** finds a few moments for friends who are having a hard time:

If a friend is in need, and I've had it up to my eyeballs—like my day has been crazy—I have such a hard time saying "NO, I can't be there for you." I would rather take off my leg than say NO—it's really, really hard.

Portrait photographer Melanie Dunea tries to accommodate her pals when their needs seem more important than hers. Changing the focus sometimes reduces her disappointment.

I got married in India on December 31. I asked a very good friend of mine who is a famous photojournalist and really in demand professionally to take the pictures. We offered to pay for her travel expenses to come. She said, "Don't be crazy, of course I'll come, and I'd be happy to do the pictures."

The day we arrived in India the tsunami happened. My friend got called by one of the major American charities saying, "If you don't get down to south India we're not going to get pictures and we're not going to get any money." She was in a huge conundrum about what to do. What did I do? I didn't say NO, I said, "Go!"

Of course when she got there, there were ten thousand other photographers, and there was no need for any more pictures, and she was really upset. She sent me an e-mail saying she felt like she'd made the wrong decision and should not have gone. She felt bad that we didn't have any professional wedding pictures. However, if I were in her shoes, I probably would have gone to the disaster, too.

In the end, we passed our cameras around and found rolls and rolls of lovely pictures taken by all different people with different perspectives.

Author Jewelle Gomez hates to disappoint her friends. She sometimes goes out of her way to avoid saying NO to them.

Usually I will do almost anything to keep from disappointing people and saying NO. That's the way women are trained. We're supposed to be able to do everything all at once and keep smiling. I think my cultural training goes that deep.

But also my mother and father split up when I was a kid, and I got raised first by a paternal grandparent, and then by my maternal great-grandmother. I think there is something that happens to a kid who gets left at that young an age, even when you do have loving caretakers. I feel like I'm always trying to keep from disappointing people because I don't want to get left. I think it's really as simple as that.

• • •

Deeply sensitive to the feeling of abandonment, **author Danielle Steel** comments on her reluctance to refuse her friends:

Having been abandoned by my mother as a kid, my fear is that if I'm not nice, or I don't do what someone wants, or I don't take a popular position, or I stand up for myself, then I'll be abandoned. I don't want to be viewed as a bad guy by my friends, and I don't want to be abandoned by my loved ones.

Women of our generation were taught to be good little girls. It's that whole "shut up and keep dancing" mentality, and also stretching yourself to fit in. I think women are programmed to not serve our own needs. It just goes that one step further where you end up doing really ridiculous things. I recently bought a bracelet I didn't want because I didn't want to hurt a friend's feelings who was the designer. I have done that so often that the only way I can protect myself from it is to stay home and not shop at the stores of friends. I am proud to say I had my secretary return the bracelet, a major victory for me.

I mean, for instance, several friends own jewelry and clothing businesses. I won't see their stuff because I know if I see their stuff, I'm going to buy some $20,000 item I don't want! I have gone to dinner parties, taken people on trips, bought things I didn't want, and taken on projects I didn't want rather than just spit it out.

It is particularly difficult being famous, because people want to assume the worst of one. They want to believe that one is nasty, spoiled, selfish, bratty, and even mean. I have spent twenty-five years of fame trying to prove otherwise, often doing what non-famous people would just blow off without a second thought. Instead I continue to try to demonstrate my kindness, decency, and humanity by bending over backwards (when others wouldn't), just to prove that I'm nice.

There are many circumstances where we give our love, energy, and support freely to special friends. Then there are times when we are bone tired or stretched thin, and a friend calls in crisis or begs for a huge favor. We may fantasize about saying NO, but it goes against our principles to bail on a buddy in need.

So what do we do? We shift into super-overdrive—wrenching out whatever's required to lend a helping hand, just as we do when a family member or co-worker or anyone else we care about asks for assistance. Sure, it's inconvenient—what else is new? We'd like to think that, if the tables were turned, the friend would do the same.

Being there for one another is what friendship is all about. We try to be considerate, helpful, and available, during the good times and the bad. As the saying goes: "A friend walks in when the rest of the world walks out." On the down side, we worry that our pals might drift away if we disappoint them. Or be less sympathetic during our next crisis. Or accuse us of being selfish. Or criticize us to others. Indeed, it doesn't take much digging to figure out why many of us find it difficult to say NO to our friends.

> *I was taking a mental health trip, much needed. I only had six days. I had already made up my mind that I wanted to go alone and I decided to stay at the Four Seasons in Costa Rica. I could afford it, and I wanted the best of both worlds—a grungy, surfer town where I could have nice amenities, and not get eaten alive by bugs.*
>
> *When this friend of mine heard about it, she said, "Oh great, I need a vacation too. I can come at the same time." My first response was like, "Yeah, great, it's going to be beautiful, you should come." And within like half a second of saying that, I really wanted to bite my tongue. Why did I say she could come when I wanted to be by myself?*
>
> **Marilyn Jaeger, Entrepreneur**

Pinocchio's NOs

When I accepted a faculty position in San Diego last year, I decided to drive my car cross country from Vermont. I saw it as an opportunity to relearn Spanish, listening to tapes as I drove. I also wanted to enjoy the scenery through my car window, which is the best way for me to do nature. And I wanted to have some quiet time before I became overwhelmed with the responsibilities of a new job.

One of my colleagues on the East Coast who's sweet but incredibly boring and a nonstop talker asked if she could drive with me. She said she was willing to split the gas with me. But I dreaded the thought of spending six days cooped up in a car with her, and I couldn't figure out how to say NO without hurting her feelings. She doesn't have many friends.

I solved my dilemma by deciding to take a very circuitous route to California to visit an ex-lover along the way. Obviously I couldn't impose on the ex-lover by bringing my colleague as well.

By the time I got up the nerve to tell my colleague that it wouldn't work out for her to drive with me, she'd forgotten that she even asked to come along!

**Esther Rothblum, Professor of
Women's Studies**

Sometimes we're so dead set against letting our friends down that we cook up a story to explain our unavailability. Concealing the real reason for a NO never feels good, but that's what we do to avoid disappointing them when we're convinced that the truth would hurt.

Sydney, a graduate student, couldn't bear to tell her roommate that she wanted to live alone. She was afraid he would walk out of her life for good if she told him it was time to get his own place to live.

Okay, so I've been trying to figure out a way to get rid of my room-mate Ethan for a really long time. He's a good friend, but I'm tired of sharing the space with him. The lease is in my name, and when Ethan moved in he promised he'd leave if I ever felt too crowded. It literally made me feel like puking when I thought about asking him to move. It's, like, really mean to tell a friend you're tired of living with him. But the problem is I can't lie.

So last week, I figured out what to do. Ethan cribs off my DSL for his work, and he can't live where he doesn't have DSL. So I cut the DSL cable and gave it to the dog to chew on. When he came home I showed him the chewed cable and said I couldn't afford to replace it for now. Ethan said he was sorry but he had to move out.

Sydney concocted this complex ruse because she couldn't convincingly out-and-out lie to Ethan or tell him how she really felt.

Sometimes we conceal the truth from our friends because talking about what's going on is simply too painful. At other times, we aren't confident they can keep a secret. Caroline was preparing to run for office when she found a breast lump that turned out to be malignant. Because she didn't want publicity, Caroline went out of her way to throw even her closest friends off track:

Five years ago I was diagnosed with breast cancer, and I made the decision to deal with it privately. I didn't want to be vulnerable at press conferences, and I didn't want my opponents to take advantage of me at a stressful time for me personally.

Other than my doctors, only three people knew about the cancer: my ex-husband, my sister, and my assistant who functions as my gatekeeper, all of whom I totally trust. I was treated at a well-known cancer hospital in another city, where I was admitted under an assumed name. I told my closest friends I was taking a break before gearing up for the campaign. I trust my friends, but I also realize how easy it is to slip up when you're trying to keep a secret.

Several times during the months I was in treatment, friends asked if they could visit. I had to make up a story about why I wasn't available. Obviously, I couldn't say, "I'm sorry I can't get together with you because I'm sick from chemo, and oh, by the way, I'm sorry I didn't tell you I'm having chemo," because they would be devastated that I hadn't told them about it.

DEVOTED PARENT

I admit, I use my kids as excuses all the time when I don't want to do something. Say a friend asks me to do something I just don't have the energy for. Instead of just saying that, I'm more apt to lie: "Oh, I wish I could, but Josh has a soccer game that day."

Laine, contractor

WHY SHE'S RELUCTANT TO TELL THE TRUTH:
I don't want my friends to stop asking me to do things, but I'm not always up for everything they invite me to. Having kids is a legitimate excuse that never hurts anyone's feelings. Everyone understands the importance of quality time with kids.

However tempting it is to disguise the truth when you're worried about what you stand to lose, it is often more satisfying to be honest. Being frank and open improves communication and strengthens the bonds between friends. The more straightforward you are, the more you and your friends can count on one another to tell it like it is.

Let's suppose your New Year's resolution is to be more forthright with your friends. How can you prepare to be more candid in your NOs?

Consider the following steps:

Step 1. Ask yourself what you're most afraid of losing.
Will your friend reject you if she or he is hurt? Might you be punished in some way? Could you be booted out of a friendship

circle? If the answer to any of these questions is YES, why do you suppose your friendship is so fragile? Is there a reason that this friend can't hear the truth? Does your friend want more from you than you're willing to give? Or is there a more deeply rooted reason for your friend's distress when she or he hears the word "NO"?

Step 2. Try putting yourself in your friend's shoes. Can you cope when this friend says NO to you?

When your friend is unavailable, would you rather listen to an elaborate overwrought tale that covers up the real reason for bowing out, or do you prefer a simple, "NO can do?" If you can handle a NO, consider the possibility that your friend may also be capable of an uncomplicated response when you decline. Or, perhaps this friend can grow with you as you become more comfortable saying NO.

Step 3. If your friend is psychologically healthy, find a good time to discuss your concerns.

All relationships are enhanced by open communication. Choose a relaxed time to raise your concern. Make sure there is no invitation or other request on the table. Explain your anxiety about saying NO, and ask your friend the best way to offer a genuine response.

A psychologically healthy friend will reassure you that you needn't walk on eggshells. She or he will point out that it isn't the end of the world when you say NO—you won't be punished, there will be no retaliation, and there will be other opportunities to say YES.

Step 4. If your friend is particularly thin-skinned and unlikely to let go of a NO, try to give an honest explanation, even if isn't the complete story.

Consider one of the following replies, as long as it's true:

Sorry, I can't.

I'm swamped.

I'm too pooped.

It's not a good time for me.

You know, I've made a commitment to do X, so I can't do Y at this point.

In the scenarios that follow, I suggest various ways to offer matter-of-fact explanations whenever you are trying for an amiable NO.

when you want to say NO, but worry about the consequences

It has always been difficult for me to say NO to friends when somebody I love or like a lot wants something and I don't want to do it. Since we're Cuban, I can say this: Cubans tend to feel free if you invite them over to dinner, to call up on that same day and say, "I ran into another friend that I would love you to meet. Is it okay if I bring her or him along?"

Vivian and I try to talk each other into calling back. We try to remember who was the "bad guy" the last time, and then we take turns. Whoever makes the call says things like, "It's too many people to fit around the table, or it's just too many people to handle as house guests." That's how we say NO.

Margarita Gandia, Board Co-chair,
National AIDS Memorial Grove

In any friendship there are times when your needs clash with a friend's wishes or expectations. If you're like most women, you're delighted to be invited but don't always care to participate. You enjoy being consulted, but not when it's inconvenient. You are happy to be in the inner circle of your friendship network—getting the dish on everyone else—but you like to be in control of your own secrets. And you feel lucky to have friends who look forward to seeing you, even though you don't necessarily choose to visit as often as they do.

How do you say NO to these pals without jeopardizing your relationship? Let's consider some typical scenarios and possible approaches.

1. Trying Times

There but for the grace of God . . .

What terrible misfortunes some people endure. Of course you want to help when your pals are having a hard time, but sometimes you wonder if you can take a break without damaging the friendship or feeling intolerably guilty.

When you are trying to juggle contradictory needs—yours and your friend's—see if you can come up with an alternative that works for everyone, at least to some extent. Ideally, you want to aim for a candid conversation with your friend in which you

---

CHARITABLE GIVING

My closest friend Lauren just finished chemo for lymphoma. She doesn't have very good odds, but she's doing everything she can to fight it. Lauren wants me to do the five-hundred-mile AIDS ride with her this fall.

My daughter just turned two, and I want to spend as much time with her as I can—especially since I recently went back to working full time. Also, I'm totally out of shape for a five-hundred-mile ride. I'd have to spend a lot of time training. I'd so much rather do it when my daughter is older and in school.

Elissa, marriage and family counselor

WHY SHE'S HAVING DIFFICULTY SAYING NO:
Duh! I could never say NO to Lauren. She may not be here by the time my daughter is old enough to go to school.

explain your dilemma. That gives the two of you an opportunity to try to figure out something else.

Lauren's friend Elissa (*"Charitable Giving"*) wants to spend time with her toddler and doesn't have time to train. Perhaps she could volunteer to go as support during all or part of the ride. Or suggest a less rigorous sporting event or other activity to benefit a charity they both care about—ideally one where her daughter could accompany them.

2. Stale Rituals

The party will never be the same without you!

Do you dread the approaching holidays because your friends expect you at their annual events? Have you fallen into gift-giving, card-sending traps that no longer mean anything to you? Have your friends already booked their weeklong stays at your home years in advance? What's the protocol for putting a stop to stale rituals?

Roll up the welcome mat? Leave town? Well, how about taking a year off to revamp your calendar?

NON, MERCI

Since my husband Ben and I live in the French Quarter, we always invite lots of friends to stay with us during Mardi Gras. In the last few years, we stopped looking forward to having a houseful of guests. Maybe we're getting older, I don't know.

Bernadette, physician

WHY SHE'S HAVING DIFFICULTY SAYING NO:
Our friends have already bought their airline tickets. As soon as this year's Mardi Gras is over, they're making plans for the next.

You'll need to plan at least two years in advance to get out of an annual event. Be sure to sow the seeds before this year's get-together, and when your visitors show up, remind them that next year is off. After your "holiday" from the annual event has come and gone, consider how you'd like to celebrate in future years (if at all), and inform the regulars of your decision.

In *"Non, Merci,"* Bernadette might say: "Ben and I have decided to travel during Mardi Gras next year. We think that we'd like to change things up a bit. If we're at home for Mardi Gras in the future, we may just have a small celebration or not do it at all. So let's look for another opportunity to visit. Maybe we can even come your way, or meet you someplace in between."

3. "I . . . I . . . I . . . me . . . me . . . me"

These are the friends who can't share the stage and can't stop talking. Every sentence begins with "I." Sure they're entertaining—in small doses. But sometimes you just miss the sound of silence or your own voice.

PUNCTUATION, PLEASE!

My dear friend Alison is a jet-setting script writer who hangs out with all sorts of celebrities. I love hearing the stories of the people she meets, and Alison's got a great sense of humor. She's a bit full of herself—who wouldn't be in her position—but she never pauses long enough for me to get a word in. It's as if she's had twenty cups of coffee.

Zoey, English professor

WHY SHE'S HAVING DIFFICULTY SETTING LIMITS:
I end up accommodating her a lot, because she's one of those in-demand people who'd probably delete me from her friendship network if I tried to direct the conversation.

Even if you're not an English professor like Zoey in *"Punctuation, Please,"* it's exhausting to have friends whose sentences run on and on. To impose limits, you must establish parameters at the outset. "I'd love to meet you for lunch—you pick the time and place. Great, that works for me, but I have a two o'clock meeting so we'll have to stop by one thirty." Or in a phone call, "I'm happy to hear from you. Listen, I need to let you know that I have to be off the phone by five thirty, so let's talk quickly."

To move it from a monologue to a dialogue, interrupt. Insert your own story or bring up something you'd like to talk about. To end a conversation, be emphatic: "I'm SO SORRY to interrupt but they're paging me for something urgent," or "One of the kids is crying," or "Oh, no—it's already time for me to go! Let's talk again soon!" Polite diversions don't work with the resolute chatterer. Plan your exit strategy in advance, execute with energy, and try to make it an authentic excuse.

4. Quid Pro Quo, Quo, Quo

How can I ever repay you?

You feel eternally grateful to friends who help you through a rough patch. Of course you want to reciprocate. But when is enough enough? When can you say NO in good conscience?

Briana, a stay-at-home mom, had a hard time when her son decided to marry a woman who isn't Jewish. Briana's rabbi connected her with Abby, another woman in their congregation, who'd gone through something similar:

Abby was extremely helpful to me because she'd had the same experience when her daughter married a Libyan guy. Abby met me for coffee every week just so I could talk about everything I was feeling.

Then Abby's husband left her a few years ago and she turned to me for support. Though she wasn't that close a friend at the time, it was the least I could do. Since then, Abby wants to spend all her free time with me. She's gotten into the habit of calling around dinner to see what I'm cooking, and then I feel like I should invite her to join us, because she always talks about how hard it is to eat alone.

Sometimes I avoid answering the phone because I don't want to deal with her.

Resentments don't bode well for friendships. If your gut tells you that you've made good on a debt to a friend, it's probably time to shift into a more reciprocal mode.

Though Abby's kindness was repaid long ago, Briana hasn't been able to set limits with her. Caller ID could come in handy here. If Briana didn't answer the phone during the dinner hour, she could still invite Abby to join them, when it was convenient. Briana could also return Abby's calls at a more relaxed time, to wean Abby from the expectation of an immediate response.

5. Love Me, Love My Mate

We'd love you to join us for . . .

Your favorite sidekick believes she has finally found the perfect match. As you see it, the man or woman of your friend's dreams is a complete nightmare. How do you say NO to invitations that now include the new mate?

Your best bet when you despise a friend's partner is to avoid complete candor. Instead of issuing a proclamation that could potentially injure the friendship, see if you can engineer more one-on-one time with your pal.

Try a straightforward statement: "I miss spending time with you alone. Would you be up for just the two of us getting together like we used to?"

Then maybe you could schedule a date for the two of you every other time you meet. If that works out, your follow-up can be: "I really love the time we spend together when neither of us brings anyone else. It gives us a chance to talk more intimately." If all goes well, eventually you will be able to state your preferences without worrying about offending anyone.

> ## TWO'S COMPANY, THREE'S A CROWD
>
> Lexie and I have been best friends ever since we were internal medicine residents together. We used to spend all our vacations and holidays together. We were pretty much joined at the hip. Whenever one of us was involved with someone, we all hung out together, and it worked because everyone liked everyone else.
>
> A couple of years ago, Lexie caught the baby bug. She decided she needed to be pregnant before her thirty-sixth birthday. She met this guy at Starbucks who is basically a big dreamer and total bullshitter—unemployed and looking for funding to start his own business—and she ignored everyone's advice and married him! Mark's happy to be a stay-at-home dad while she works her butt off in academic medicine.
>
> Here's my problem with the situation: I don't want to hang out with them, because Mark drives me nuts. He's one of those in-your-face guys who expresses his insecurity by being very argumentative and know-it-all-ish. Lexie doesn't even ask, she just brings him whenever we get together.
>
> *Vera, physician*
>
> WHY SHE'S HAVING DIFFICULTY SAYING NO:
> I'd never tell my best friend that I can't stand her husband. Then she'd be forced to choose between us.

6. Relentless Badgering

Of course you want to. Don't you realize how much fun you're going to have?

If you don't stand your ground with friends who are accustomed to getting what they want, they'll steamroll you.

Whether their arm twisting is in seriousness or in jest, these pals love a good tussle. Forceful friends are comfortable get-

NO KIDDING?!

Two hours before some of my girlfriends from the Garden Club were supposed to come over for lunch, my neighbor Dixie called to make sure I'd gotten the warning about the sewer repair.

She said: "Hon, you wrapped your toilets with Saran wrap today, didn't you?" I told her I didn't know what she was talking about.

"Dear God, sweetie, didn't you get that flyer from the sewage commissioner? They're flushing the sewer lines in our neighborhood today and there could be a back-up of toxic fumes—or God knows what else. We are supposed to cover our toilets with Saran wrap, and put plastic on the floor around the toilets, just in case."

I asked what I was supposed to do if somebody needed to use the toilet.

"Sweetie, they set up Porta-Johns on practically every corner. You obviously haven't been outside today, 'cause you can't miss them. Listen, I have to make one phone call and then I'll come over and help you wrap."

The whole thing sounded bizarre. I looked out my upstairs window. I couldn't see any workers or Porta-Johns. If Dixie hadn't insisted, I probably would have closed the bathroom doors and taken my chances.

By the time she arrived, I'd covered each toilet. Dixie asked to see one to make sure I'd done it properly. When we walked into the downstairs bathroom, she burst out laughing, practically collapsing onto the floor. She'd made the whole thing up!

Cathy Lee, homemaker

WHY SHE DIDN'T SAY NO:
That would have seemed so rude. I mean, essentially I'd be calling her a liar. I could never do that.

ting in your face in a way that may really put you off. Your only chance of having a say is to be as persistent as they are.

You might want to take advantage of this opportunity to practice your most adamant NO. Nothing is more stimulating to insistent friends than the challenge of circumventing a roadblock. They're not likely to take your NO personally, because they plan to ignore it anyway.

So when badgering friends pressure you to do something you don't want to do, use your most resolute NO. They can handle it, and you'll find the practice helpful for other situations in which you're struggling to express your wishes and, once you do, to stand firm.

7. Special Dispensation

I hate to ask but . . .

When a long-suffering friend asks for something that's outside your comfort zone, can you say NO in good conscience?

Let's look at a common scenario.

Five years ago, Francisca, an accountant, was pregnant when her husband lost his job. About six months later, he was hit by a car when he was riding his bike, and he hasn't had a job since. On three different occasions, Francisca asked her friend Carla for a loan. It was a sticky situation for Carla.

Of course I loaned Francisca the money each time, even though she hasn't paid any of it back. I worry that these loans have driven a wedge between the two of us. I feel more frustrated with her husband than Francisca, because he hasn't made much effort to get a job.

Loaning money to friends is complicated, because friendships often don't survive the failure to repay a debt. People feel embarrassed when they have to ask for money, and they can become resentful if you ask for your money back. They probably wouldn't have asked you in the first place if they didn't think you could afford it, and they feel humiliated when they have to justify their needs all over again.

If you want to help a pal who's having a financial problem, and you don't want to lose the friendship over an unpaid loan, here's what I suggest. First, write up an agreement that specifies the loan amount, interest to be paid (if any), and terms of repayment. Second, hand over the funds and forget about them. Make a private decision to consider the money a gift. If things work out, your friend will pay you back. If not, pat yourself on the back for helping your friend during a difficult time, and let it go. Also, prepare your NO in case you are asked for more and you have reached your limit.

When Carla said that she wasn't able to offer more financial assistance, Francisca asked for a letter of recommendation.

Last night, Francisca called to ask me to write her husband a letter of reference for a job he's applying for. She was hoping I could fudge and say he'd worked for me in the past. Now I feel even more on the spot.

What's the equation here—the friendship versus Carla's integrity? Let's try for a solution where Carla holds onto both.

Since Francisca's request compromises Carla's credibility and principles, Carla could express sympathy for Francisca's dilemma as she draws the line: "I know you're in a bind and you could certainly use a second income to support your family. But I don't feel comfortable saying your husband worked for me when he didn't. I'd rather he ask his former employers for references." If, instead of accepting the refusal, Francisca persists and asks Carla to write a character reference for her husband, Carla may feel cornered.

Before agreeing to something you find objectionable, try to buy time. "Let me give this some thought and I will get back to you." Consider your options. Consult with others you trust about possible responses.

Here, Carla may decide that writing the character reference is preferable to disappointing her friend. Or, she may feel that the friendship can sustain a NO. In that case, it's best to keep it simple: "I'm sorry. I just don't think I'm the best person to write a letter for your husband." If your friend asks for reasons, just stay on message and repeat yourself. "I'm really not the right person for this." Sometimes explanations can ease the pain, but too much information can also be perceived as adding insult to injury.

> *I once lost a good friend because I said YES and then I said NO. It's much more hurtful and harmful when somebody's asking you for something to say YES and then NO. If you have any inkling you're going to say NO, then say it in the beginning. Otherwise, people doubt your integrity. If you say, "NO, I don't think I can, but if things change I'll let you know," and then things do change, they're delighted. But the reverse never applies.*
>
> *I have a house that I rent out that was available when a friend of mine was looking for a place to live. She needed a greatly reduced rent, and I felt bad for her, so I said YES. Afterwards, I had a talk with [another] friend who's very business-savvy, who advised that this wouldn't be a good idea down the road. I heeded his warning, went back and said NO to my friend, and that ended the friendship. It was quite a loss, and still is.*
>
> *I learned from an old friend, when people are coming to you for whatever and you know it's going to be draining you financially or emotionally, or time-wise or energy-wise, the best thing to do is to establish your boundaries and tell them what you will do for them. And then when they want more, you can say, "Well, I told you this is what I'm doing."*
>
> **Stephanie Zimbalist, actor**

8. Broken Record

I know I've said this before, but this time it's different.

Enough already! These friends don't seem to get it that the same old drama is driving you nuts. You understand why it's difficult for them to dump the dude or ditch the job, but they just can't seem to make it happen. Whenever you try to change the subject, they find a way back to it. Can you set limits without seeming uninterested in the focal point of their lives?

STAGE MOTHER

I love kids. I have two of my own. What parent doesn't like to tell stories about their kids' greatest accomplishments? But my friend Aileen is over the top. She wants her daughter to make it on Broadway. The kid's not that talented. She's mainly a tap dancer, but she takes ballet and music lessons and acting classes, and that's pretty difficult on Aileen's meager salary. Aileen takes her from audition to audition, and I hear about every one—what she wears, what she sings. Aileen can't stop talking about it—it's like an obsession for her.

Brenda, teacher

WHY SHE HAS DIFFICULTY SETTING LIMITS:
Believe me: I recognize the syndrome of parents who live vicariously through their kids. Trust me, these people don't appreciate it if you point it out to them.

If you tell a friend he or she is boring, boring, boring, that's sure to end the friendship. I suggest a different approach: make your interactions more activity-based than conversation-based. How about a film? You could meet at the movies and grab a cup of coffee afterwards. Discuss the film as long as possible.

And when the friend starts in on his or her favorite topic, interrupt periodically with questions or diversions: "So what's going on in the rest of your life?" "Tell me about you ... your job ..." "Hey, I've been meaning to ask you, what do you think about ..." "Oh, I've been meaning to tell you ... (something about you!)" It's more work for you, but hey—the conversation will be a lot more interesting if you bump it out of the familiar rut.

9. Passive Aggressive

You can absolutely count me in—I'm down with that and I'll be there.

These pals are good on promises, poor on follow-through, and rarely straightforward. How long do you tolerate it before you realize it's time to put the friendship on a more even keel?

You know that a friendship is sadly out of balance when you're constantly in the giving and waiting position, and you feel like you've been putting up with your friend's excuses far too long. It's hard to admit that this friend is just not there for you, so for a time, you allow extra latitude.

Eventually, you reach your limit. You realize that whatever you're hoping for is either unlikely to materialize, or not worth the frustration of being put on indefinite hold. You'll feel better

---

PROMISES, PROMISES

I invited my friend Barbara to co-chair a benefit for foster care. I explained the various responsibilities, and Barbara said she was thrilled to do it. Barbara is a partner in a corporate law firm, and she said that her firm would underwrite the event.

I prepared the event announcement with Barbara's name and firm at the top. Then all of a sudden, Barbara started cancelling meetings at the last minute, and once she didn't even show. When I reached her afterwards, she'd say the firm was for sure committed, sorry she was so out of touch, she's just swamped with a case. Guess what? She didn't show at the event and the firm's check never arrived.

Monica, headhunter

WHY SHE COULDN'T SET LIMITS:
Barbara is—or should I say "was"—my friend. Frankly, I wanted to use the firm's name and I needed their money.

---

if you communicate your disappointment directly, even if your friend's response is a litany of justifications.

Monica (*"Promises, Promises"*) was reluctant to call Barbara on her broken promises, because Monica didn't want to jeopardize the firm's underwriting of her event. When it became apparent that Barbara and her firm were no-shows, Monica had little to lose by speaking her mind.

At what point do you give up on a passive-aggressive friend? My advice: three last-minute cancellations or missed deadlines without a clear apology and a credible excuse, and this friend is out the door. How can you trust this person again after a series of disrespectful incidents? You don't have to take a hit to your self-esteem just because he or she is unable to be more direct with you and say NO.

10. No Reciprocity

When they drain and don't sustain.

Who would have thought that having a lot of friends could be a hardship? When you're fun to party with, everyone wants to be your pal. But it's problematic if they always show up empty-handed.

Samantha, an engineer, decided when she turned thirty-five that it was time to get rid of two-thirds of her friends, because she couldn't say NO to any of them.

I had about thirty friends—I mean, I'm a pretty energetic, likeable person—but I'd say only about seven of them were the fill-up-your-tank kind, and the rest were like sponges. You know the type—you get together with them, they kvetch, they whine—you leave feeling completely drained.

Of course the sponges are the ones who book you up months in advance, so your calendar is full of dates with these depressing people. There you are at the end of the month, totally drained, on the path to becoming a sponge yourself! Anyway, I made a decision:

ditch the sponges. The problem was figuring out how to do it without lying or being mean or hurting their feelings. After giving it a lot of thought, I came up with a super plan that totally worked. I decided to run a marathon. So when the sponges called to ask me to do something, I explained that I was training for a marathon, and couldn't get together unless they could meet me at the track and run five miles with me. That did it! They stopped calling.

When you're feeling dragged down by friends who don't give back, it might be time to reallocate your energy. First you must decide if you'd rather discontinue the friendship or see the friends less frequently. Culling the best and dumping the rest is tricky. How do you make the cuts without being hurtful?

Samantha's strategy made it seem as though her friends had dropped her, rather than the other way around. And she got in shape, to boot!

It's sometimes easier to lie than to come up with an honest excuse, but an all-purpose truthful response has a longer shelf life: "You know, I realize that I never schedule enough time for myself. Instead of getting together this month, let's book a date next month (or later)."

Nobody can argue with the need for self-care in our all-consuming world. As you expand the intervals between visits, your nonreciprocal friends may look elsewhere for support. You may appreciate them more if they're less dependent on you. Or you may decide that your life is more enjoyable without them.

All in all, friendships are more fulfilling when we can comfortably set limits. But most women hesitate to express our preferences until we're pretty sure our pals can handle a NO and we can cope with their unhappiness when we do. The more confident we are in a friendship, the less elaborate our explanations need to be. Between trusted old pals, "I'm so sorry, but I just can't" is acceptable and probably won't ruffle a feather. Communication is so much simpler with those we NO well.

chapter five

opportunity . . . NOts

(when saying NO at work doesn't

work for you)

*Hiring people is very difficult for me. I've been so bad at it
that I've stopped doing it. I get others to refer people to me,
because my judgment is so bad.*

*Once I hired someone who just basically had a list of
things she wanted me to do for her. Another person I hired
put mail in bags and hid them. And then got sober and
came back and did her amends and brought me the mail.
It was two years old by that time.*

*I am better at hiring plumbers and electricians and
people like that. I don't have a problem saying NO to those
people—possibly because I came from a class of people
who were those people.*

Dorothy Allison, author

Are you inclined to pamper or indulge your employees? Do you
hesitate to comment on poor performance? Do you speak up or
do you keep it to yourself when co-workers fail to do their part?
Can you say NO to your boss, when you really need to, without
losing your job? Are you able to fire an employee whose skills
aren't up to par or whose behavior is reprehensible?

The ability to say NO in the workplace is a function of two elements—personality and power. If you are comfortable expressing your preferences and you are authorized to do so, establishing boundaries and setting limits may be easy for you. But when you're not in charge, or your job security is linked to your willingness to do whatever is asked or expected, you have to choose your NOs carefully. Even if you have the power to determine policy and to make or enforce rules, sometimes you may decide to back off—by going easy on an employee who has a sick relative, or by taking a cut in your own pay to avoid layoffs—because that's the considerate or compassionate thing to do.

I informally surveyed my female friends and colleagues about the most difficult or complicated NO they'd faced as employers, employees, or co-workers. I asked each woman to tell me how her style of setting limits has evolved by specifically considering two questions: (1) Have your experiences as an employee (i.e., a subordinate on the career ladder) influenced your own management style? (2) When you are in charge, what personal issues help or hinder your ability to be assertive?

Some women told me that they learned to say NO when their employers treated them unfairly or abusively. In a few instances, women wanted to say NO, but felt powerless to preserve their jobs or careers if they did so. Women who said NO as employers remarked at the different kind of angst it brought up: they recognized the need to set boundaries and struggled to figure out where, when, and how to draw the lines without losing rapport with their employees or damaging their overall morale.

saying NO as an employee

Childhood experiences can have a profound impact on your response to injustice in the workplace. A well known British film star hired my friend Lucy as his personal assistant. When he became abusive, it seemed familiar to her because she had grown up with violence: ·

OK, so this was a really big deal for me to be working for X. I mean, he's one of the biggest names in film. He was so-o-o nice to me at first. I wanted to do a good job, so I worked really hard. Like, when he'd call me in the middle of the night having a panic attack, I'd go to his house and massage him and hold his cigarettes for him.

But his being nice to me didn't last long. He was f——ing nuts! I'm from a really screwed up family and I've been smacked around plenty. I thought, "Here I go again." He abused the shit out of me. I don't even wanna repeat some of the things he said and did to me.

Not only that, but he had a lot of guns, and that was really scary.

The decision to leave was complicated by fear for her own safety.

Well, it took me more than a year to get up the nerve. I had to think about it really hard 'cause I was gonna be on the street without a job. But I realized I was different from every other chick he met—I didn't wanna sleep with him and I didn't wanna be an actress. If I told him to stop, he was either going to shoot me or fire me, and either way, I'll be better off.

Well, X was having this meeting. He told me to serve tea. I brought it in, polite as always, "Here you are, sir." He started screaming it wasn't hot enough. I'd made up my mind I wasn't going to take one more insult. Before I knew it, I picked up his cup and poured it in his lap. "Get your own damned tea," I said, and walked out of the room.

If she had it to do all over, would she have said NO earlier or gotten out quicker? Probably not. Lucy describes the experience as one of life's lessons. She needed to put together the jigsaw pieces of being abused as a child with being mistreated as an employee. This helped her figure out that she had a choice—even though the choice felt life-threatening. Lucy couldn't imagine short-circuiting a process that taught her she had a right to set limits. "Now I don't take shit from anyone," she says.

Quitting when the boss becomes abusive frequently seems

out of the question for women who are supporting children. My colleague Beverly was a year from completing her training when a supervisor began sexually harassing her. "He'd say, 'Hey Black Beauty: Here's my credit card. Go rent us a room.'" She was afraid to ask for another supervisor. "I didn't say NO. I just turned away when he shoved that credit card in my face, trying to do the best work I could, never responding to that degradation." Beverly rode home on the bus each night in tears, and she developed asthma and a skin rash that wouldn't go away. "I kept showing up each morning because I was trying to make a better life for my kids. I grew up on welfare so there was no way I was going back to that."

Beverly sometimes regrets her decision to stay. If her children ever found themselves in a similar circumstance, she'd advise them to quit. "That's what I've done with my anger—I have taught them how to be respectful and I have prepared them to fight injustice." She feels lucky to be self-employed and independent now. Nevertheless, many years later, the training incident still smarts: "I hope that guy gets his karmic retribution in this lifetime!"

Paradoxically, career-boosting opportunities can reduce our negotiating power. To avoid a NO from someone who can help us, we sometimes remain silent when we disagree. Isabelle, a sculptor, was raised in an upper-class family in El Salvador. Her big break came when she was invited by a prominent Miami gallery to participate in a special exhibit on Central American artists. The curator offered Isabelle an exclusive contract with the gallery. If she agreed, she could no longer sell to her private clients without the gallery taking a percentage.

You know, this was my dream! I have to be honest with you. I want to be famous! I know I am going to be famous. I mean, I already have so many people who love my work, and I didn't want them to pay more for it because the gallery has an exclusive contract. And I have to tell you, I went in to tell them I couldn't sign the contract, and I thought I would have a heart attack, because I'm so afraid they wouldn't use me if I didn't sign the contract. So I signed the contract.

When Isabelle examined her reluctance to negotiate about the exclusivity, she had to acknowledge that the income from the gallery sales made it possible for her to quit her day job and sculpt full-time. She decided to postpone the contract renegotiation until she had saved enough to go solo. "I mean, I know I can do it, and I'm going to do it soon," Isabelle said, "but I'm just a little bit afraid still."

Lucy, Beverly, and Isabelle describe themselves as self-confident women who felt unable to say NO to their employers because of the potential consequences. Being subordinate clearly limits options. Sometimes saying NO can get you fired or deprive you of opportunities. Yet, knowing that you have a choice makes you feel more in control—even when you're dealt a rotten hand. Lucy took a big risk in stopping X's abuse; to her surprise, X didn't shoot her. Beverly knew several trainees who'd quit when they were harassed, but they weren't parents. When Isabelle has a large enough clientele, she plans to renegotiate her contract, or, failing that, to leave the gallery.

Few people are able to say NO to superiors at work when the potential consequences seem unacceptable. By remaining silent, we hope to avoid:

> Career limitations
> Economic downgrades
> Family hardships
> Unemployment.

In a time-limited situation, such as an internship or training period, the immediate or anticipated benefits of acquiescing are sometimes worth a sacrifice. But if you find yourself repeatedly relinquishing your best interests over the long term, you need to take a hard look at why. It's crucial to draw the line at serious abuse or exploitation—which can have lasting hurtful effects on you.

saying NO as a co-worker

Women define ourselves in terms of relationships and connection. We bring qualities of sensitivity and thoughtfulness to the workplace. We keep track of co-workers' birthdays and plan the holiday parties. We collect for the retirement gifts and charity funds. We buy baby gifts when co-workers are expecting and condolence cards when their family members pass away. In so many ways, we reach out to make our work environments more like communities, less alienating.

At other times we feel stuck—we'd like to say NO, but we worry about the fallout. We drag spouses or families to work functions we'd rather skip. We wrack our brains for a delicate way to handle associates who want to befriend us or collaborate with us when we don't want to. And sometimes we overextend ourselves when saying NO would mean that women like us wouldn't be represented on a panel or committee.

Jean, an anthropology professor, believes that she is asked to serve on many academic committees out of tokenism. "It's two birds in the hand with me: a woman and a person of color." Yet saying NO means that some committees might not be as thoughtful about race, class, sexual orientation, or other issues of diversity:

Heck, I have a committee meeting every night of the week. I don't get promoted based on the number of meetings I go to, but I hate letting those boys meet on their own, if you know what I mean. There's no telling how much damage they can do.

Jean also does more than her share when collaborating with other academics. Rather than missing a deadline because of others' excuses, she prefers to do the work herself:

I can't send a substandard manuscript out the door, yet some of my research associates are, quite frankly, flakes. Earlier in my career, I'd sit those people down and have a heart-to-heart about why they weren't doing what they were supposed to do. Then I'd get all caught up in whatever their personal issues were and, you know, at some point I realized I probably could have finished the entire project myself by then. Just going ahead and doing it is my way of saying NO to dealing with all their personal stuff.

Now, whenever I agree to work with someone, I know I could very well end up doing most of it myself. But that's a lot simpler than dealing with excuses, asking them to step down, or turning out a piece of junk.

Saying NO to a fellow employee also raises concerns about not being a team player. Dana, a biotechnologist, has a hard time saying NO to so-called "optional" meetings:

Nobody thinks twice about men skipping out on bag lunches, but I worry about the message it gives if I don't show up. For women in our business, attendance is equated with enthusiasm. If we're not present, it's assumed that we have some personal issue or priority—like a family—that we care more about than our jobs. If one of the guys doesn't show, he must be working on something important.

Our relationships and families are important to us—sometimes more important than our jobs. Saying YES to an optional lunch meeting means less time to check on the kids, organize the car pool, or speak with an ailing parent, but for many women, a no-show is just too risky.

Women sometimes end up doing double duty on the job because of the tacit expectation that we're there to provide personal support as well as professional expertise. It's not easy to shut out distress signals when our colleagues are needy or hurting, though "social worker" or "shrink" is not part of the job description. As Dana says:

I'm a highly skilled and well paid technologist, but I do a lot of on-the-job hand-holding: I'm a cheerleader for the project, a shrink during the divorce, a stroker of fragile egos, a shoulder to cry on. In many instances, I'd rather duck out and get home to my kids sooner, but, I figure, I work with these people sixty hours a week, and there's just a certain amount of give-and-take that goes into creating a positive work environment.

Lacey, a researcher, has ten-year-old twin girls. She has become a de facto expert on parenting for three other colleagues with younger sets of twins:

It seems like everyone is having twins these days—probably because of assisted reproductive technology. I work with two women and one guy who also have twins, and they often pop into my office to get my take on things or ask for advice. Like yesterday, one mom spent an hour talking about private schools for her boys, and the father of two-year-old girls was asking last week how I deal with competition between my girls. I'm happy to share my experiences, but I'm always behind in my work.

In theory, hanging the "DO-NOT-DISTURB-ME-WITH-YOUR-PERSONAL-ISSUES" sign on the office door would be tough. It might seem disloyal, harsh, or hard-nosed. We worry about resentments—losing a sense of camaraderie. What if we're having a crisis? Who will cover for us when our kids are sick? We believe in "paying it forward" . . . doing unto others . . .

As co-workers, we say YES more often than we'd like for so many reasons: to advance careers, to show commitment, to be team players, to be charitable, to be kind, to be liked, to show compassion, to preserve relationships, to demonstrate loyalty, and to be represented. Such choices involve contributions of energy and sacrifices of time. We don't feel good about ourselves if we refuse to help out, but sometimes, if we want to leave at a reasonable hour, we need to cut down on the caretaking and focus on our own work.

saying NO as an employer

> *I had a nanny I wanted to fire, but just didn't have the
> guts. I thought of just leaving her the kids, the house, my
> husband, rather than explain to her I wanted her to get
> out. So I told her I was leaving my husband, giving him
> the kids, and he didn't want a nanny, so she had to go. She
> believed me! She was quite amazed, was sorry to hear our
> marriage was on the rocks and that I was giving up the
> kids, but of course she left.*
>
> *I could of course have done something subtler, like burn
> the house to the ground or move to another state. It's utterly
> amazing, in retrospect, the lengths to which one will go,
> rather than say the dreaded word NO.*
>
> **Danielle Steel, author**

My friend Marny is an accomplished psychotherapist who specializes in helping people set limits. She lives in a state of (to her)
organized chaos—a living room strewn with printouts, notes,
and clippings, a refrigerator full of old take-out food, dirty laundry nesting wherever it lands. Household maintenance isn't
important to her, but she wanted someone to handle the basics.
So she hired Gisela, "the queen of organization" to pay the bills,
deposit checks, and run errands.

As it turned out, Gisela paid Marny's bills, and also a few of
her own—with Marny's credit cards. One day Marny opened a
Visa statement with several large charges from Macy's. She mentioned it to Gisela, a spiritual person who purportedly valued
"integrity," who admitted she'd been using Marny's credit cards to
pay for her own food and clothing. Marny was taken aback—both
by Gisela's larceny and her admission of guilt. She told Gisela that
she needed some time to think about what to do. She hated the
idea of disciplining Gisela, because overall, Gisela had been a terrific employee. Marny's friends thought she was nuts.

A week later, Marny asked for Gisela's input. "I think you should fire me," said Gisela. Reluctantly, Marny let her go.

Another friend of mine, Lisa, is an incredibly busy ob-gyn and single mother of three, who hired an assistant to market the software programs she developed:

I interviewed several candidates and ended up hiring Florence, this sweet, middle-aged woman. She had previously done public affairs for an animal rescue group I support. Her dog had just died, and she was planning to adopt another. Her references commented on her integrity, punctuality, and reliability.

Florence's first day on the job seemed to be going smoothly until I picked up my telephone messages. Many of the names she'd written were missing critical vowels, and the phone numbers she'd copied had only three or four digits. It turned out that she was hearing-impaired and dyslexic. She hadn't worked the phones at previous jobs, so her employers never knew. Florence assured me, tearfully, that she would try harder to be accurate.

Earnestness, tearfulness, and a dead dog—what better qualifications for employment in my office? Basically, we did a re-org—changing her responsibilities to things she could handle, and I hired someone else to do the marketing. Florence is always willing to house- and dog-sit when I'm gone, so I found a way to make it work for me.

Marny's and Lisa's predicaments are not all that unusual. Many of us dislike being employers, but we need help to run our businesses. We hope our generosity will be matched by honesty and loyalty on the part of our employees. If we find disciplining adults difficult or distasteful, we may be overly lenient with those whose work is unsatisfactory. And some of us—I am a prime example—are so accustomed to being caregivers that we find it hard to switch roles when we're in charge.

When I went to medical school, I figured out pretty quickly that you can get a really bad reputation by saying NO to a superior. To be successful in medicine, it's best to be compliant—however purposeless an assignment might be. Dodging even the most trivial task is tantamount to saying "I don't care about patients, or saving lives, or human welfare." I witnessed so many senior physicians exploiting and demeaning the staff—screaming at nurses, throwing instruments in the operating room—that I couldn't wait to be my own boss. I resolved never to allow mistreatment of subordinates if I had the power to prevent it.

When it was my turn to give orders, I chose a less dictatorial style—punctuating requests with "please, when it's convenient . . . thank you!" What I hadn't counted on, once I became a psychotherapist, was the liability of being a huge magnet for people in pain. Forlorn folks are drawn to me, and sometimes, compassion clouds my judgment.

My first assistant was a very efficient self-starter. She kept things running smoothly for a year or so before succumbing to mental illness. One day, as I entered her office, I noticed boxes of baking soda near the computer, fax, and copier. Each box had a skull and crossbones drawn on it.

"What's with the baking soda?" I asked.

Cautioning me not to touch the boxes, she explained that they soaked up radiation emitted by the office equipment.

Over the next few months, she became progressively delusional. I got her a good shrink, but I didn't have the heart to fire her, because I know how incapacitating mental illness can be. With her doctor's help, this employee acknowledged that she was no longer able to do the job. Subsequently, she resigned and admitted herself to a psychiatric hospital. I felt good that I had not let her go before she was ready, and she appreciated my support.

Suyin, an internist in a women's medical practice, believes that most female healthcare professionals have a hard time terminating psychologically impaired employees because it's our calling to relieve suffering. At one time, Suyin and her partners met as a group to interview each job applicant. Eventually the partners realized that their hiring strategy had brought them so many high-maintenance and problematic employees that a single physician could probably screen just as poorly.

Suyin told the story of a receptionist who was a nightmare from day one. Her attendance was poor, and she had many personal crises during busy clinic sessions. The docs in Suyin's group would have continued to accommodate the troublesome receptionist if a patient had not recognized her as a thief and blown the whistle:

A patient flipped out when she saw this woman behind the desk. Apparently our receptionist had stolen thousands of dollars through social security numbers at the hospital where she used to work. We did some checking, and it was true. That hospital never had enough evidence to arrest her. They also never mentioned it when we checked her references.

Still, firing the receptionist wasn't easy. "We drew straws because nobody wanted to be the one to do it." said Suyin.

I relate to this head-in-the-sand approach. The first time I terminated an employee—twenty years ago—I obsessed about it for weeks before asking him to leave.

When my spouse Dee was a medical intern and I was a young Harvard professor, we rarely had time to prepare meals, so we hired a cook. Although the first few meals were edible, we soon realized that we'd made a terrible mistake. The guy had no sense of taste (how could he—smoking two packs per day?) and no talent for seasoning. Did we complain? Of course not. We ate out.

When he asked for a raise, our friends said unequivocally, "Fire him! You've been *ripped off!*" They presented us with a mock "WANTED" poster with the cook's photo on it—hoping to nudge us into dumping him.

We hesitated. The problem was that we felt sorry for him. His cooking sucked, he couldn't find a lover, and he had poor social skills. We didn't want to give him a raise because he didn't deserve it, but we dreaded causing him more heartache by firing him. He was a sweet guy with a sense of humor—something I appreciate.

Nevertheless, we decided to let him go—and to tell him together. As Dee and I explained that we no longer needed a cook, tears welled up in his eyes. Watching him remove our house key from his keychain and walk out the door felt like breaking up with a lover.

To my surprise, by the next morning, I was relieved that the cook was gone. I'd always dreaded hearing about his failed love affairs when I returned home at night. I realized that it was a mistake to have allowed my emotional resources to be depleted by someone we had hired to make our lives easier.

Many women can relate to these struggles to set limits with employees. We worry about what's fair and appropriate. We don't want to be demanding, micromanaging, inconsiderate, or oppressive, because we know how it feels to be at the receiving end of such behavior. We try to be thoughtful so that we can get the job done in a mutually respectful atmosphere. But sometimes we need to say NO, and here are some examples of how to do it.

when the pain ain't worth the gain

It's possible to avoid saying NO at work almost indefinitely—as long as the benefits (feeling good about your generosity; maintaining your self-image; holding onto economic security; advancing your career; steering clear of resentments; being a team player) are greater than the sacrifices you make. Inevitably, with the passage of time, your needs shift, and you're forced to change your priorities. You may find that you're more frustrated, impatient, or angry at employees who take advantage of you. Or you have an elderly parent who is ill and asks for more attention. Or a teenage child who is acting out and requires more supervision. Or a new lover. Or a book to write.

So how do you prepare to set limits?

Here's what I recommend:

Step 1. Seek the advice of neutral, uninvolved parties

It is always important to hear other perspectives when you're trying to make a change. Friends who have had similar problems can
share strategies that worked for them or help you role-play conversations that you have been avoiding. The more practice you
have speaking up in a nonthreatening environment, the easier it is
to talk when you're face to face with the person you need to confront. The practice session gives you the chance to hear the kind of
reactions or arguments you may encounter. Afterwards, you can
discuss which of your points were most persuasive and effective.
Be sure to switch roles so you have a chance to play both parts.

When I was trying to decide how to deal with my delusional
employee, I spoke with several friends who were also therapists.
They thought it would be a bad idea to suggest a medical leave
when her world was falling apart and she wasn't getting treatment. They urged me to find her a psychiatrist before she dete-
riorated further. I did, and it was a big relief to both of us.

Step 2. Form a women's support group

Rarely are you the only one who is having trouble setting limits
at work. See if you can interest trusted colleagues or co-workers
in a regularly scheduled gathering to discuss relevant topics: How
can the work environment be improved? What is the best way to
handle disagreements on the job? What prevents employees from
saying NO when they need to? How can co-workers support each
other around inequities in the workplace? Establish guidelines
concerning confidentiality (nothing you say to each other leaves
the room). Invite outside speakers to address common concerns.

My friend Jean, the anthropology professor, organized
monthly potlucks for minority women faculty. Because there
were so few women of color on the faculty, it seemed impossible
to avoid being overcommitted until they were able to bring more
diversity to the university. But after several women experienced

early burnout, they hired a consultant who helped them establish guidelines for taking time off and taking better care of themselves so they'd be around long enough to achieve their goals.

Step 3. Enroll in a women's empowerment course
Among the many assertiveness-training opportunities, self-defense courses (see Chapter 9) are top-of-the-line confidence boosters. They teach you how to pack every NO with maximum power.

Several years after she was sexually harassed, Beverly took a full-contact self-defense course for women's empowerment. Every time she was attacked, she conjured up her former supervisor: "It helped me clobber the attacker in the padded suit. I loved screaming 'NO' at the top of my lungs. Not only did I work out all the pent-up anger I felt toward my old boss, I also now feel strong enough stand up for myself if anything like that ever happens again."

Once you are ready to say NO, make sure you:

Step 1. Select the appropriate moment.
Set up an appointment. Choose a quiet moment when there isn't a deadline or crisis looming.

Isabelle, the sculptor, set up a meeting with the curator at the end of the day, just after the gallery had closed.

Step 2. Speak in the first person, using "I" instead of "you" statements.
Explain what is not working for you and how you'd like things to be different.

Isabelle practiced her speech in preparation for the meeting: "I am very grateful that you chose me for the exhibit and I appreciate the attention it has brought to my work. I would like to renegotiate my contract, which has now been in place for a year. I would like to be able to sell to private clients without the gallery taking a percentage." She didn't say, "You need to stop taking a percentage."

Step 3. Avoid blaming.

Notice that Isabelle refrained from claiming that her contract wasn't fair, or criticizing the curator in any way.

Step 4. Hear each other out.

Hold your ground, even if your NO prompts an ugly response.

The curator initially seemed irritated. He said Isabelle's visibility had skyrocketed when they decided to feature her work. Did she really want to be on her own again?

Isabelle had made up her mind to leave the gallery if she couldn't negotiate a new contract. Calmly, she explained why the initial contract no longer worked for her. When the curator realized that she was prepared to leave, he agreed to consider other options.

Step 5. If your target audience is receptive to your NO, congratulate yourself on a well-timed, well-executed NO.

Occasionally, your boss, co-worker, or employee may surprise you with a mature, healthy response to your limit. Here are some examples:

"I had no idea you felt that way. Give me a few days to think it over. I'd like to find a way to deal with this."

"Well, nobody likes to be criticized, but you have a valid point. Let's bring this up at our next staff meeting."

"I'd rather hear directly about your dissatisfaction than have you talk about this behind my back. My perspective is different from yours, but I don't want your unhappiness to affect our work together. Let's continue our conversation after I've had time to consider all the options."

If you find that you are frequently reluctant to speak up at work, another strategy is to organize an employment empowerment group. One of the strongest influences on my decision to fire our cook was the chorus of friends' voices urging me to cut him loose. In a similar fashion, an empowerment group helps to propel you forward when you are hesitant to say NO.

In my recent search for a new office assistant, I decided to do just that.

hiring muscle

When I began advertising for a new assistant, several friends—including retired **Police Chief Jan Tepper**—volunteered to help me screen applicants and filter out the shrink-seeking/needy lot. My first assignment was to critique the humorous help wanted ad they'd written for me, mocking my previous overly generous employment practices:

WANTED: OFFICE ASSISTANT FOR WOMAN PSYCHIATRIST

Full benefits. Flexible hours, including paid time off for:

PMS

Menopause

Holiday shopping

Bonding with pets

If interested, specify salary requirements and send resume to:

no-NO-nanette@job-op.com

Then, getting down to business, we defined the essential skills needed for the job and developed a list of interview questions. They pointed out that in the past my interviews had been more like real estate disclosures—in which I felt compelled to inform applicants about why the job might seem repetitive or tedious, rather than discuss their qualifications.

Next, I was encouraged to do background checks on the top candidates. I had a bit of difficulty with this one—because I didn't want to give the impression that I didn't trust folks. I eventually agreed, but put my foot down on credit checks. (At least I said NO to my friends.) Even though employees have access to my financial data, how they manage their own money is a private matter.

Finally, my empowerment team explained the importance of requesting letters of reference on company letterhead from the company fax machine, to prevent fudging by friends who pretend an applicant has worked for them.

Under my coaches' watchful eyes, I carefully screened 173 applications, and invited the top three candidates to interviews. Candidate #1 seemed like a "go" until she explained that she couldn't fundraise for our nonprofit, because it conflicted with her obligations as a Jehovah's Witness. And, by the way, would I mind if she canvassed door to door for her church during lunch?

Candidate #2 was drop-dead gorgeous, overly qualified, very self-possessed, six feet tall, and highly intimidating. I figured out pretty quickly that she might end up telling me what to do, rather than the other way around.

My coaches agreed with taking a pass on #1 and #2. I had to wait several days before meeting #3, so I drafted a condolence email to the first two. Only as I was typing did I notice Candidate #2's email address: TIGRESSA@carefree.com!

Fortunately, Candidate #3 was a perfect match—talented, bright, enthusiastic, with a delightful sense of humor and an appreciation of boundaries. Of course you can't ask about prior therapy, but Amalia has never looked to me for that. Whatever I've asked her to do she has been able to handle. On the rare occasion when Amalia has asked for something that I couldn't accommodate, I say NO, give an explanation, and we work it out. NO BIG DEAL.

I know I'm not alone in finding it challenging to set limits at work. There wouldn't be much of a market for self-help books, talk shows, or shrinks if saying NO were easy for women. But instead of belittling our compassion, let's acknowledge and appreciate the ways we reach out to make interpersonal interactions count.

Instead of being self-critical about our reluctance to set limits, let's explore our options when we feel powerless. In the following chapter, we hear from eighteen accomplished women who explain how saying NO at work has paid off for them.

chapter six

no-nonsense NOs

(saying NO at work)

Hey, on the seventh day even God said NO!
Reverend Dr. Susan Newman

The "I'm not looking to have you like me—I need you to respect me" approach seems to work very well. When I'm hired, they know the party's over.
CEO Cheryl Traverse

Believe it or not, there are women who can say NO at work and mean it. It isn't always easy or natural for them, but they've learned how to do it. I spoke with eighteen such women who have perfected the art of on-the-job NOs. Most had done stints as YES-women before converting.

Are these women hardwired with an assertiveness gene that others don't have? I doubt it. Most women, with enough determination and practice, can become effective limit setters. Indeed, the more successful we become, the more we are expected and invited to do, and the more we must say NO.

Yet, very often women are held to a higher standard when we lay down the law: it's okay to say NO as long as we do it nicely. But if the NO isn't warm and nurturing, we lose points.

For most women, finding just the right mixture of firmness and thoughtfulness to score a good, clean, Olympic-class NO takes training and practice.

In this chapter, the highly assertive women I interviewed share inside tips on how they learned to say NO, how it feels to say NO, what they sometimes lose by saying NO, and how saying NO allows them to say YES when choices that are more meaningful emerge over the long run. A few even tell us how to win friends and influence people while saying NO. What a breath of fresh air for women who fear making people angry!

Let's take a look at these various types of NO.

keeping it simple

Have you ever felt like kicking yourself for being too chatty as you try to justify your unavailability or unwillingness to do something? Oversharing is definitely a bad idea when your job takes you behind bars, as **Jeanne Woodford,** former **director** of the **California Department of Corrections,** points out. Woodford honed her NOs as **chief warden** at **San Quentin Prison,** where long explanations don't work with hardened criminals who push the limits.

I always tell people in corrections that your NO has to be a NO. As a woman with Christian values, that used to be difficult for me. I was not raised to say NO to people in the assertive way that you need to when you're working in a prison. You really have to define your lines and let your NO be your NO and your YES be your YES.

I came straight from college right into the prison system. I'd have hundreds of inmates around me and they would ask me for this or that, or "Can I go here?" or "Can I go there?" My tendency as a woman was to try to explain myself.

Well, very quickly I learned I didn't have time for those kinds of answers. I had to be very clear about, "The rules are this and so therefore the answer is NO." Or, "I don't have time right now, come

back and see me later." The inmate would try and push and say, "I
need my light bulb now." I'd reply, "I'm sorry, right now I'm watch-
ing an inmate, so, NO. Come back in an hour." You learn that in
order to survive within a prison system you have to be very quick to
assess the situation and make a decision and give a brief explana-
tion, but there can't be a long dialogue.

This approach might be a good strategy in rowdy classrooms
and other situations in which demands for immediate attention
pile up quickly.

compassionate NOs

Boston's first woman **Police Commissioner Kathleen O'Toole,**
who recently became   **Chief Inspector** of Ireland's **Garda**
Inspectorate, values a team approach to management in non-
emergency situations. When she has the luxury of time, she
favors a softer style. If it's life or death, she doesn't hesitate to
use her authority to make decisions and give orders. But whatever the circumstances, she has learned she can be tough without being loud.

Well, I'll say this humbly—probably my interpersonal skills are my
greatest strength. I had a chief of staff who once said I was the only
person he knew who could fire someone and have that person leave
my office thanking me. I think that's because I've always tried to
be very straightforward and honest with people, but compassion-
ate at the same time. I don't hesitate to break bad news, but I try
to do it in a humane way. Whether it's saying NO to a request
or having to disappoint or fire someone, I try to be consistent in
terms of my delivery.
I learned early on that to yell and scream didn't work. There's
a way to convey a message that can be more effective and more
constructive. I went to a military-type police academy that was
a very rigid autocratic environment. In that type of environment

people will do just enough to get by, but they won't necessarily be inspired. So I've kind of acquired a different style, which is more democratic.

*I'm a situational manager. In certain situations when it's a life or death decision, I'm an autocrat—I'm very decisive and I say, "This is the way it's going to be, end of story." It's really easy to say NO or YES, or to make a decision in a split second, because one really doesn't have a choice. You don't have time to worry about hurting people's feelings. **But in situations where I have the luxury of time and it's not a public safety emergency, I'd much rather involve my team and get input from as many people as possible.** My style is very different from situation to situation.*

You know, that's what true leadership is all about—not just dictating to people, but inspiring people. And being a team player. I like to inspire others to be part of a team as well. That's when I've seen the organizations I've worked for realize their true potential—when people have really been inspired.

I think it's easy to say NO or make difficult decisions when you make those decisions based on principle—as painful as that can be politically. I think every decision has to be made on principle. I have to make tough decisions every day that make some people happy and disappoint others. But I've always felt strongly that if I can go home at night and look at myself in the mirror knowing I truly tried to do the right thing, then I sleep well.

fearless NOs

As a "serial turnaround" **CEO, Cheryl Traverse** doesn't have time to worry about being liked when she's hired to streamline a company. Cheryl attributes her on-the-job assertiveness and overall chutzpah to growing up in a family where no challenge was too great.

I take over troubled technology companies, restructure them, fix them up, and sell them. I've taken over five companies and sold four. I have to be really, really fast. To keep pace in the technology time frame you need to keep ahead in three-month time frames— or maybe six-month, max.

When venture capitalists hire me I say to them, "If you're looking for someone to be nice to your employees and coddle them and have a touchy-feely kind of company, please don't hire me, because I don't have the time to do that and I won't be able to do what you want me to do." I tell them I am very goal-oriented and I deal with people in a rough, tough way or we're not going to be able to get to where we want to go.

Sometimes it's painful, because people like to be liked. It can be very lonely, but I have to remind myself that I'm not there to make friends. You just can't look for that as a CEO. I have very good friends outside of work. When I come home with a couple of million bucks after selling a company, that's nice. My coping mechanism at work is just to put aside that whole personal part of myself. I think early on I really was very torn between getting a job done and having people like me. But the desire to achieve was so strong that I just got over it. In most cases—as a CEO—people don't like me.

In my family, I have successful businesswomen as role models. In the early to mid-1900s, my great-grandmother was considered one of the most successful women in northeastern Pennsylvania. She took over her husband's trucking company when he died in 1912 and converted it from horses to trucks. She ran it until she died in 1954. My grandmother—my mother's mother—ran it with her. With a trucking company, being nice is not part of the deal. The employees were a pretty rough bunch of union truckers.

My father built homes as a hobby. Every weekend it was like, "Well, shall we do plumbing this weekend or electrical?" There are always successes and failures when you do those kinds of things. I was never afraid of taking on new challenges. That was the way I was brought up. I never worry about failure. Failure to me is nothing to be ashamed of if I have really tried.

supermom NOs

With a successful career, it's impossible to create space for motherhood if you can't say NO. When the desire to be a good parent overrides the concern about disappointing co-workers, setting limits is easier.

I heard from three high-profile women who found that 24/7s on the job weren't in the best interests of their children.

Author, presidential speechwriter, *Wall Street Journal* contributing editor Peggy Noonan explains that being clear about her own goals has kept her from being swept along by the force of someone else's agenda. Sorting out what she must do and what she likes to do helps her make decisions without worrying so much about disappointing others.

It's very important to know how to say NO. You have to learn how to do it. You have to discipline yourself to do it. You have to make sure you don't, at the same time, stop learning how to say YES. **Both NO and YES are important in life! NO to meeting the assertive agendas of others, YES to meeting the joys and pleasures and fun of life; NO to requests that do not seem to you at a given time to be appropriate or legitimate, YES to those requests that are serious, that reflect serious needs that you can meet.**

Here is a general way I think of requests for my time.

1. *Do I want to do it? That is, will the experience give me pleasure, satisfaction, happiness at having done it?*
2. *Do I have to do it? That is, does the doing of it assist me in meeting my responsibilities as mother, home supporter, friend, Catholic, citizen?*

The first is usually easy to answer. I know or can guess what will make me feel happy. The second can be tougher. If I don't want to and don't have to, it's easy: I don't do it. If I want to do it, I try hard to do it. If I have to do it, I do it.

As an example, if I am offered a substantial amount of money to cross the continent to make a speech, I don't really like to leave home, and I don't like to leave my son, but I do have to support him and myself, so I will likely make the speech. And have a good time doing it because I like people, like to meet them, and also feel it's emotionally impractical to not enjoy what you're doing. It's no good to not turn it into fun.

One thing that is hard for women, or I think in general harder for women than men: feeling that you are disappointing people by saying NO. When I first became well-known as a writer I was engulfed with requests for appearances to help this group and that, this candidate and that. I didn't have my "Do I want to, do I have to" worked out yet. I hadn't heard of the word "boundaries." I thought I should help everyone because they asked me.

About ten years ago a woman running an impressive and worthy woman's congressional campaign in the Midwest called and told me if I came out there and campaigned for the woman she would likely win—it was fifty-fifty, all she needed was a well-timed boost from me. I said, "Gee, I understand and I would love to help, your candidate is terrific, but I have a little boy and I'm a single mother and . . ." She said, "Bring him!" I said, "NO, he has school, and little kids don't like it when you yank them out of their lives so you can go to a strange place with strange people." She said, "It's the U.S. Congress!" I said, "Gee . . ." She said, "We need you!"

Suddenly I realized: She doesn't care about my son. My son is not her agenda. Winning is her agenda. But my agenda is my son. Her agenda is crucial to her; my agenda is crucial to me; they are not the same agenda. I told her I just couldn't do it. And I know I not only disappointed her, I think she went from a person who admired me to a person who thought I didn't get the big picture. It took me a while to realize: that doesn't matter. I have my own big picture.

But it also had taken me, by that point, a few years to under-

stand that in all too many cases people who ask for your time for some professional purpose don't care at all about your familial reality or responsibilities. They care about their needs. That doesn't mean they're bad, it's just something you have to know to operate in the world realistically.

Marti Morfitt, president and **CEO** of **CNS, Inc.** in Minneapolis, imagined that she could squeeze motherhood into an already overloaded work schedule. The YESes that played a role in her early success evolved into NOs when she wanted time to be with her son. Prioritizing was the key to saying NO with ease.

Probably the fact that I didn't say NO for a long time was a huge contributor to my successful career. In the early days of my career I was relatively indiscriminate about how I worked. It was just all the time—mostly at the expense of everything else.

And then one of my bosses actually gave me a gift.

I was pregnant for the first time in my late twenties, and I found out I'd be having a C-section—scheduled for a Tuesday—I told them I'd be back the following Monday. "Don't take any meetings off my calendar. Maternity leave is for other people, not me."

My boss said, "We don't pay you for what you do with your arms and legs. We pay you for your knowledge and your experience and your judgment. So you actually don't have to show up here the day after you deliver for us to know you're committed, and the world isn't going to come to a screeching halt because your patch of the rice paddy didn't get picked."

The other thing that happened came with my son's birth. There is a force of nature that possesses you and makes you love these little babies like nothing else. It's like I will throw myself in front of a train for this kid. So for the first time in my career, I became incredibly adept at prioritizing—which is the most important part of saying NO. Up until that time, my work was always a little chaotic. I'd save all the really big

important stuff to get done on the weekend. When my son was born, I
made a commitment to myself that the sky would have to be falling for
me to work weekends.

At this point in my business life it's really easy to say NO. The
priorities are clear. There are rational reasons for just about every-
thing. So saying NO, and making good, balanced decisions that
lead to NO, are pretty straightforward.

Kelli Conlin, executive director of **NARAL Pro-choice,** New
York, also developed new skills in organizing when her children
were born. She has become an expert at rank ordering everything that's essential, from donors to diapers.

The tipping moment where I felt empowered to say NO was when
my twins were born. That gave me more of an ability to set bound-
aries without feeling like I am abandoning people or rejecting
them.

Being able to set boundaries and saying NO are two distinct
tracks. *The first is the ability to be highly structured and scheduled.*
In some ways, it's easy to say NO if it doesn't fit your structure. The
other is where we worry about being mean or rejecting if we say NO.
They both intertwine, especially for really busy people. You become
much clearer about your own abilities the more you have on your
plate. The higher up the totem pole you go, the more demands you
have on your time—be it family demands, professional demands,
personal demands.

You have to have clarity about what's important or you get
eaten alive. *There is no personal organizer that can give you that*
sort of intuitive knowledge about how to prioritize. For me, there
are usually five things at the top of the platform that have to be
done. One of them might be going to get diapers, but it's at the top
of the platform. If I have to deviate I will, but I've become better at
sifting out what can be jettisoned versus what can't.

Now, am I always successful at that? Absolutely not. I think that the more power someone has over your life, the harder it becomes to say NO. For me, it's easy to say NO if a staff member says to me, "Oh, I'd like you to be on this conference call at two thirty." But if a major donor calls me and says, "I'd like you to be on this conference call at two thirty," it's much harder. I have to assess where the person is on my power structure, how they can help my career or my organization. Saying NO professionally gets hard for me when we're growing our organization and our circle of individual contributors becomes bigger.

For me the major piece that was cathartic is that it's nothing personal when I have to say NO.

impersonal NOs

Don't take it personally . . . Let it go . . . Sage advice that would put psychiatrists out of business if it were that simple to follow. Yet it does take some of the sting out of a NO if we know the reasoning behind it, or if we know that other similar requests are treated the same way.

According to **Maria Elena Lagomasino,** former **chair** and **CEO, J.P. Morgan Private Bank,** one way to take the sting out of a NO is to depersonalize it. Maria crafted a corporate identity that provided a frame for saying YES or NO. Then, if requests didn't fit into the bank's overall strategy, NOs were less likely to be taken personally.

I've never had a conversation about setting limits with a male executive—even though I have more male executives report to me than women. I talk about saying NO fairly frequently with my women executives.

It's easy for me to say NO to protect our business or our clients. I have been extremely effective in that. When we were building our business strategy, the first thing I had to do was decide who

we weren't going to be. That meant that I had to say NO to a lot
of people. We spent an awful lot of time crafting our target mar-
ket, our mission, our vision, what we were all about, because that
would give everybody the frame in terms of what to say NO or YES
about. In order to be great in the business, I had to be sure that not
only could I say NO, but my staff could all say NO.

The key is to make these things not seem personal to people.
When people personalize issues, it's very difficult to hear a NO.
If people understand the frame under which you're saying NO,
then it doesn't become personal, and even though they might
have liked another outcome, they don't take it personally, so you
don't destroy a relationship.

My mom has a hard time saying NO. She tries to please every-
body, hates to disappoint people. So actually, I had to unlearn what
I learned from her. At one point I also had to tell myself that my
goal in life was not to be the most popular person, but to get the
things done that I set out to do.

Pitzer College President Laura Trombley avoids autocratic decision making in the university setting. She sticks to the rules of
governance when students want to make an end run around
them. Not everyone has a clear-cut code to fall back on, but any-
time there are existing guidelines or established procedures, they
help clarify our options and frame our explanations.

I'm most effective and most comfortable saying NO when people
want to bypass appropriate process, and ask me for immediate
decisions. I tell them that there is a process that they need to
respect and that I respect, and that it needs to be followed. The
way we do this within our system is through a particular series of
interactions.

Last year I had a group of students want me to ban smoking
on campus—just ban it for everybody. I said, "You know, while

certainly I appreciate your concerns and the health and litter and socioeconomic concerns, you need to understand that we have a system of governance here. While this may seem like a pretty clear instance of doing something appropriate, you don't want a president with that kind of power."

Sometimes students say, "We don't know whether we can trust the process." My response is, "You need to try it first. If it's a flawed or problematic process, then we need to fix that. But without having tried it, I can understand your doubt, but you need to at least go through it."

self-preserving NOs

Health-conscious **Faye Wattleton, president** of the **Center for the Advancement of Women,** stresses the importance of self-care on the job. Her nursing training has helped her keep cool and focused under pressure. If her inner signals tell her to slow down, she's learned to listen and make changes.

It's really hard for successful women to say NO, because a lot of the drive that has made it possible for us to succeed is rooted in a profound sense of inadequacy or the need for approval. This is a pattern that is common among successful people—especially among women. You find yourself in a constant chase to achieve to the level of satisfaction that will give yourself permission to say NO.

I was told something really early in my career that I've not forgotten: "You have to take care of yourself because no one else will. People will consume you without meaning to, without malevolence, but at the end of the day if you don't take care of yourself, you are the one who is the loser." I try to listen to that voice; I play that tape over and over again when I feel that I am taking on too much. I try to listen to my body and my own psychological signals about taking on too much.

My professional education was in nursing. In healthcare, you're trained to keep alert for long hours, because the safety of patients is on the line and a mistake can be costly, if not deadly. I learned to concentrate even under stress. What that training has done is to convey the appearance of not being stressed when I am.

When I'm not concentrating well, or feel disorganized, or not attending well to the responsibilities to which I've already committed—then I know that it's time to either cut back or to cut out some things.

I have been fortunate to be trusted on a national platform that gives me the opportunity to be influential more broadly than one on one. I try very hard to expend my energy where I will get the best and the broadest audience. I try to exercise a fair amount of caution before I accept invitations to organizations about which I know very little.

A lot of the time I simply turn down requests, because I can't afford to get involved in something that could be harmful to the work I've done. I've spent forty years building a professional reputation and thirty-five years working for a cause; affiliating with the wrong group could tear down the results of years in a minute. I'm very respectful of the fragility of success.

valuing NOs

Beth Grupp is an **organizational development consultant** in Washington, D.C., who advises nonprofit corporations. Her expertise is invaluable to an organization's strategic planning and fundraising efforts. Beth has no trouble saying NO to nonprofit groups who ask her to provide services without payment or for a reduced fee. She believes that modeling her own worth challenges the organizations she works with to act as though they also deserve support.

I've consulted with a lot of groups in which there is a real hesitancy about taking power and raising money because they feel more com-

fortable in the underdog role. That nonprofit poverty mentality—
"We don't have enough money to pay ourselves well so we can't
pay you well"—just doesn't serve us well in the progressive social
justice community. I'm not willing to work for cheap because it's
not a healthy value. I explain [to my clients] that they don't expect
the phone company to give them a break, so let's not expect that of
ourselves or our experts—the most precious resources we have.

When somebody says they don't have money to pay, it's a state-
ment about priorities. If they are just starting out and they're all-
volunteer, okay, they probably don't have any money. But in estab-
lished organizations, when they say they can't pay for something,
they're really saying they can't prioritize it higher. They put it in
financial terms, when it is really a values choice.

considerate NOs

In the nonprofit sector where doing "good" is as important as doing
well, **Mills College President Jan Holmgren** is cautious about over-
burdening her staff by overextending herself. She has learned to
pace herself and, in effect, the people who work for her.

When you are running an institution of higher education, it's very
important to have people working with you to screen requests before
they get to you. It's a delicate balance, because these gatekeepers
have a really big responsibility and you don't want to overburden
them or over-empower them. They usually end up not being as well
liked as you are, because they are the watchdogs at the door.

Over the years I've learned to be fairly cautious about saying
YES, because I don't like to put my energy into or name on some-
thing that I don't have enough time for. In the past, I overestimated
the amount of time and energy I could put into various things.
I've learned to be more judicious, both about choosing to say
NO to things that I don't want to do and to things that I don't
think I could really do well. Those are the two criteria that I try
to apply.

There is a definite difference, I find, between the for-profit and the nonprofit world. In the business world people are much more willing to say NO because they are looking at the bottom line. They are focused on success in a fairly well-defined way. In the nonprofit world, the concept of doing well and doing "good" are both part of what you are asked to take on, and the boundaries aren't as clearly defined.

I have a tremendous capacity for taking on work but it often has a negative effect on the people who work for me—because they end up having to carry too heavy a load. So I've learned that it can also be a kindness to them for me to say NO.

culturally appropriate NOs

When we don't share a common language or culture, our intentions can be misinterpreted. A NO that seems polite to some people may seem rude or hostile to others.

Marti Morfitt found that her Canadian directness didn't go over well when she moved to Minnesota. Now, when she doesn't have time to "gift-wrap" her NOs, Marti sometimes begins her sentences with an apology.

I would say that **people's orientation, whether it's their own personal style or where they come from, makes a huge difference in how you say NO. In my company, there are some people for whom a two-by-four works just fine. And then there are other people who require fur lining to be able to hear hard things.** So for them, a NO may just take more planning. I think that we're just a microcosm of what people's individual styles or their backgrounds lend themselves to. For instance, our sales guys probably hear NO 75 percent of the time. So for them you don't have to gift-wrap it. But you have to expect they'll come back and ask you again. That's their job, that's how they got to where they are.

I'm from Toronto originally, where people communicate quite directly. If I think you made a mistake I say, "I think you made a mistake." When I moved to the Twin Cities about twelve or thirteen years ago, I did not understand that the communication style here in general is far less direct than that. I was lucky enough to have a young woman working for me who followed me around and every time we left a meeting she would say, "Okay, so here are the four people you offended in that meeting and here's what we're going to do to fix it."

One of the things about how indirect we are in this part of the country is that you never know when you've offended somebody. So how you say NO here becomes pretty important.

Actually, when I'm feeling impatient or don't feel like I have the time to think through how do I say something really sweetly, I just start off sentences with, "I'm not from here, so . . ." with a preemptive apology.

Faye Wattleton, on the other hand, finds cross-cultural communication more effective when she can be direct.

I do think that there are cultural patterns that are unique to the way that we are socialized. As an African American woman, I was socialized to be straightforward and direct. I'm really bad at being circuitous. I'm sometimes awestruck by how clever people can be in saying NO without people thinking they have said NO. On the other hand, I feel that there is something dishonest about being circular about one's intentions. I've been on the other side of that, in which I'd like to have a YES or NO answer so that I have clarity to know where I'm going. The limbo stage is, I think, akin to purgatory.

Maybe it has something to do with the way I was brought up. My mother was a fundamentalist minister who was very direct and strict and the rules were clear. Right was right and wrong was wrong.

African American language codes tend to be much more direct.

When I go to Africa, it is ratcheted up to another level of directness in the way that people communicate. **Being direct can be misinterpreted in the majority culture as being defiant and difficult, when in my conditioning, being direct is being honest.** *Being indirect is not an honest way to communicate. It is misleading and may give people the wrong impression, which can be very hurtful and very harmful.*

I've traveled all over the world. I find that people will trust you much more quickly if you're direct—if they sense that there is an integrity and an authenticity about your directness; it's not hostile or intimidating, just direct and honest.

Everyone has had the experience of wondering what it means when someone in a position of authority says, "I'll get back to you," and then doesn't. Initially you're hopeful, but eventually you feel devalued. You hate having to ask more than once. So when it's your turn to say NO, giving a clear response in a timely manner conveys respect for everyone involved.

NO to inequity

Betty Dukes, lead plaintiff in the gender discrimination class action suit against **Wal-Mart,** learned to say NO to anything that threatened her ethics or sense of self. She will not tolerate abusive or demeaning behavior.

When I decide to make a stand—"NO, you can't treat me this way"—I'm determined to take it to the absolute end. I do have a great ability to focus when I set my mind to something, and my resolve keeps me afloat.

I became determined because I got tired of abuse over the years. Coming up as an African American, there are a lot of obstacles one has to face. I was out on my own at a very early age and I had to learn to survive. A lot of surviving is just saying, "NO, I'm not gonna do that."

I am most effective at saying NO when my YES would be detrimental to me or to others, or when my YES is going to affect my spiritual development and growth and stability. I will say NO if it involves dishonesty. I have self-respect. And I will not let anyone attempt to tarnish that.

At Wal-Mart a lot of women—especially hourly associates— put up with a lot of stuff that they wouldn't normally put up with if they were better educated so they could change jobs when they are treated unfairly. I saw a lot of disparity in treatment of us lower level employees. Wal-Mart hires a lot of uneducated people who don't have a lot of avenues to empower themselves.

Don't ever allow fear to get under your feet: it will carry you where you don't want to go.

showbiz NOs

On Broadway, in film, and in the recording industry, people "in the business" make it their business to morph their clients into something they are not. When someone is young and impressionable, hoping for a big break, the image machine may be the first adversary, so it's important to establish clear limits around the marketing of a professional image.

The entertainers I spoke with all faced tough choices when they were first starting out.

Stephanie Zimbalist, actor, producer

Our YESes and NOs make us who we are, and guide our lives. When I first dipped my gamine toe into my chosen profession, a producer dangled a peach of a movie role in front of me if I would sleep with him. I blasted out of that room and never looked back. I believed in myself, somehow, and knew I should never betray that belief.

Donna McKechnie, Tony Award-winning actor, singer, dancer

I was a young actress when I was interviewed by Otto Preminger for a film he was doing. Later, I got a call from my agent, who said, "Well, they want you to do it but you have to go topless running down the beach in one scene." Because I was born in the Bible Belt and raised as a Lutheran, I just couldn't imagine doing that. I was also very inhibited—a lot of dancers are. As much as I wanted the part, I said NO to being topless, assuming I would lose the part.

Well, sometimes when you say NO you get more. I got a call back from the agent who said, "Well, they really want you to do it so they have a better part for you, an acting role." That was a major victory—a good lesson for a girl who has a hard time saying NO.

Also I think it's important to be personal about saying NO. I prefer to speak for myself. It's like signing my own checks. I once asked a really wealthy friend for advice. He said, "Never let anyone sign your checks." I feel that way about saying YES or NO. I like to deal with things in a personal way.

When you work with agents, sometimes it's more difficult. It's their job to say YES or NO. But I insist on knowing what they're going to say and how they plan to say it, because how you say NO to people in business is very important. One shouldn't be cavalier about it.

Lisa Loeb, Grammy-nominated singer/songwriter, actor, TV host

I learned to say NO through mistakes—through people saying, "You look fantastic in that dress," or, "It doesn't sound stupid when you say those things." Then I see myself on TV or in a video and I realize that it didn't look like me and I didn't listen to myself, because it seemed like there were experts around me who knew better. I've learned to trust my own instincts. Sometimes it takes counting to ten and just saying NO. Just like counting "one, two, three" and jumping off the high diving board, you say NO because you know it's right.

One of the first times I did a photo shoot for People *magazine, there were stylists who ended up having me wear a red spandex dress with cheddar cheese-yellow flowers, tights, and Mary Jane shoes. When the picture came out, I looked like a cartoon. It was a really superficial cutesy image that wasn't me. That happened at a time when I was trying to ingrain the fact in people's minds that I was a serious songwriter, even though I already had a number-one single. I realized I'd rather wear a simple black shirt and really great makeup than Mary Janes and a red spandex dress.*

When it comes to creative situations, **I can now say NO very easily to something that misrepresents me**—*especially if it's the kind of thing that we can't go back and edit.*

affirmative NOs

Offering helpful suggestions or alternatives when turning people down creates a win-win situation: you feel good about being generous and they appreciate your support.

Judy O'Brien, the only woman to be cited by *Forbes Magazine* among the "**Most Powerful Dealmakers**" five years in a row (2001–2005) and the top woman on *Forbes*'s "**Midas List**," has a negotiating style that helps her succeed in business by saying YES.

My strategy for saying NO is a positive strategy. It's a YES-based approach. [As an attorney] I said YES to the other side in all kinds of ways that didn't matter to my client. I always got what I wanted because the other side liked me so much. I've had a number of clients who have told me that I had one of the least confrontational, most friendly, and most effective negotiating styles that they'd ever seen. Most of the successful women I know have learned to use collaboration and cooperation to help others in ways that make them successful.

At this point, I say NO a lot. I'm not afraid to say it. As a venture capitalist, you have to look at whether a company can pay you for your services and how successful they are going to be over time. Is it worth allocating time to this company? Most of them aren't going to be successful anyway. It's something I've had to adjust to, because I tend to want to help everybody—it's my nature.

I always try to be helpful when I turn companies down—to give them some advice about building their business so they will look back at the conversation from a positive perspective. This is a give-and-get concept. *You help them and they'll help you some way in the future—perhaps they will send you somebody else, and maybe that's the next Google.*

Estelle Freedman, the Edgar E. Robinson Professor in U.S. History at Stanford University, watched the pendulum swing from all YESes to all NOs before she found her own set point. Now she takes time to consider her response to requests before answering, and when declining, suggests another person who might help.

Once I became a professional, it took me quite a while to realize that it was an issue to say NO. I teach women's history and interdisciplinary feminist studies, and my mission when I entered academia in the 1970s was to integrate women into the profession and women's history and the study of women more generally into the university.

So after quite a few years of saying YES to all opportunities—"YES, I'll speak to your class; YES, I'll give a guest lunch; OF COURSE I'll do another honors section; YES, I want all the grad students I can get"—I realized I was overextended and that I had not really had much training in how to say NO.

The models that I had were total YES or NO, and not a lot of process in between. When I realized I was overextended, at first my tendency was to go to the opposite extreme, which was to just say

NO. What I had to learn was that **there is a middle ground—both in making decisions and how you say YES or NO.** For me, the middle ground—which is much more satisfying than YES and taking on more than I can, or NO and cutting people off—is buying time—"Let me get back to you on that"—then making lists of priorities, thinking about the rewards and costs of the things I'm agreeing to. If a colleague I trust says it is really important, I am more likely to say YES.

When I say NO, I don't say "I'm too busy," but—I've learned this from the way people have said NO to me in terms of what feels better or worse—I say, "That is a great idea, and I wish you the best in your project." That affirms the request and that's what I mean by the middle ground.

I learned some of this from colleagues. When I started teaching we would share stories about what it was like to be some of the first women teaching at Princeton, and I began to hear how other women managed their lives and their time. I was surprised to hear that they said NO. It was actually quite upsetting to me when they said NO to me. ("I am available, I can come at any time, I'll read your work. And you're saying NO to me?? Where's the sisterhood?")

Years later we had potlucks for women faculty at Stanford, and as we sat around and shared stories, some of the women who had children would say, "I have to draw these boundaries because of the children." Well, not having children, I didn't have that automatic or legitimate family boundary. But I did learn from other women faculty not to make a snap decision no matter how appealing it is. I always have a list in my mind or by my phone of the other women on campus who might be available if I can't do something. I try to suggest someone who will meet that need—and ideally, someone who might welcome the opportunity.

At this point I'm known for being very clear about boundaries, and I feel comfortable telling people what they are. I find it extremely difficult when someone does not say NO when he or she *needs to—which leaves me in the position of not knowing whether I need to ask someone else, whether I've offended the person I've asked, or whether he or she has even gotten my message. NO can be a really useful response, and sometimes we need to hear it.*

Over the years, **literary agent Frances Goldin** has learned to avoid the demanding divas whom she fears she may never make happy. But she believes strongly in offering encouragement along with any NOs. She makes the answers to her most frequently asked questions available and sends out referrals and instructions along with her good wishes.

I've been in the literary business for forty-eight years. What I've learned is when I either don't have the answer or don't want to say YES, to refer them to others.

I've become the referral agency of the Lower East Side. People call me and I might not be able to help them, but I know someone who can. People thank me a lot for sending them to others who can help. There's not a week that goes by that people don't want a lawyer, or an agent, or another agent—since I generally don't handle children's books. If they want a children's book agent, I have a form that gives eight good children's book agents. I just put it in the envelope and mail it to them. I've also developed documents, like, "How to write a good query letter," that I make available.

It is important not to discourage people. Even if someone should never be a writer, I say something good about their writing. Like I'll say, "Your family needs this book. Put it in writing, replicate it one hundred times and make sure that it lives for posterity."

Being generous and helpful and encouraging in our NO is important. A standard response from me might be, "This is not my genre, but it is a saleable book. I hope you find an agent who represents you well. Good luck." I can do that in thirty seconds. If I can, I'd rather send them somewhere else or encourage them than say NO. Then I don't feel so bad.

What conclusions do we draw from the collective wisdom of these no-nonsense naysayers? First, we need to know what our priorities are. Additionally, we need to understand that learning how to say NO is often a lengthy process. Finally, each of us must create a unique mixture of decisiveness and flexibility to fit the demands of our professional responsibilities.

So when you are asked to do something at work that you're not sure about, what steps can you take to clarify your options?

Here's what I suggest:

Step 1. Before responding, take time to ask yourself if you have to do it and what you might lose if you say NO.

Is what you are being asked to do within the parameters of your job description? Does your job, livelihood, or promotion hinge on saying YES? If your career is not on the line, will agreeing to the request be a hardship for you, your family, or other important relationships?

Step 2. Ask yourself if you want to do it.

You don't have to say YES or NO right away. Give yourself time to think about it. Does the request fit within your priorities, is it part of your personal agenda, will it bring you closer to your goals? Will you be happy or fulfilled if you agree to the request? Are you being asked to do something meaningful or substantive? Can you do it well? Is someone else better suited to handle the responsibility?

Step 3. If you decide that it is not in your best interest to say YES, state your NO clearly and decisively.

A clear NO is usually easier to deal with than a mushy non-answer that leaves the requester in the twilight zone.

Step 4. If you choose to explain your reasons, be succinct.
Clarify why the request doesn't fit within your priorities, strategies, or prior commitments. Try to place it within a preexisting frame to let the requester know that the decision is not personal.

Step 5. When turning people down, be as encouraging as possible.
Acknowledge the requester's need by suggesting others who could help or alternative ways of getting it done. It's always better to be helpful when you can.

nice and nasty NOs

It never occurred to me as I launched this book project that I'd be rejected as often as I was by women I hoped to interview. When Nancy Snyderman suggested that I talk to accomplished women about how they learned to set limits, I jumped at the idea, undaunted by the prospect of negotiating with their ferocious gatekeepers.

I'm usually fairly adept at avoiding situations that make me feel bad—like asking for things I won't get. When I began the first round of calls for this book, I hadn't experienced a big-time rejection in quite a while. Naively, I expected an enthusiastic response to the topic, since setting limits is something women deal with every day. Besides, I told myself, I'm a good listener and a nice person, and most people enjoy talking with shrinks (judging from my experiences on airplanes).

Guess again! Cold calls and e-mails don't work with high-profile women. I scored an interview with women I didn't know only when a trusted intermediary pitched the project for me. I collected so many NOs from my cold calls that I sorted them into categories: nice NOs, fade-out NOs, wishy-washy NOs, and nasty NOs.

Here are my observations about these various NOs.

nice NOs

I learned something from the nice NOs. They transmit a gentle affirmation that makes the disappointment more palatable. Instead of imagining that I'm being turned down because someone thinks my idea is idiotic, I'm given a send-off with best wishes for a successful mission. I like the idea of encouraging other women, so I've changed the format of my own "I'm sorry I can't help you" response. Now whenever I say NO, I also wish people good luck on their projects.

Some of my favorite nice NOs:

From a former university president: *Your background sounds quite impressive, and I am sure that your book will be helpful to a number of people. However . . . I'm deeply enjoying being on sabbatical . . . so I must regretfully say "no," even though you didn't want me to at this point. Best of luck, anyway.*

From the staff of a prominent politician: *Thank you for inviting [the politician] to participate in an interview with you. Unfortunately, due to [the politician's] schedule, she will not be in a position to participate. Please accept her wishes for a successful project.*

From a museum president: *I am honored by your invitation to participate as an interview subject for your upcoming book on assertiveness in women. Your longstanding research into the ability of women to say "no" and set boundaries for themselves is certainly fascinating and clearly very valuable in these times of constant and widening demands.*

I regret that I am in the awkward position of proving your point, which is to say that I am indeed a woman who can say "no" when I must. As you suggest, I receive many such inquiries for very worthy projects—indeed, many more than I can possibly accept, and I am sorry that I must decline yours.

I hope you will understand my position and accept my very best wishes on your book. I look forward very much to reading it when it is complete.

From a minister's assistant: *[The minister] requested that I respond to your gracious request for an interview for you upcoming book on saying "no." [The minister's] time constraints with speaking and writing, as well as family responsibilities, are such that she will have to exercise that prerogative to say "no," even to such a unique opportunity.*

We pray God will bless the work of your hands and heart.

Hey, if you don't ask, the answer is always NO!

fade-out NOs, wishy-washy NOs

Don't keep me dangling! Spit it out. It may wreck my day, but I can handle it!

Here's a typical fade-out NO:

Hi Nanette. I did receive the materials you sent about the "NO Project"—so to speak. I'm in Florida now on a speaking gig, and I'll be returning to Washington tomorrow. I'll get back to you in the next few days, assuming I can think of something interview-worthy to say on this topic.

Despite intermittent, gentle prodding I never heard from her again.

And a wishy-washy NO:

That seems like a fascinating project. I'm leaving tomorrow for Bali, but just as soon as I get back we can find a time to talk.

Four months later:

I'm sorry I have to cancel our interview again, but some-thing's come up. Unfortunately, my travel plans call for me to leave for Europe tomorrow. Check with my assistant about rescheduling.

[The assistant was reluctant to schedule without the boss's okay.]

There is nothing more frustrating than being on indefinite hold, with the pseudo-possibility of a YES. I don't want to be a nudge, and that puts me in the position of calling back at intervals that are widely spaced enough not to be irritating. Wishy-washy and fade-out NOs rarely turn into YESes, and when they do, in the interim, I've become so frustrated that I've lost respect for the person.

I say, "Tell it to me straight and get it over with!" We'll both feel better in the long run.

nasty NOs

Don't get me started. I mean really, what is the point of being nasty? Have I injured you by admiring you enough to consider you interview worthy?

Just as the sweet NOs add a little bounce to my step, I've been upset by unnecessarily hostile replies. I'm a psychiatrist. I know that many people get up on the wrong side of the bed—some-times every day—but even at the worst of times, it's important to keep your negativity in check.

For instance, I invited a distinguished scholar (whom I'll call "Professor S") for an interview. A mutual friend promised to lay the groundwork for me. This was Professor S's reply:

I must maintain a very narrow focus in order to complete my manuscript. I'm saying NO to everything that could distract me, and your project seems a bit baroque to me.

Baroque?! What was that supposed to mean? I had studied baroque *architecture* during college. Was she telling me that the topic of saying NO is ornate to the point of being ridiculous?

I called my friend **Esther Rothblum,** a professor who grew up in Vienna, city of "baroque," to get her take on Professor S's NO.

"At least she didn't call it 'rococo!' " scoffed Esther, the author of more than 120 publications. "You know," she continued, "reviewers say all kinds of hostile things about my manuscripts, and I just blow them off. Once somebody called my writing 'clunky and pedantic,' and that felt bad for a day or so until my lover at the time told me all Germanic people have a clunky and pedantic style. The only thing that gets me down is when our women's basketball team loses."

I would like to report that I learned to take the hostile replies in stride as my stack of rejections grew higher. But the truth is that I sometimes took it personally when I received a particularly unfriendly response. On the other hand, all the fade-out, wishy-washy, and frosty communications taught me to appreciate those nice, no-nonsense NOs.

chapter seven
---

saying NO when the president calls

(saying NO in public service)

As the wife of a former president, I can't think of a time I've ever said NO to something important. I've lived in thirty homes in seventeen years following my husband's political career. It's a life I chose, and I choose to like life.

Barbara Bush, former First Lady

In government service, most decisions you make are open to public scrutiny. When your NOs have local or global ramifications, you expect to be accountable for each and every one. Today's NO could be tomorrow's headline. Tomorrow's NO could save lives or affect the well-being of thousands of individuals.

So how do women handle the challenges of saying NO in public service? Do they set limits differently than their male counterparts? Can women in government service say NO to superiors? Do women question policies or defy directives that they think are wrong? How do highly visible women maintain any semblance of privacy?

Women in public service are wise to consider the pros and cons of every NO. They realize that their choices will be measured on a yardstick that's calibrated specifically for women leaders: Is the NO compassionate or cutthroat? Accommodating or hard-nosed? Is it derived through consensus or conflict? Will the NO be admired or resented?

I interviewed nine prominent women about saying NO in government service. These women talked about learning to say NO and what saying NO means to them. They addressed moral dilemmas on the job and why it's important to be accessible to constituents, even though they can't possibly accommodate every request. And several women described their determination to achieve specific objectives, even when people tried to throw them off course.

pushing the limits

Most women in public service start their climb up the career ladder at or near the bottom rung. But for many years, women aiming for the top were told to give up the idea of becoming a leader because "it was a man's world."

Susan P. Kennedy, Governor Schwarzenegger's Chief of Staff, and **HIV/AIDS activist Mary Fisher** began their government service by breaking the gender barrier. Before they could issue any official NOs, they had to vault over the NOs that blocked their way.

When **Kennedy** was shut out of tactical meetings during a political campaign, she turned up day after day until the men in charge finally opened the door.

A long time ago, I was a field organizer during a political campaign when it was still a rarity for women. The people running the campaign were all men—consultants, managers, staff. I wanted to be in the strategic meetings, and they said NO. When I showed up, they literally would not come down and answer the door. So I got really fired up and told myself I would not take NO for an answer. I showed up the next day and the day after and the day after, until they finally got tired of it and let me in.

That was a confidence-builder early on in my career, because I refused to succumb to the humiliation. They were upstairs, they could hear me knocking, and they just let me stand there. I was proud of myself for turning my frustration into anger, and turning that anger into determination. It was hard to go in there the next day and see the smirks on their faces, but ultimately I earned a lot of respect. I learned that I didn't have to take NO for an answer— even when they added a dash of humiliation to it. By persevering, I came out stronger in the end.

Before she became a noted **AIDS activist, artist,** and **author, Mary Fisher** worked as a producer for ABC television and, later, as an advance person for President Ford. For both positions, she had to convince the men who were doing the hiring that she had the right stuff.

Early in my career I was working in television, and I wanted to work as a producer for ABC in Detroit. They told me that ABC had never hired a woman producer. I said, "So what?" I sort of forced my way in, starting as a secretary. I just kept working my way up as other people left. Eventually, I was the only one there, and all of a sudden I was the first woman working on the morning shows.

The other significant time I refused to take NO as an answer was when I was working for President Ford. I didn't realize that they'd never had a woman as an advance "man." When Ford became president he really had no staff. He needed people for every office. I said I'd like to apply for the job of advance "man," and they said that a woman had never done that job. Again I said, "So what?" "Well," they said, "You'll be traveling with all men." I said, "So . . . ?"

I could see that this was not going to be one of the easiest hurdles to get over, because it was really a man's world back then—the field of security, communications, all the things that go into how you travel with a president. Not to mention that they were not accustomed to taking orders from women. But I persisted and I got the job. I never was told I did a good job, and I never got paid the amount of money I deserved. But I loved the job and I loved the president. It was something I really loved doing.

Recently when I've been in Washington or seen people from the White House, the advance women come up to me to thank me for paving the way.

According to **U.S. Air Force Colonel Patricia Rose**, officer training school is designed to drive out the wimps. Since she had a family to support, she refused to be disqualified.

Sometimes the best way for me to succeed at something is to have somebody tell me I can't do it. In officer training school, I was having such a difficult time. I didn't think I was going to make it. Then one day I realized they were actually trying to make me quit by what's called "self-induced elimination." They try to weed people out by making it so miserable and giving you so much to do that you can't possibly do it all, so you end up getting punished.

I joined the military because my father was dying of cancer and I had to support my family. The stakes were too high for me to fail. I became more determined than ever when they tried to weed me out.

Women who had to circumvent obstacles in their own careers sometimes make a special effort to be fair when they hold the power. Or, they simply feel better about themselves when they can be evenhanded, or when they can open doors for other women to follow.

The first woman named to the Supreme Court, **Justice Sandra Day O'Connor** had a crucial role as the pivotal and deciding vote on many landmark cases. On the bench, Justice O'Connor had no trouble saying NO.

Justice O'Connor also has the reputation of being extraordinarily generous to women who hope to follow in her footsteps. Her law clerks became members of her extended family, learning not only the work of the Supreme Court, but also the importance of health, fitness, and leisure activities. Moreover, Justice O'Connor found time to meet and counsel countless students who studied and worked in Washington. A popular speaker on the lecture circuit, she always has far more invitations than she can accommodate.

Does the Justice who can say NO with impunity in important legal decisions have difficulty saying NO outside her professional capacity? You bet.

I caught up with Justice O'Connor at a Stanford women's honorary society dinner where she was the guest speaker and asked if she had a hard time saying NO to the many requests for her time and attention. Justice O'Connor replied: "All the time. I'm thinking about hiring someone just to say NO for me."

refusing to pull rank

Rank has its privileges, but some of the women I spoke with use it only as a last resort. They prefer to take a little extra time with their explanations. As **Colonel Margarethe Cammermeyer** points out, when it isn't a life-or-death situation, it's good to be considered thoughtful and helpful, so that a feeling of camaraderie will carry over to times of crisis.

I am one of those whose philosophy is not to say NO. My father's automatic response was always NO, without any discussion. Those automatic NOs devalued me, and as a result my own world view is, "Why not?"

The influence of that growing up experience has permeated

my entire way of being. When I was in the military and gave a directive, I would always couch it in the reason why, so that people would understand that it was not just an arbitrary decision for saying NO.

Unless it's an emergency, **Colonel Rose** is never too busy to give an explanation for her orders. She is a leader who listens and considers the options. Whenever possible, she communicates why she is saying NO.

I can certainly say NO to subordinates who want things that I feel are contrary to the overarching goals of the organization. I don't have any trouble with that. I try to be fair and hear them out and meet their needs as much as possible. But if their needs and the needs of the organization don't jibe, then I am okay with saying, "NO, I can't do that for you," although I try really hard not to have to get to that point.

In the military, it's more fashionable to not have your authority challenged. The whole rank structure is such that if the officer says NO—then it's NO. I think it's somewhat of a failing if I just resort to saying NO because I'm wearing the rank that outranks you and therefore I can. In the Air Force, the enlisted folks wear their rank on their sleeves—they wear chevrons—and officers have, depending on their rank, various symbols, bars, and eagles. Some officers point to the rank on their sleeves to enforce an order. The message is: rank has its privileges. I have never done that.

It would be a really bad failing on my part if I had to resort to pulling rank. I prefer to think that the orders I give or the tasks that I assign have some basis and merit. And that if I've explained what we're trying to accomplish well enough—that I can pretty much ask people to do something and they'll do it. My personal belief is that nobody's ever died from too much information.

A lot of people think that the military is a bunch of mindless zombies who just follow orders without question. In combat, you do want to have a level of discipline where orders are followed. That results in lives being saved. In the heat of battle when you're being told to do something, you don't say, "Let's put together a task force and talk about the consequence of what you're asking me to do."

But outside of combat—in day-to-day military operations— it's imperative to be perceived as fair. Once that perception is gone, you're very ineffective. If subordinates don't feel like you're fair, you're toast.

not copping an attitude

Retired **Chief of Police Jan Tepper** was the first woman to ride patrol in Santa Cruz County. She wasn't tall enough to push people around, so she had to develop her own technique of setting limits. Jan Tepper figured out how to diffuse tense situations with conversation and humor. Her tactics helped her avoid physical confrontation.

Riding in a patrol car and responding to calls and trying to prevent crime in a certain coverage area or beat is what you think of as frontline police work. During the first three months I was on patrol, I trained with various senior officers. These guys were used to training men, and their style didn't work for me. My first training officer was six feet, four inches tall, and all he had to do was show up and take the sunlight out and people responded to him because he was a big guy. Obviously, I couldn't do that because I'm not that tall. So I had to figure out my own style.

One style I developed was to use humor whenever I could. If somebody was threatening, I tried to diffuse the situation by looking at the situation from the other person's point of view, instead of going in chest-to-chest. I tried to find a way to appeal to that person, instead of challenging him head on. Or I would change my body language—turning slightly to the side—so I wouldn't be physically in his face.

I tended to do well with drunks and crazy people. Other officers called me in when they were having difficulties with these people because my way of saying NO was more effective. I didn't treat these people like they were bad. I tried to understand what they needed.

Nobody's face got smashed in with my approach. A lot of it took more time, and some of the guys were often more impatient. Their style was to go in, get in somebody's face, yell at them, use physical intimidation, get it resolved, and get out. **My way wasn't quick—I had to reason, let them vent, keep a safe distance, and sometimes after they'd vented they'd just give up.**

Research has shown that **women in law enforcement get in far fewer physical altercations and use verbal skills more than physical skills, and from my perspective, that's a better outcome—to avoid escalating the situation, but still get the job done.** *Obviously, if somebody has a knife to another person's throat, if it's a life-or-death situation, that's a whole different ballgame.*

Very often, it's the considerate gestures that count. Former **Boston Police Commissioner Kathleen O'Toole** believes that it is important for government officials to create and maintain a public image in which they can take pride. The way she sees it, her jobs entail both law enforcement and community service. For Kathleen O'Toole, being available to her constituents often means saying YES rather than NO.

When we were just starting the Democratic National Convention planning, a police officer's dad—a retired fire lieutenant from the Boston Fire Department—was dying in a hospital down the street. His son—our officer—was on the list for promotion to detective, but it was clear that his dad wasn't going to live long enough to see the formal ceremony. Somebody suggested to me that it would be kind of nice to get over there and see the dad. So we staged his promotional ceremony as a surprise for the father, who died shortly afterwards.

How could you say NO to situations like that? Those are the things that not only bring me huge satisfaction in my job—those little things, those human things, but also the things that I think have helped me in terms of my credibility. Because I think people know that I care. I do dozens and dozens of this type of thing every week.

Now I remember in my very early days of being a commander, when I was thirty-two years old, every so often I'd hear about a good arrest, or I'd hear about a nice gesture performed by a police officer. I liked to scribble out a little note of appreciation in my poor penmanship on my stationery that said my name and title, and I'd send it off to that person.

One day, probably a year after I'd sent one of these notes off, I walked into a district station. There was a police officer on the verge of retirement who was sitting at a desk. I did a second take when I saw the note that I'd sent him hanging on his wall. I told him I would have used better penmanship if I'd known he was going to post it. He laughed and said it was the only time in his entire career that anybody ever acknowledged anything good he'd done in his job.

I love my job. I think that people can tell that. I'm in a business that people think of as law enforcement. Well, only a small percentage of it is law enforcement. The vast majority of it is service to others. It's just really important to try to be as compassionate and caring as possible.

It takes time to be accessible, to hear people out, to consider all possibilities, and to explain the reasons for your NO. The women in public service whom I interviewed believe that this is time well spent. They prefer to lead rather than command, to make an extra effort to celebrate or commemorate a special event, and to be respectful even as they set limits.

But how do these women deal with public curiosity about their private lives? Or with invitations to events that might encroach on family time? Are off hours off limits? Reporters are not known for respecting boundaries when it comes to public figures. If any situation might bring out a no-nonsense NO, protecting your own privacy might call for it.

saying NO when your private life is public property

According to **Chief Jan Tepper,** when you're a prominent official, every decision you make, whether as a private individual or a public servant, must be evaluated in terms of how it would play if a reporter got hold of it. Indeed, the personal is political when you're in government service.

How can we enforce the laws if we don't follow the laws personally? We have to be above reproach.

There were awkward situations that I would have to say NO to because I was a public figure. I always had to have in the back of my mind, "How would I explain this to the local newspaper if they wrote an article about this or found out about this situation I'm in now?"

An example—I was invited to a birthday party outdoors in a back yard, with lots of people there of all ages and from all walks of life. I walked into the party and I was there about three minutes before I smelled marijuana. Even though only a couple of people were smoking, I had to turn around and leave the party. It would be ridiculous to go up to the person and say, "Put that out." But if it came up somewhere that I was at a party where marijuana was being smoked, how do you deal with that in the press? My integrity and reputation and standing in the community were at stake.

My way of saying NO when it's outside the line of duty is to go out the side door instead of being a party pooper and confronting it head on.

• • •

Chief Tepper points out that it's also very stressful to work in an environment where every citizen considers himself or herself your boss—especially when you are called on the carpet for something a citizen thinks you should have handled differently. In those circumstances, Tepper felt she didn't have the option to say NO: it was her job to listen to the complaints and to handle them diplomatically.

Saying NO as a public servant is completely different from saying NO in any other profession, because I'm accountable to the public in one form or another. It's a huge pressure. The public considers themselves our bosses—an officer is driving along in a marked patrol car, and back at the office there is a call from a citizen complaining that the patrol car ran a red light. As chief, I got those calls all the time. "What's your officer doing over here?" You're constantly in the spotlight and open to public scrutiny.

saying NO in politics

When the job calls for efficient and effective NOs, how do women government officials boost their game? Do they model themselves after more experienced colleagues? Were they lucky enough to have mentors? **Susan P. Kennedy,** who has worked for two different California governors at the highest levels and for Senator Diane Feinstein, shares some of her most meaningful training experiences.

Mentoring is really, really important. I watched Senator Feinstein say NO, and that's where I learned it most forcefully. I learned how to say NO, and I learned what it felt like to be on the receiving end. The thing about the senator is that she's crystal clear, doesn't hesitate, and is just blunt. She's not cruel. She's just firm. She'll look you in the eye, and she'll be absolutely direct with you.

I watched grown men cower when they had to go in to tell Senator Feinstein something she didn't want to hear. I learned that giving criticism or saying NO doesn't have to be personal. I learned to walk through fear, walk through discomfort, walk into the spotlight, go through it, and walk away. Senator Feinstein actually respected me more because I could do that and I could take it. Eventually I realized that **being told NO is not so painful,** and that **saying NO is something you can learn.** It's not something you're born with.

When I was cabinet secretary for Governor Gray Davis, I dramatically strengthened my NOs. I became very comfortable with saying NO in stressful situations—having no choice but to be blunt and unapologetic, but kind. Because I had to say NO so often, it took a lot of the pain out of it, because I had to practice so much. I was in charge of preparing the budget for the governor, and my job was to say YES or NO to every agency secretary, every single program that had a constituency group or state staff or legislator behind it, every department head, and every department within the government that wanted funding for a particular program. I was constantly barraged by lobbyists for various programs, and saying NO was a daily part of my job.

Learning how to say NO without alienating was extremely important. My job was to get the job done for the governor, but also to protect him. I had to learn to look people in the eye in a way that conveys respect when I said NO, and then explain why I was saying it. It was important to **make people feel heard and understood, even when saying NO to them.**

My policy was: don't delay and don't demur. Delay creates anxiety, and conveys a sense of disrespect. Delay conveys uncertainty or lack of confidence, so people aren't sure if they should press you harder or whether you don't really understand. So I learned that you need to say NO upfront and **be clear and honest** with people. People respect me for that.

· · ·

If your job is to say NO for your boss, you'd better make sure he or she will back you up, as **Susan P. Kennedy** learned while working for Governor Davis.

In 1999, we had just signed an enormous sweeping package of HMO reform bills. Governor Davis was worried about its effect on premiums, so he told me to tell legislators not to send health-related bills that session, because he would veto them. There were four bills related to cancer research, and one of the legislators who was very powerful—someone I respected and considered a friend—said, "Screw you," and sent a bill down.

Well, this particular bill dealt with prostate cancer research, and it had some of the most powerful men in the country behind it. When that bill reached the governor's desk, I had to convince him to veto it. He had sent me upstairs to say NO; if he did not back me up, I would never be able to say NO to another legislator again. I would be completely undermined. Governor Davis actually got on the phone with CEOs of some of the major companies in the United States who were passionately behind this bill.

Governor Davis told them, "I'm sorry but I have to back Susan up." He convinced them that we would be able to do something more comprehensive at a later time. Then the governor vetoed the bill. It was enormously important, because my credibility was at stake.

Is there a paradigm for saying NO in public service? We know that you can't stay connected to constituents if you are inaccessible. You must keep an open door and still be able to say NO, when necessary. So how do you find just the right blend of engagement and effectiveness?

Here is what I suggest:

Step 1. If possible, find a mentor who can help you develop your ability to say NO.

There are prominent women in all branches of our government.

Look for someone who seems approachable and who sets limits in a way that you admire. Ask if she might be willing to mentor you. If she is extremely busy, suggest that you meet over coffee or lunch once a month. Be prepared to accept something less often. (Remember, she is going to teach you how to set boundaries!) When you get together, present a couple of cases in which you've had trouble saying NO. Ask if she can suggest the best way to set limits in each scenario.

For instance, if you're reporting to two superiors of equal rank, sometimes you're expected to be in two places at once. A mentor can help you figure out how to prioritize your supervisors' requests; she can also suggest ways to say NO without jeopardizing your position.

Step 2. If mentors aren't available, don't be afraid to develop your own style of setting limits.
Each woman we heard from in this chapter figured out what worked best for her and then followed her own path. And each feels proud of her style—especially when it's more effective than the way her male counterparts say NO.

Step 3. When you are asked for something, if it's not a life-or-death situation, take time to hear people out.
Listening to the concerns of your subordinates or constituents makes them feel validated and you feel connected. Don't shortchange yourself or the other party when you are gathering the facts.

Step 4. Don't feel obligated to answer immediately if the matter isn't urgent.
Indicate the date and time when you will respond. Remember that it's preferable to let them know as soon as possible. Keep your word. People feel angry and manipulated if they don't get an answer when promised.

Step 5. After you consider all the possibilities, state your NO clearly and directly. Explain the reasons for your NO.

Look people in the eye as you give your answer. Don't waver. Convey a sense of confidence in your decision. You are less likely to be pressured for a different answer if you make it clear that you have considered the matter carefully. It helps to highlight the determining factors. Be succinct.

Step 6. If you are pressured, don't back down.

After you have come to a decision based on the best available evidence, hold your line. People respect consistency. If they sense that you are hesitant or ambivalent, they will challenge your NO—especially if it's their job to talk you into something.

Step 7. If you are saying NO *for* a superior, make sure that he or she will stand behind your NO.

Explain to your superior that you will lose your effectiveness as the NO-sayer if she or he fails to back you up.

moral dilemmas in public service

What happens when your conscience dictates that you break rank? Can you say NO to a superior?

After rising to the rank of colonel in a distinguished twenty-six-year career in the U.S. Army, **Margarethe Cammermeyer** said NO to serving her country in silence. During an interview for top-secret security clearance, she acknowledged that she is a lesbian. She was discharged. When she decided to fight for her right to retain her position, Colonel Cammermeyer became the highest-ranking officer to challenge the ban on homosexuals in the military. "Integrity was the basis of everything I stood for in my life and career," she said.

Colonel Cammermeyer's NO paid off. A Federal District Court ruled that her rights had been denied and that she had been unfairly discharged. The colonel was reinstated and returned to service, although her case did not set a precedent throughout the military.

Earlier in her career, Colonel Cammermeyer learned that she had the fortitude to stand up for what she believed when she said NO to a superior officer.

The military does have a certain hierarchy in which somebody gives an order, somebody else follows through. What is particularly difficult in the military is if you're a subordinate and somebody gives you an order that you think will do harm to someone else, then you have to take a moral stance about how you're going to deal with that.

When I was a young lieutenant, I was indoctrinated that your superiors gave you an order and you could be court-martialed or shot if you refused. On one occasion, I was a nurse on night duty, and I had seventy-six patients including four who were in critical condition. They'd had heart attacks, and this was before the days of intensive care units, but we had a room where they were monitored closely. I was the only nurse on.

Around five in the morning, I got a phone call from my superiors, who told me to report downstairs, that we were having an alert and I needed to come down and sign in. This was a direct order. I said that I really could not leave my patients, but that I would come down as soon as I was relieved. They were furious. Three times they called back to say that I needed to report. I refused because of the condition of my patients. After a while there was no way in hell I was going to be going down regardless of what the threats were. When I was relieved I went downstairs, expecting to be admonished because I had refused a direct order. They ended up apologizing because they hadn't realized how sick my patients were at the time.

What that taught me, more than anything else, was that I did have the intestinal fortitude to stand up and say, "This is not the right thing to do." I would defend my patients rather than worry

about being told to do something that I thought was inappropri-
ate. Sometimes you need those sorts of challenges to your integrity
and to what you stand for to know whether or not you're going to
buckle or whether you're going to do the right thing.

And when you decide to say NO by registering a complaint
within a closed system, what are the chances you will get a fair
hearing? **Colonel Cammermeyer** comments on sexual harassment in the military.

For women in the military it is particularly difficult to say NO to
a male superior—both because of gender and because of the power
of superiors. There are many stories of women subordinates figur-
ing that it was easier to have sex than to lose their career, either by
being called a lesbian for saying NO, or by not cooperating with
a superior. Until recently, the same chain of command that you
were part of for your day-to-day work was also the chain of com-
mand that you would raise a complaint with in a case of sexual
harassment. So the fact that the military has you confined makes it
extremely difficult to say NO.

    I tried to be much more distant in the military. I did not social-
ize with the people I worked with. Because I'm tall, I'm also rather
formidable-appearing and people felt somewhat intimidated.
Being reserved allowed me to have a social distance. I rarely got
close to people. By not getting close, that also meant I didn't have to
deal with some of the social sexual innuendos that are easy to fall
prey to. And before I came out I was married, which also gave me
some space and distance.

Colonel Ann Wright, a veteran of the **United States Army and
Army Reserves,** has been forthright about her objections when
she concludes that the U.S. foreign policy is detrimental to our
country.

I got in trouble with the Clinton administration when, as part of the United Nations operation in Somalia, I was head of the UN's Justice division, which was charged with reestablishing the police, the judicial and prison systems. In June 1993, the U.S. military unilaterally went after one of the Somali warlords, General Aideed, who had earlier ambushed and killed thirty-four Pakistani UN troops. The U.S. military helicopters blew up a building where they thought General Aideed was. But in the building were at least eighty Somali elders from various tribes who had gathered to discuss how to broker a ceasefire between Aideed and the UN military forces. All were killed. As chief of the UN's operation in Somalia, I wrote a legal opinion that the U.S. military's action was a war crime. Many people in the Clinton administration were angry that I dared to question the U.S. military's operational tactics.

During her 16 years as a diplomat, Colonel Wright served all over the world. In December, 2001, she was in Afghanistan as part of the team that reopened the U.S. Embassy. Later, hers was one of the few voices inside the State Department raised in protest of the war in Iraq. When she had exhausted all official channels through which she could voice her dissent, Colonel Wright resigned from the U.S. Diplomatic Corps so she could continue to speak out.

Having been in international relations for well over thirty-five years in eight different administrations, I felt that the decision of the Bush administration to invade and occupy an oil-rich, Arab, Muslim country that had done nothing to the United States was going to jeopardize U.S. national security, not increase it. I was also concerned about the unnecessary curtailment of civil liberties in the United States following September 11.

As a federal employee, my job was to implement the policies of each administration elected by the people of the United States. However, I felt I could not represent these and many other policies

of the Bush administration. Since I had exhausted all official chan-
nels within the system with my dissent, I felt I had to resign so that
I could speak out about my objections as a private citizen. I think
probably 95 percent of the people in the State Department were
against invading Iraq, but only three of us diplomats resigned.

The issue of political parties has nothing to do with my decision.
My resignation was over what's good for America. If a Democratic
administration had decided to invade Iraq, I would have spoken
out as well. I believe in speaking up and saying NO to any admin-
istration whose policies are bad for America and for the world.

Even when it's your job to enforce laws that you believe in, you
are allowed some discretion. There is a difference between the
letter of the law and the spirit of the law. Painful personal experiences can also influence your choices about detaining or arrest-
ing people, as **Chief Jan Tepper** points out.

Basically I agreed with almost all the laws I was ever required to
enforce. It would be nice if the laws could be as simple as: (1) you
can't purposely hurt another person; (2) you can't take something
that doesn't belong to you; and (3) you can't mess up other people's
stuff. I agree with all three, but the laws are often much more com-
plex than that.

Officers are given a lot of discretion in the field. Though some
think the letter of the law is the only thing that matters, I'm a per-
son who thinks the spirit of the law is very important. Sometimes
we have to ask ourselves if we are taking too much liberty with the
discretion we're given, or are we in fact more qualified to make
those decisions because we are at the scene and we can see what the
dynamics are.

Don't get me wrong: when it comes to sociopathic torturers,
I'm happy to have them out of the gene pool. In those situations,
saying NO is very easy for me. But in everyday law enforcement, I

thought a lot about equity and fairness, what it meant when a kid made a stupid mistake, when to give somebody a second chance, and how to accommodate human frailty.

Officers exercise discretion every single day with every single call they get. We all bring our stuff to the work we do and every decision we make. If somebody I love had been killed by a drunk driver, I would never have let anyone anywhere near the legal limit off.

When my brother was dying and he had severe seizures and unmanageable pain, his doctor told him to use medical marijuana, which helped him in a way none of the medications he was given did. My brother was a productive member of society who wasn't hurting anyone. I'm glad I never had to arrest anyone who was using medical marijuana, and I hope the laws will be changed so that medical marijuana can legally prescribed with quality and quantity controls for people who need it.

If, as a public servant, you disagree with an order, policy, or regulation, how can you bolster your resolve and confidence to say NO *to* a superior?

I recommend the following steps:

Step 1. If you have time, consider the pros and cons of making a stand.

What might you gain from saying NO? An increase in self-confidence? The possibility of protecting others from harm? The chance to avoid a costly mistake? The knowledge that you won't betray the well-being of others for personal gain or your own safety?

And what might you lose? Could you be fired? Demoted? Could you be expelled from the inner circle?

In your experience, would you describe your superior as psychologically healthy or troubled? If he or she is in tiptop shape, psychologically speaking, your chances for a favorable outcome are greater. Superiors who are narcissistic (see Chapter 2), passive aggressive (see Chapter 4), thin-skinned, or short-fused need to be approached carefully. It's always better to have allies when dealing with personalities like these.

Step 2. If possible, consult with people you trust.

Talk with friends, family, or a counselor about your dilemma. Ask for their guidance and support. Listen to their perspectives. If they agree that it's important to stand your ground, discuss how you might respond if your worst fears were realized. Are you prepared to file a grievance? Are you willing to consult an attorney? Do you have the strength and stamina to pursue the next courses of action, whatever they may be?

Step 3. Document everything.

Even if you decide that the risks of setting limits in a particular case are too great, keep a record of all conversations and observations related to the incident. This record may be useful at a later point if you decide to confront a similar situation of wrongdoing or neglect. Be sure to include dates, times, and the names of all individuals involved. Write down everything that happened before you forget the details.

Step 4. If you decide to confront your superior, practice your speech in advance.

Choose your words carefully, speaking in the first person. Role-play with trusted allies to develop responses to the kind of arguments you may encounter.

A concise, straightforward statement might be: "I am unable to do _____, because I believe it is not in the best interest of _____ for me to do so." As we saw above, Colonel Cammermeyer refused to report for a drill because she thought it would jeopardize her sick patients. And Mary Fisher wouldn't back down from her belief that women were as competent as men for the jobs she wanted to do.

Step 5. After you have presented your case, listen carefully to your superior's response.
If your superior disagrees with your decision, ask if he or she might suggest other ways to handle your objection. Ask if he or she would be willing to think about it and discuss it again at a later time.

Superiors who are psychologically healthy may ask for more time to consider your concerns. You might be asked to state your objection in writing, delineating the reasons for your refusal. Or, you might be encouraged to raise your concerns at a future meeting of all interested parties.

Healthy superiors understand that it's important to pay attention when trusted subordinates are unhappy. They do not want to ignore potential problems. Even if they dislike your choices or feel that you've brought them up at an inconvenient time, they don't punish you for speaking up. You are likely to leave the encounter feeling as though you have been heard, regardless of the final outcome.

It's important for government officials to be attentive to their constituents. The constituents, in turn, want to feel well represented. This style of give-and-take serves our country well. According to the women in this chapter, to stay connected when you say NO in public service, you must have: (1) a commitment to being accessible; (2) an ability to listen to the concerns of all parties; (3) a desire to understand the purpose of a request; and (4) a willingness to explain the reasons for a NO.

Government officials work for the public. Private citizens also contribute to the common good when we serve our communities. In the next chapter, we look at the complexity of saying NO to the disadvantaged in our society.

chapter eight

NOblesse oblige

(saying NO in the community)

If you asked me whether I'd trade being compassionate for having an easier time saying NO—if I could somehow stop letting the pain of the world in—I'd never do it. That's what life is about—really letting yourself feel the extremes. I wouldn't want to be the person who could just turn over and go back to sleep after hearing about a tragedy.

Marilyn Jaeger, entrepreneur

Poverty, disease, war, hunger, and violence are everyday realities for far too many people on our planet. Whether we witness these misfortunes with our own eyes or learn about them through the media, our hearts go out to the victims. How do we choose among the many solicitations for time and money to help those in need? Is there a compassionate way to say NO? How do women maintain a good balance between tending to others and taking care of ourselves? What's the best way to deal with the guilt from feeling that we haven't given enough?

In this chapter, I discuss empathy, generosity, and compassion as we relate to the hardships in our local, national, and global communities, and why most women find it so painful to say NO when we are asked to help.

saying NO in the streets

"Excuse me, ma'am, do you have five minutes to save our planet?"
"Pardon me—can you take a moment to help inner city youth?"
"Are you doing all you can to stop global warming?" "Could you
spare a quarter for a cup of coffee?"

Whenever I walk from my home to our neighborhood super-
market, at least three or four people approach me for money. I
store up free coffee coupons to give to the homeless folks, but I
don't always have time to improve urban conditions or save the
planet. And I feel guilty when I reply, "Sorry, not today."

For starters, I know how it feels to solicit strangers who
aren't in the mood for an interruption. When I was in college, I
worked the streets as an environmental activist. Even now, during elections, I go door to door to get out the vote. I've felt the
sting of being yelled at, or having doors slammed in my face, by
people who couldn't come up with a nicer way to say NO.

Beyond empathizing with activists, I generally support the
various causes that street solicitors are asking me to consider,
and I don't like giving the impression that I don't. I'm particularly sensitive to the tragedies of homelessness. When I try to put
myself in the shoes of chronically mentally ill people who live
on the streets, I can't imagine having the resilience to cope with
inadequate healthcare, food, clothing, and housing. It breaks my
heart to know how much they suffer, largely in silence, day after
day. And though I spend two evenings a month providing free
psychiatric services to homeless people, it's not nearly enough to
make a dent in the suffering I witness.

But I do have other responsibilities, including a family,
teaching, a psychotherapy practice, and a research project. I also
need to take care of myself. So how do I cope with the discomfort of refusing street solicitors whose causes I support or whose
needs are painfully apparent?

Recently, I came up with a way to say NO that reduces my
distress.

Since I already make annual contributions to several environmental groups and I volunteer my expertise to the homeless, I've started referring to these gifts when asked to make others. If, say, I'm hit up for a contribution to an environmental cause, my NO sounds like this: "I give to Heifer International. That's the group I choose to support." Or, if somebody asks me to contribute to a shelter, I reply, "I volunteer at Caduceus Outreach Services." Then I thank the solicitor for her or his involvement, and very often, he or she says something like, "Back at ya." **It feels good to say NO in a way that indicates respect for the solicitor and support for his or her cause.**

I've spoken with many women who have a hard time setting boundaries when people on the streets ask them for help. **Professor Esther Rothblum** has no difficulty saying NO to students or colleagues, yet she'll generously chauffeur a complete stranger all over town:

Last week, I was standing in line at the Department of Parking to get a guest parking sticker. There are usually about a hundred people in line. You're there for such a long time that this feeling of solidarity develops: people start introducing themselves, saying why they're there, and it begins to feel like a group process.

I was standing there in a semi-trance when a woman came up and attached herself to me and started telling me her life story. About an hour into it, she told me why she was there. The police had impounded her car because she had forgotten to pay her tickets—even though she was on disability for mental illness.

"Can you drive me to pick up my car?" she asked. I didn't have a looming deadline, so I told her I would if I got through the line before dark. People really help each other out when they're dealing with the frustration of that bureaucracy.

I drove the woman to the tow place and waited for an hour while she dealt with documents there. Then I drove her to another agency, so she could stand in line and deal with more paperwork, even though she had lost the receipt she'd just stood in line to get.

I didn't say NO, because she seemed so desperate. I'm sure it's difficult to live with that degree of impairment.

Homeless folks often ask for handouts from **executive chef Monica Pope,** owner of Houston's T'afia restaurant, and Monica is happy to help out. Only when people make unreasonable requests of her is she comfortable setting limits.

Both personally and professionally I find it a struggle to say NO. There are other chefs who find it extremely easy to say NO. That just doesn't work for me. I will never be that person. As a kid, I wanted to go to work with Mother Teresa. I didn't, but I end up feeding the masses in a different way. And I like being generous.

But I can say NO if somebody asks for something that's really inappropriate. Like not so long ago when I got a call at the restaurant from a homeless guy I'd given a meal to. I find it difficult to not take every call where somebody says, "I'd like to speak to Monica." So I got on the phone and this guy says, "This is John Williams. You may remember me—you gave me a meal when I just got out of prison." I had no clue who he was. I asked why he was calling me, and he said he needed five dollars. I was like, "NO, I'm really sorry." He says, "Okay, well, hey, how's business?"

Many spiritual traditions advise the faithful to be on the lookout for prophets in humble garb, seeking handouts and testing for compassion. If you believe that anyone who asks for help could be a prophet in disguise, it's even more challenging to say NO. Charmaine, a nonprofit administrator, has struggled with this concept for years:

I grew up in an ethos where I was taught that Christ was in every person who asked something of me. I don't even go to church these days, but I'll tell you, I'm still afraid to say NO to somebody who is obviously in need. I can't unscript what I learned growing up. What if I say NO and it's really Jesus at the door?

Many women are conflicted about the best way to assist the poor and mentally impaired people we encounter in the streets. We'd like to give within reason and decline without guilt. When we're able to support the food programs or treatment facilities that benefit at least some street people, we sleep better at night. Still, if we compare our lifestyles with theirs, it's easy to feel distressed that we don't offer more.

One way to handle that discomfort is to select several worthy causes where you can make a significant difference—then focus your efforts there. Often the most meaningful contributions come from feeling connected to people who need assistance or to the organizations that provide effective aid. Let's take a look at contributing in an intentional manner.

choosing your causes

No five-year-old child should have to worry about being raped—again. Our hearts just shattered when we learned about the growing epidemic of child rapes in South Africa. We knew we had to do something to help after we'd been there and met so many little girls who had been raped.

We don't have that many resources, and we have a lot of expenses since all three of our children were adopted from severely abusive foster care situations. But we got $20,000 out of refinancing our home and started a nonprofit to build a sanctuary to provide a safe space and treatment facility for South African children who have been raped.

Tammy Hanks,
"Beyond 12" Family Services

Everyone has limited time and money, and it's easy to feel overwhelmed by the number of requests you receive. It's also challenging to figure out how large a contribution would allow you to feel generous. If you're not proactive about giving, you may end up agreeing to something before you have considered all your options. Planning involves matching your heartfelt values to your choices, instead of responding with a knee-jerk YES to any request.

All appeals are designed to draw you in, and none of us likes to seem unsympathetic. **Vivian Stephenson,** the former **COO of Williams-Sonoma,** points out that knowing exactly what you are being asked, and how that fits into your priorities, can help you make a meaningful contribution without overextending.

I think we all like the fact of being asked to do something. We feel valued and respected. When you're asked to do something, it's because someone considers that: (1) you can do it; (2) you've done it before, and obviously you've done it well enough that they want to enlist you to do it again. So in a way it's counterintuitive to say NO. I'm always tempted to say YES, but I really can't say YES to everything I'm asked to do. I try to narrow my focus to two categories I am interested in: women's leadership and education, and the fight against AIDS.

I am candid. If I do say NO, I share my whole process in getting to a NO answer. Typically I try to help the people or the organization in some other way, whether it's financial or trying to find someone else I think could fit the bill. It's very difficult for me to say NO to community outreach. So if I say YES, I make it clear that I'll only be able to attend 20 percent of the board meetings, if that is the case.

Fairly recently I learned to say, "Look, I don't want to give you an answer right now. I want to know more about the project. I want to really understand the time commitment and then I'll get back to you with whether or not it's possible for me to insert this next level of commitment or project on my schedule."

I try to give myself some space and time to really think it through. If I really want to do it, I sort out my schedule to make sure that I can accommodate it, as opposed to saying YES and then trying to fit it in.

SUPPORTING OUR TEACHERS

I have difficulty saying NO to people who want me to speak to organizations like Alcoholics Anonymous or a teacher's organization. I have such a passion about those groups and the work they do. I almost feel guilty telling them NO, because they volunteer so much of their own time, and are so unselfish with their time. I rarely say NO to those organizations. I somehow manage to fit it in.

Jeanne Woodford, former director,
California Department of Corrections

Though she enjoys being helpful, former **First Lady Barbara Bush** no longer has the stamina to attend every charitable event that she's asked to support. She tries to limit her contributions to the issues at the top of her priority list.

The wife of a former president can raise a ton of money for people, and we like to help out whenever we can. My husband is traveling all over the world for things like tsunami relief. I'm saying NO more often because I get tired traveling so much.

I get over fifty invitations a month. I try to focus on the issues that matter to me—literacy and cancer.

When we do say NO, we can do it in a positive way. **Pitzer College President Laura Trombley** tries to be considerate of those drumming up support for community projects because she appreciates how tough it is to make a pitch. She cultivates a style of being approachable that includes an explanation for her NOs.

I ask people to do things all the time. I know that it takes something to ask and that it can be difficult to find competent people. So having been there and having to do that, I respect the dynamics. Having an insider's view makes it sometimes difficult to say NO. When I'm asked to do certain things that I know are important, and I am being asked because they know me or my reputation, and it's a request based upon professional respect, that's difficult for me.

__When I say NO, I give a reason.__ I can't just say the Donald Trump, "You're outta here." __I try to practice gentleness, no matter whom I'm dealing with, to be clear and encouraging.__ Sometimes maybe I'm a bit too encouraging. I don't want to give people false hopes, but I don't want to turn them off to the process.

I do want people to come in and ask me for things—I want to feel needed and useful and productive. So I try as much as I can to have a productive conversation. Sometimes people will be frustrated because I won't tell them YES, but what I hope for is that at least they will understand why.

close to home and heart

Focusing on what you care about is not selfish. Noted **AIDS activist, artist,** and **author Mary Fisher** receives a constant stream of invitations to speak, write, fundraise, and lobby in an effort to stop the pandemic. As much as she'd like to assist everyone who needs it, she says NO whenever the request isn't specifically related to AIDS. After Mary contracted HIV herself, saying NO took on a whole new dimension.

Having lived with the certainty that death was imminent for the first five years of my diagnosis of HIV—before the medicines, before the anti-retrovirals—changed me in a number of ways. One thing that really became clear was that I needed to act on what was most important now. I couldn't put off until later things that really mattered because I didn't expect to have a later. I'm grateful for that lesson—to do what matters now, act on priorities. Knowing what the limits are has forced me to say NO and helped me to say YES. It's taken my diagnosis and living with AIDS to bring things right to the top.

The only thing all of us have that is equal is time. Every day we get equal amounts of it. The only way I can use it wisely is to say NO so I can have enough time to say YES to the things that I really want to do.

If you are a compassionate person, the struggle to say NO whenever something new and very compelling comes up is like being a recovering alcoholic every day. You say, "I'm not going to drink today," just like you say, "I'm going to reaffirm my priorities today."

When I can't do something I'm asked to do, I've learned how to affirm their mission, and—if it's something that's near and dear to my heart and I'm just torn about it—maybe give a speech for them or offer to do an event for them or help them find someone else who can do it.

Dr. Susan Love has dedicated her life to eradicating breast cancer. She'd like to support every women's health advocacy group that asks her to speak, but she can't, so she frequently makes a complimentary appearance when she has a well-paying speaking gig nearby.

There are so many breast cancer and women's health advocacy groups around the country that feel a special connection to me because they've read my books. Often they can't pay even my transportation to do the fundraiser they've invited me for.

Ultimately, I have to make a decision about what I'm going to do and what I'm not going to do. I make a list of my goals for each year. If I have a new book out, maybe I will do more free talks because that sells more books. Or, if we're doing research at the Dr. Susan Love Research Foundation and I need more subjects, I'm more likely to do talks in Los Angeles for free because I can recruit women. So I have my list of priorities and I match it to the invitations that come in.

Until recently, I had an assistant who said NO for me. I've been trying to go it alone, but having to say NO so often may just be the thing that pushes me into hiring another assistant. What I say when I do have a personal assistant is, "I don't keep my calendar, I don't know if I'll be free. Call my assistant." That way I'm not saying NO exactly, and I can be charming, and then I let my assistant say, "I'm sorry, she's not available."

BROADWAY BENEFITS

It's very, very difficult for me to say NO because I like to please. I like to make people happy. For example, I'm going to do a benefit at the Symphony Space tomorrow, first thing in the morning. I'm singing a very difficult song—"Here's to the Ladies Who Lunch" for Steve Sondheim's birthday. I've got a terrible allergy. I'm running from eyes, ears, nose, and throat, and it would be nice to stay home and put my feet up. But I'm going to perform, because it's very difficult for me to say NO. And I rather like myself much better than those I see on the boards today, who stay home at the drop of a hat.

Elaine Stritch, actor

Our passions usually come from our own experiences and we're most likely to support groups that touch us personally—our alma mater or religious congregation, an organization that advocates for a group we identify with, or a research facility working to find a cure for a disease that afflicted a loved one.

Very often we overextend when the need is urgent; even so, it helps to make that a clear choice. And when we do stretch to say YES, it's far more satisfying to focus on the rewards of being kind than the irritations of taking on so much.

Reverend Dr. Jennifer Hughes, an **Episcopal minister,** takes a Zen approach to compassionate giving:

In my congregation I often agree to meet with people when my schedule is overbooked because I have compassion for them. For example, there is an elderly widower who makes appointments to see me every week, and he just wants to talk. He doesn't have anything specific to talk about—he's just lonely. Sometimes I end up spending an hour with him even though that means I'll have less time at the end of the day with my child.

One thing I'm very clear about: I don't rehash any frustration I may feel about the lost time when I reach out to people who are hurting. Really, I say NO to rehashing or reprocessing, unless there is something I feel I can learn from it. If I agree to meet with somebody who needs me, then I do it and it's done. I try to be Zen about it.

women's ways of fundraising

It's difficult for women not to personalize a NO when potential donors decline to contribute to a cause that is close to our hearts. As **nonprofit organizational development consultant Beth Grupp** points out, taking NOs to heart makes it harder to ask. Beth says that a NO in response to a solicitation means: "Your organization and I are not a good fit." It does not mean that you or your cause are unworthy.

Because women are more inclined to feel as though we shouldn't refuse and that we should always give, in the philanthropic world, women start out from a position of being hesitant to ask for money because we are more sensitive to the degree of imposition. We understand how hard it is for others to say NO to us. Men don't typically feel that same tension around asking.

Successful fundraising uses the strengths that women have, and that's the ability to listen to what the donor wants and what the donor's interests are—to be focused on the donor rather than the fundraiser. Women are good fundraisers because we're good at building relationships and understanding what other people want. The best fundraisers I know are good listeners rather than glib talkers.

Beth makes it clear that, if you are a fundraiser, a NO from a potential donor does not mean you have failed. The flip side— for the person who is being solicited—is that your NO is not a heartless dismissal, but rather the result of using your own priorities to guide your decision making.

women's ways of financing

Nancy Barry has a knack for turning seemingly insurmountable NOs into profitable YESes. As **president of Women's World Banking** (WWB), Nancy helped low-income women throughout the world escape poverty by providing the financial services they needed to establish business enterprises like growing vegetables and marketing crafts. As the standard of living rose in places where women-led microfinancing organizations were active, women entrepreneurs were increasingly recognized as the foundation of the economy. Bankers took notice, and they teamed up with other microfinance institutions in the WWB network to grant small loans—averaging $250—to over 20 million low income entrepreneurs in forty countries. Today, WWB boasts a near 99 percent repayment rate on these funds.

With collaboration and compassion, Nancy is changing the way the world works. During her sixteen years at WWB, she encouraged the teaching of leadership skills to microentrepre-

NOblesse oblige   161

neurs. Since retiring from WWB, Nancy has launched a new initiative to mobilize the private sector to support entrepreneurial solutions to poverty in Asia, Latin America, and Africa.

Microfinance is about women's empowerment. Some people call microfinancing "capitalism with a human face." It's helping people help themselves. The global-local network building at WWB is all about connectedness. Our full mission is to open up women's economic access, participation, and power.

The WWB network has at its heart mutual accountability for results based upon standards built by women-led organizations. WWB has global meetings every two years. Women leaders from all over the world meet to build or revisit our mission, vision, principles, performance standards, and ways of working. These are articulated in a fairly elaborate consensus-building process. We consider things like, how much should we weigh the poverty of the women we're reaching versus their repayment, performance, efficiency, and profitability. By the end of these meetings, there is total ownership of the principles. So if an organization subsequently gets disaffiliated, they have to acknowledge that they created the rules and it was within their power to meet these standards; they didn't, so they will have to meet those standards to get back in.

The WWB network also builds leadership standards. You're expected to contribute to the knowledge, service, and policy change agenda of the network. You're also expected to use what you know and share it with others, often creating your own competition. This is very different from the competitive model. The ripple effects of small women-led organizations with integrity have been just enormous.

WWB is a very successful model of self-monitoring and collaborative decision making that respects and reflects the needs of all parties. When you hear, "NO, you didn't meet the requirements," it is easier to accept because the rules are defined by the participants' consensus. It is much more difficult to accept a NO that comes from faraway, unknown arbiters and seems only to serve their interests. By saying YES to self-determination, WBB has avoided many NOs.

preventing burnout

If you want to help, you have choices: you can go to where the trouble in the world is—like the Middle East or New Orleans—or you can go to a demonstration about it, or you can become an armchair activist—the best kind of which is the kind that sends money. Or you can become a click activist, where you sign every petition and send a letter to your elected officials about every issue that every group you ever gave your e-mail address recommends. You can literally spend hours just clicking away.

After spending a couple of years as a click activist, I decided this was not the way I wished to heal the world any longer. I was becoming massively depressed at the state of the world and click activism didn't seem very effective. Everything in the world only seemed to be getting worse, including my personal state of mind.

I mentioned this to my psychiatrist, who said that if I was feeling so guilty about not showing up at demonstrations or fundraisers or delegations to meet elected officials— because these organizations ask you to do a lot more than just click—I should get off the lists. She pointed out that I certainly didn't need a dozen reminders a day about all the things I wasn't doing.

Still it took me a month to say NO to all the lists. But I sure feel better not being reminded by e-mail every hour of every day of all the good I'm not doing for the world.

Meg, software salesperson

I spoke with a number of high-profile women who discovered that being overly generous took a toll on their well-being or livelihood. At this point, they try not to jeopardize their ability to do good by taking on more than they can handle.

Author Jewelle Gomez found it difficult to stay focused on her writing when so many worthy causes beckoned. She had to learn to say NO so that she could divide her time between her own writing and fostering others' development.

I think that **maturity is figuring out the difference between giving generously and giving yourself away.** *In the past, if anybody called me to say, will you MC this event? I'd say, "Absolutely." Would you help edit this magazine? "Absolutely." Will you be my writing coach? "Of course."*

I had to come three thousand miles to start saying NO. I figured out if I were going to have a really serious and focused writing life I had to get out of New York, because that was where I had developed as a writer and part of the thing that I did was donate my time constantly. I never said NO. I thought if I moved across the country to a place where my reputation for generosity didn't precede me, it would be a little easier.

Even now, when people ask me to do public things, that's the hardest NO for me, because it always seems like it won't take up too much time. In the last couple of years I have started telling people, "NO, I cannot, I'm finishing my book." Or, "NO, that's my writing time; I cannot give it to you."

I learned to do this by working with a life coach who was fabulous. She had me make appointments with myself to write. So when someone would ask me to do something, I would look at my calendar and it would say, "writing." I would then say I couldn't because I was booked. Of course, you'd think I could have figured that out myself. But until my life coach had me book time in my calendar for writing, my writing time seemed so amorphous. I gave the time away because it was a blank space on my calendar.

• • •

Tony Award-winning actor, singer, dancer, and author Donna McKechnie said YES to so many community benefits that she had no space on her calendar for paid work. Donna had to learn to say NO because doing good was getting in the way of earning a living.

In our business—musical theater—there are so many benefits for very good causes. But at one point a couple of years ago it started really bothering me that I couldn't say NO. It was reaching a point where it was costing me: I was losing out on paying jobs because I was doing so many benefits and free theatre. It was as if I was on some list of people who always say YES.

So I demanded of myself that I say NO for a while—and only accept jobs where I was being paid. Then all of a sudden, I started getting paying jobs again and getting the work I wanted and feeling very fulfilled, and now I'm able to really pick and choose.

I feel like I'm taking better care of myself. Now that I can say NO, it's wonderful to be able to say YES because I really like doing something good for other people.

With fame came an overwhelming onslaught of invitations that **author Dorothy Allison** found difficult to refuse. Eventually, health constraints forced her to say NO.

I lost a year of work after becoming famous, because I had no clue how to say NO. I had to have gatekeepers do it for me. My agent, who has a lot of the same political and emotional convictions that I have, would say NO for me.

But then I would somehow run into the people my agent had said NO to, and end up doing a freebie, because I couldn't handle that she had said NO. Some rape crisis center from Des Moines wanted me to do a benefit, and my agent had said NO. And then I met the woman from the center in the airport, and I was so over-

whelmed, the next thing I knew I was paying for my own flight to Des Moines to do the freebie.

It just about broke me. I got pneumonia because I was going all the time, working all the time, not getting my own work done, but not being able to turn people down.

Why was it so difficult for me to say NO? Because I felt kissed by God, and I felt I had to repay that blessing. I know people who are gifted artists who never get any recognition or money. There is no justice for artists in terms of fame or money or sales or awards. Knowing all that made me feel that I had no right to say NO. The only reason I could say NO was if I was genuinely on death's door. So I pretty much worked myself to death's door, repeatedly.

I am learning to say, "If I do that I'll have pneumonia. I can't afford to get pneumonia again this year." But to say that to someone who is troubled and needs the kind of help you can provide feels bad.

It has taken me thirteen years to get to the point where I can leave the mail in my assistant's hands, rather than write an apologetic letter myself that will invite them to ask me again, because that's what those apologetic letters do. For me to say NO, I really literally have to take a deep breath and grit my teeth and clench my fist and that's the only way it works.

I'm insanely jealous of the people for whom it's cheap and easy, but I don't want to be them.

In a career that combines pastoral work with public service, **Reverend Dr. Susan Newman, advisor on religious affairs** for the former mayor of Washington, D.C., looks to the scripture for guidance on giving herself a break.

In the midst of all this hurricane Katrina stuff, I'm running to the armory every day, sometimes at eleven o'clock at night, trying to get over a thousand clergy in Washington scheduled to offer pastoral care. In the middle of the day two days ago, I turned both of my cell phones off, and I got a manicure and a pedicure. And then I went back to the armory. Because if I am totally spent and exhausted, I have nothing left to give to anyone else, see?

I strongly believe in the proverb that says there is a time and a season for everything under heaven. I believe there's a time to say YES and there's a time to say NO. As religious people and people of faith, we preachers have what I call the Messianic complex—that if we don't save folk, it won't happen.

But then I say to myself, if God had to take a day and take a nap in creating the world, why is my behind running around here trying to do everything seven days a week, twenty-four hours a day, 365 days a year? So I create for myself a Sabbath. It might not be on Friday or Saturday or Sunday, but I find my Sabbath in there.

I have come to the point that in order to be sane and fulfilled and whole, I have to have a balance in my life. There is a certain amount of public service that I have to give, and as a minister, especially because of being a compassionate person, I will sometimes overextend myself. But then I will find the balance somewhere else. And for me it's all about choices and consequences—what I choose to do and what the consequences will be if I make a particular choice.

There's one particular passage I love in the scriptures. Jesus went to this one particular town where he had been performing miracles, healing people, walking on water, just doing everything. And there was this one particular day when he said, 'I can't do any miracles.' Now if the Creator of the universe realizes that He needs to get away, He's burned out, He's going to rest, there's a lesson for all of us. Jesus would get up early in the morning and stay up late at night just to have some time for Himself. All of us could be of better use to people, and ourselves, when we learn to say NO and take care of ourselves like that.

• • •

Lifelong activist and Buddhist teacher **Sylvia Boorstein**, a **co-founder of Spirit Rock Meditation Center**, is learning to say NO to outreach because she doesn't have the energy she had when she was younger. A friend and Zen teacher helped Sylvia come up with a gentle way to say NO.

When people ask me to do some community event that I feel passion-ate about, especially a thing I know I can do well, I would love to do it for them. Like somebody saying, "You want to come give a talk at this peace rally?" Of course I do. I might not have time to do it, but if I can, I squeeze it in. I feel disheartened when I can't respond to someone's need. I wish I could make it happen.

*Yvonne Rand, who is a Zen teacher with whom I discussed my difficulty saying NO, seven years ago told me that **I don't actually have to say NO, I just need to say, "It doesn't work for me to . . ."** **It is a kind way of responding,** and I use that phrase often when I can't accommodate a request.*

I feel tremendously fortunate to have been gifted with good health. I'm nearly seventy years old and I'm not sick. I do feel older, and sometimes I have noticed that I'm feeling tired for the first time in my life. I think it's a wise thing for me to start noticing and changing the way I plan my schedule, based on my growing aware-ness that heroism is nonsense at this point.

These women have crafted personal equivalents to "first put on your own oxygen mask," so they can sustain themselves and still be able to help.

collective compassion

Rabbi Sheila Weinberg, who is currently at New York's **Institute of Jewish Spirituality,** has made a career of community service. When she was a congregational rabbi, she answered every call and helped out whenever asked. Eventually, she realized that she needed guidance to decide when it was appropriate to say NO. She now meets with six other rabbis to figure out how best to allocate her time among many areas of need.

I have a conciliatory personality. And I have a genuine desire to be there for people when they call on me. And yet how do I discern when I need to be protective of myself, when I really am able to help them, or not? In a way, it's easier in a congregation where there are certain things you respond to. Someone dies, you respond. It doesn't matter what else is going on, basically, you don't say NO to that.

In the congregation, I formed a group whose main purpose was to help me discern what was the best use of my time. In my current position, I work with six other rabbis in a collaborative way, and we talk about when it's appropriate for me to do something that I'm asked to do, where the person is coming from, where's my ego.

I really believe in doing social justice work. But of course the more you're asked, the more you say YES, and the more you take on. It's taken me many years to learn that I'm most effective when I deliberate—when I don't answer YES or NO right away when I'm asked to participate in something, however important it seems. I **allow myself some space to contemplate what the motive for me to say YES would be. Am I doing something because I feel that I'm really going to be significantly useful? Have I made a commitment that I have to honor? Is the project directly related to my own goals?**

Joan E. Biren, a **photographer** and **documentary filmmaker** and long-time political activist, belongs to a women's empowerment group, Freelance Radicals, that specializes in helping its socially conscious members lead a balanced life. They are learning what it means to be compassionate toward themselves as they serve their communities.

The Freelance Radicals ("Free Rads" for short) are self-employed women—black and white, lesbian and straight—who are dedicated to progressive social change. The group was initially formed to provide support around work-related issues at the interface of the personal, the political, and the professional. What surprised the members is that the group has become a forum for supporting each other in saying NO. You might find that you can use their group as a model to start one of your own.

The women meet for a two-hour lunch, once a month. The meeting is divided into three segments:

1. SUCCESS STORIES (30 minutes)
Each woman shares a work-related success story about saying NO (applause and tremendous praise follow each story).

2. GENERAL DISCUSSION (45 minutes)
The group discusses a generally relevant topic, such as who is the "perfect" client, how much money is enough, or being an effective social change agent.

3. QUEEN FOR A DAY (45 minutes)
One participant raises a particular concern—often related to a difficulty setting limits. The group gives feedback about the problem.

The Free Rads have found that encouragement to say NO is far more powerful when it comes from a chorus of voices than from a single ally. Members typically shout out: "Are you crazy?!" "Let it go, girl!" "You can't do good work if you don't take care of yourself!"

The animated group support—whooping it up whenever someone reports a limit-setting success—provides the incentive to practice self-preservation within social justice activism. As each woman has become more effective at setting limits on projects that are likely to take a toll on her physical and mental health, the group has learned more about what NO means:

1. You can't say an authentic YES unless you can say a real NO and mean it.
2. When you say NO to one thing you're saying YES to something else. (Saying NO to one social justice project gives you time for another.)
3. Sometimes the YES is to the unknown that isn't there yet. (Living with uncertainty requires having faith that something good and creative will come of it.)
4. Sometimes saying NO is modeling a NO for clients who are also doing social change work and have their own struggles with limits.
5. Saying NO means getting to a greater YES. (It's important to do good work, love what you do, and be healthy and sane.)
6. The **death of superwoman.** (We all have to give up something to do good work and have reasonable lives.)

The Free Rads support each woman in saying NO, leading a balanced life, and holding onto her self-esteem. This is particularly important for compassionate social justice advocates who are liable to equate self-care with slacking off on more important commitments. Even full-time activists must learn to say NO in order to regroup, replenish, and avoid burnout.

budgeting your YESes

If you would like to translate your compassion into a meaningful contribution, what is the best way to balance your desire to give and your need for self-care? How can you say YES without overcommitting and say NO without feeling guilty or selfish?

Here's what I recommend:

Step 1. Choose your causes before they choose you.

Map out a plan for giving so that you can direct your support to the people you are most committed to helping. Begin by deciding which issues you resonate with the most. Does your heart go out to foster children? Would you like to be involved in famine relief? Are you angered by infringements on civil rights? Are you worried about the environment? What are you most passionate about?

Select one to three causes in priority order. It's far more satisfying to choose than to feel cornered into a commitment because you can't say NO.

Step 2. Don't make a snap decision.

Research the various groups and organizations that work on the issues or causes you have chosen. Decide if you want to work at the local, regional, national, or international level.

Giving money: It's harder to give money when you don't know how much discretionary income you have, so educate yourself about your assets and income. Understand your own financial resources and needs so you can avoid the anxiety that what you give will leave you without enough. Usually, the more you know about your own financial situation, the easier it is to give appropriately and without worry.

Look back at charitable checks or cash donations from the last two or three years and see if you need to re-budget or concentrate giving in some areas and eliminate others.

Decide how much you will give annually. You can choose a fixed dollar amount or a percentage. Set aside a portion of this amount for spontaneous giving (when you just can't refuse the person on your doorstep). Intentionally allocate the rest. Decide if it makes you feel better to give a few larger donations or many smaller ones. Stick to your budget throughout the year.

Giving time: Before you meet with anyone from a group or organization, figure out what you're going to say so that you don't agree to help before you've considered all options.

For instance, you might say: "I like what I've read about your organization and I'm considering volunteering to help. I wanted to meet with you (or talk with you) to find out about the possibility of matching my skills and availability with your organization's needs."

Make sure you have a chance to ask questions. Don't commit to anything on the spot. At the end of the conversation, praise the organization's efforts and express appreciation for its accomplishments. Explain that you will let them know what you decide.

If you are pressed for an on-the-spot commitment, buy yourself some time to consider the situation. One way to do this is to say: "I need a while to think about how this might fit in with my other obligations. I will get back to you in one week." Then think it over and respond punctually.

If you decide that you and the organization aren't a good match, and you have a hard time saying NO directly, consider e-mailing your response. Compliment the organization's efforts before you explain why it's not a good fit for you. Hardworking community volunteers appreciate verbal support, even if you can't offer more.

Step 3. When you select an organization, be specific about how you plan to contribute.

Do you intend to give money, donate your time, or share your expertise? Check out the various ways of giving. Do you want to make your financial contribution as an outright gift, a challenge or a matching grant, or a planned gift?

Do you have specific skills that match the needs of the group? You might enjoy working in the area of your expertise. Or you might find it more satisfying to contribute in some other way. For instance a lawyer might like to help with media relations and a photographer might prefer doing legal aid work.

Take a good, hard look at your calendar before you make any promises. Make sure you carve out personal time and family time in addition to your work and community service. Try not to overcommit: it breeds resentment and takes the pleasure out of being generous.

Step 4. No automatic renewals. No upping the ante.

If you offer your services or expertise, indicate the length of time you will be available to avoid feeling trapped in a never-ending obligation. You might begin with a three- or six-month commitment, then evaluate whether your contribution seems worthwhile at the end of that time. If you choose to renew, again specify the length of time. If you are asked to do more, be prepared to reply, "This is all I can commit to for now. If I am able to do more, I will let you know."

If you make a large monetary gift, clarify whether it is a single or renewable contribution or if there are conditions which must be met for you to renew. If your donation is significant in the budget of the group you are supporting, it is better to talk with people there about your intentions.

Step 5. Remember your priorities when asked for other contributions.

Though it's difficult to dodge direct solicitations from individuals who have been trained to appeal to your generosity, narrowing your focus to a few specific areas of need makes it easier to say NO to requests that don't fit within your guidelines. For example, if you are strongly committed to increasing literacy, your response to other solicitations might be: "I only support educational programs."

Invitations that come via mail or phone don't require an immediate response. If they are generic solicitations for issues that aren't on your agenda, you are not obligated to answer.

Keep a record of your spontaneous contributions. When you reach your predetermined limit, and you are asked for a contribution, you can say: "Sorry, I'm tapped out this year." Or, "Sorry, I've already given all I've budgeted for this year." You can always add, "But thank you for your contribution to this very important cause." Again, it's nice to express appreciation when you can't offer more.

Step 6. Form a women's empowerment group to help you maintain a good balance between giving to yourself and giving to the community.

We have groups to discuss investment in the stock market, why not have one to share thoughts on investing in the common good? It's a trap to believe that there is one right way to be socially conscious and responsible. Bouncing things off a group that shares your values is a wonderful way to avoid unnecessary self-criticism. Sometimes we can understand our own tendencies more easily when we observe them in other people. A group can help you figure out when enough is more than enough.

Step 7. When you do say NO, remind yourself that your goal is to contribute in a way that makes you feel good about what you've done.
Prioritizing your giving reduces the reactive, scattered contributions whenever someone writes, calls, or knocks at your door. Your NOs have more conviction when you say: "I'm sorry, it's really not part of my giving plan." There is nothing wrong with having fun with your YESes.

Pace yourself. Overcommitting leads to anxiety and depression. Having an organized plan for your financial contributions and volunteer efforts prevents unhappiness and burnout. As Mother Teresa said, "We can do no great things—only small things, with great love."

Doing good feels good. When it comes to healing the world, we like ourselves better when we do our part. By creating a plan for giving, you contribute consistently and consciously in ways that are meaningful to you. Intentional giving is more satisfying because it allows you to avoid the knee-jerk YESes or NOs that you later regret. Then when you do say NO to requests that don't fit within your priorities, your generosity comes full circle as you practice compassion for yourself.

chapter nine

NOt on your life!

(saying NO to assault and harassment)

Before I began martial arts training I was always afraid whenever I was alone anywhere, day or night. The news is full of stories about men raping women, and I'm not very big. I was especially frightened when I was using public transportation.

Martial arts training has developed my confidence to the point where I walk differently and talk differently. It has affected every part of my life. I can say NO when I need to. I don't worry as much about being attacked. Through my years of training, I have developed a so-called bag of tricks, with several techniques to use, depending on the situation. I could protect myself in almost any situation where I was a target.

Susie Brodsky, third degree black belt, Tukong Moosul

What would you do if a man standing behind you on the bus started rubbing up against you? If a group of frat guys pulled you into a bedroom and barricaded the door? Or a former boyfriend forced his way into your apartment? Or your husband hit you? If a stranger grabbed you and pointed a knife at you, could you scream NO at the top of your lungs? Could you kick, hit, and scratch to defend yourself against assault? Could you fight for your life?

Violence against women is pandemic. It affects all women— even those who have never been directly victimized—all the time. It makes us feel so unsafe that we constrict our movement and limit our choices. Many women never feel secure and worry about being raped or assaulted whenever we are alone in isolated areas. As a matter of routine, we double-check the locks, listen for unusual sounds, and feel frightened if footsteps unexpectedly come too close. We stick to busy subway stations, avoid poorly lit stairwells, and peer into the back seat before we get into our cars. But street-wise precautions offer no protection against assaults by the men we know intimately.

Almost every woman I know has been harassed, abused, or assaulted at some point in her life. For many of us, the first incidents occurred when we were children. When I was seven years old, two sixteen-year-old boys put a .22 rifle to my head and molested me in their tree fort. Contrary to popular misconceptions about sexual assault, this didn't happen in a high-crime community. I was raised in sunny, suburban Santa Barbara; my teenage assailants were the sons of the physician who lived next door.

When I got to college, I lived in an all-women dorm. We were admonished not to ride our bikes to the library at night because of the rapes that had occurred, and we were cautioned to keep our dorm rooms locked to prevent predators from slipping in unnoticed. I never felt safe unless I was with a large group of friends; I was hypervigilant, guarded, and anxious.

All that changed when I took a women's self-defense course as a senior. Confidence replaced fear as I was taught to shout, hit, and kick; to smash the nose and gouge out the eyes of an assailant; and, most important, to trust my own instincts. I learned that if I felt unsafe, I needed to take action. Never again did I hesitate to cross the street if the other side was better lit or I sensed that something was just not right about where I was.

Research has shown that a very effective way to prevent assault or to diminish its psychological impact is to resist—to say or enact a NO. And, according to the self-defense instructors, martial artists, and police officers I interviewed for this chapter, being able to defend yourself against physical attacks is one of the most effective ways of empowering women to say NO in all aspects of your life.

In my "Psychology of Women" classes, I ask students what they do on a daily basis to avoid getting raped. Here's what they say:

FOR FEMALE STUDENTS, STANDARD PRECAUTIONS:
1. Carry pepper spray.
2. Walk in pairs.
3. Talk on a cell phone to a friend who can call for help if the student is attacked.
4. Publish only her initials and last name in the telephone directory.
5. Have a male friend leave an outgoing message on her voicemail saying, "You've reached the home of Susan and Arthur (Arthur is the name of her dog)."
6. Carry a backpack instead of a purse so she can run.
7. If she has to use the bathroom during a party, have a friend stay with her drink so nobody can slip a sedative into it.
8. Avoid evening classes.
9. Put in a burglar alarm and install extra deadbolts.
10. Call campus security for transportation to her car.
11. Use a deep voice when answering the intercom to her apartment if someone rings the bell.
12. Keep pepper spray by the bed.

FOR MALE STUDENTS, STANDARD PRECAUTIONS:
None
(One male student said, "Avoid prisons.")

Professor Esther Rothblum

---

protection from the one you love

What's the difference between rape and sex? The difference is consent. If you can't really say NO, then you can never really say YES to sex or to relationships because your YES is compromised by the fact that it's not a choice.

Lauren R. Taylor,
Defend Yourself/DC Self-Defense
Karate Association

Self-protection begins at home. Most violence against women is perpetrated by men (therefore I use the male pronoun in reference to abusers in this chapter), most of the perpetrators are known to the victims, and one in four American women is in an abusive relationship at some point in her life. Intimate partner abuse does not discriminate by socioeconomic class, ethnicity, or educational background. In many cases, the victims are left with long-lasting psychological scars.

Abuse by an intimate partner rarely begins with a full-on attack; more often, it starts with verbal degradation, controlling behavior, or explosive anger that gets worse over time. The abuser uses criticism, fear, and intimidation to gain power over his partner. His comments about her appearance or behavior are often demeaning and deeply hurtful. He isolates her from friends and family who might help her retain a sense of her worth. Even if he never lays a hand on her, his threats can be terrifying and paralyzing.

Your best chance of preventing or stopping abuse comes from valuing yourself enough to draw a line at unacceptable conduct. That means paying attention to your gut feelings after a spouse or partner says something that makes you feel bad. If you feel frightened or hurt, you need to figure out why, and then explain clearly and emphatically that you don't want it to happen again.

Many women have difficulty deciphering the differences between appropriate expressions of anger and verbal abuse. In dysfunctional families, anger is acted out through deliberate cruelty—verbal or physical. Disassociating love from violence can be challenging for women whose parents were cruel. Often, women from dysfunctional families are drawn to relationships that replicate the unhealthy ones they had while growing up.

There are mean and clean ways of expressing anger. Psychologically healthy people express anger cleanly—communicating their disappointment about another person's *behavior,* instead of condemning a person's *character.* In clean anger, there is no name calling, no profanity, no overgeneralizing (using words like "always" or "never"), and no threat of abandonment.

Clean = *I am angry because you promised to pick up my suit from the cleaners and you didn't do it.*

Mean = *You're such a* loser. (= global condemnation) *I don't know why I'm still with you.* (= threat of abandonment) *I ask you to do one simple thing and you're such a lazy slob you can't even do that. I'm not even attracted to you anymore.* (= cruelty)

Psychologically healthy people try to find the source of the hurt that is fueling the anger. Identifying the cause of the pain can short-circuit a fight—particularly if the other person acknowledges the inconsiderate behavior and offers a sincere apology.

Explaining the pain = *Tomorrow I'm doing an important presentation and I want to wear that suit because it's comfortable and looks good and I want to make a good impression. I feel hurt that you didn't help me out by picking it up at the cleaners like you promised.*

Conflict resolution = *I'm really sorry—I didn't realize you needed it tomorrow. I'll get up early and go get it when they open at seven. I'll be back in time for you to wear it to work.*

· · ·

Just as important as keeping anger clean is the ability to say NO to demeaning comments. **Lauren Taylor, a Tae Kwon Do black belt** and a Washington, D.C., self-defense instructor, teaches women to set limits as soon as any mistreatment starts.

If women want to be able to make choices and have power in our lives, we must be able to say NO. Without the ability to say NO, we have no boundaries, people make choices for us, and they can violate us at will. Our NO may not always be respected, but if we can't say NO, it definitely won't be.

If your potential boyfriend hit you on your first date, you probably wouldn't go on the second date. But most violence in a relationship starts with more subtle behavior, and if you can say NO at these earlier stages, then you have a chance of preventing the vast majority of assaults. Even though the responsibility always rests with the perpetrator, you might be able to stop something before it becomes a full-on attack and you need to use your physical skills.

Demeaning comments damage your self-confidence. Repeated insults erode your self-esteem. According to Lauren, before enrolling in self-defense classes, some women have been so degraded that they feel powerless to take protective action.

Some women are afraid to hurt somebody's feelings, never mind hurt someone physically. You can teach women to hit all you want, but if they don't feel like they're worth defending and they don't feel like they have a right to hurt somebody else in self-defense, those hits don't matter. They're not going to defend themselves if they don't feel their worth.

In class, women feel sadness or outrage on each other's behalf. Hearing that feedback from each other helps women value themselves enough to say NO. NO takes all forms. It could be a serious look, a one-word answer ("NO"), a directive ("Take your hand off me"), leaving an abusive relationship, a loud yell, or a strike that disables or distracts an attacker long enough to get away. We need all of these kinds of NOs because we face all kinds of situations in life.

The peer support in Lauren's self-defense classes helps women learn to be more assertive about behaviors that others see as warning signs or as unacceptable. One woman might say that the worst thing her husband has ever done is slam her into a door, but she's not worried that he will beat her up. Another will say that pushing is never okay; she thought it wasn't a big deal until her boyfriend shoved her down the stairs. In these exchanges, women encourage each other to take better care of themselves and to believe they deserve respect.

Before you can muster the courage to speak up about a partner's unacceptable conduct, you must face your fears about losing the relationship. As I discussed in Chapter 3, letting go of a partner is enormously painful, even when you realize that nothing good can come from staying together.

What can you do to reduce the fear of losing your relationship?

Here's what I suggest:

Step 1. Tally your losses.
It's important to take stock of the losses that have already occurred. Your self-esteem and self-confidence have been damaged. You may have lost contact with family and friends. You may already have suffered some physical abuse. You are constantly on guard. If you have children, you're concerned about their safety as well.

Step 2. Ask yourself how your life might be improved if you set limits.
Would you feel less frightened for yourself and your children? Do you welcome the prospect of being more in control of your life and well-being? Would you spend more time with friends and family who appreciate you if you weren't worried about making him angry?

Step 3. Tell yourself that you deserve a healthy, mutually respectful relationship.

Ask your friends to tell you what they like about you. Write down what they say. Review this list every day. Whenever you think about losing your partner, say to yourself: "I deserve to be treated with love and respect. I will not tolerate degradation or abuse of any kind."

If you don't have anyone you can ask, this may be an indication that your partner is keeping you isolated. An outside perspective is imperative if you feel cut off from friends or family.

Step 4. Find support. Enroll in a self-defense class or assertiveness training. Get into therapy or a self-help group. Call a hotline.

Do this at a time when your husband or partner is working. Keep it to yourself. Consider it your private commitment to your well-being. Self-defense classes and assertiveness training build confidence and self-esteem; they teach you skills that will enable you to stand up for and defend yourself. Therapy, support groups, and hotlines validate your concerns and help you develop strategies to protect yourself.

Step 5. Remind yourself that your goal is to regain your self-worth and to prevent further damage.

Think back to a time when your life was happier. Remember how it felt to wake up looking forward to your day. Tell yourself that you will feel that way again—if you value yourself enough to say NO to your partner's demeaning comments, or to walk out, if necessary.

It is important to prepare for all possible outcomes before you initiate a conversation with an abusive partner. If you feel that it is safe to confront your partner about his unacceptable conduct, what is the best way to go about it? These are my recommendations:

Step 1. Develop your personal safety plan.

You must individualize your safety plans. Before you say anything to your partner about your relationship, inform a friend or family member about the situation. Give this ally an envelope containing copies of your (and your children's) important documents—driver's license(s), birth certificate(s), passport(s), bank account statements, insurance policies, deeds or leases, income tax records (yours and your spouse's)—whatever you would need if you had to leave. If you have medical or police records of past incidents of abuse, take them with you. Call the National Domestic Violence Hotline for help in developing a strategy that suits your situation. Call the hotline even if you're not sure your relationship is abusive: 1-800-799-SAFE (7233) or 1-800-787-3224 (TTY).

Plan to have the conversation with your partner at a time when your ally is available and, ideally, when your children are at the home of someone you trust who knows what's going on. Ask your ally to call you an hour later, if she or he hasn't heard from you. Make up a code word that you give to your ally. If you say this word, your ally should seek emergency help for you.

Step 2. Prepare your own exit strategy.

Just in case you need to leave, situate yourself nearest the door. Have your wallet, cell phone, keys, and the addresses of safe houses in your pockets. Without being conspicuous, unlock the door before you initiate the conversation.

Step 3. Pick a good time.

Choose a quiet moment when you and your partner are not in the midst of a conflict. Explain to your partner that you'd like ten minutes of his time to discuss a problem in your relationship. The time limit is important because psychologically unhealthy people balk at problem solving. Keep the conversation short.

Step 4. Select one or two recent incidents to illustrate your point.

As an example, you might say:

Last night when I was making dinner you called me an idiot for overcooking the vegetables. It hurts me when you call me names or swear at me because it feels disrespectful. Please don't do that again.

Step 5. Speak in the first person and don't generalize.

Use "I" statements as much as possible. Don't pull out the laundry list of the things he's done that you don't like, or you'll end up in a mud-slinging free-for-all. Stick to your point and repeat it as often as you need to.

Step 6. Expect resistance.

Psychologically unhealthy people become defensive when they are criticized. They lash back, often cruelly. Try to stay focused. If your partner starts complaining about your behavior, you might say:

Right now we are talking about treating each other respectfully. I'd like to make an agreement that there will be no more name calling or swearing or demeaning comments in our house.

Step 7. Be prepared for him to walk out.

Unhealthy partners often threaten to leave when confronted with their objectionable conduct. "I'm sick of your complaining," he might say. "I'll go find a girlfriend who likes me the way I am."

Don't let the threat derail you. Be prepared to counter: "I'm not talking about breaking up. I am talking about treating each other respectfully."

If he walks out, try to stay calm. Don't plead with him: he's testing you. Chances are that he will return when he realizes that you won't beg him to come back.

Step 8. Trust your instincts.

Pay attention to your gut as you set limits. If you begin to feel more anxious about your safety, leave as soon as you can. If he becomes violent or you fear violence, go to a shelter or the home of a friend your partner doesn't know so he won't be able to find you.

Making the decision to terminate an abusive relationship always takes longer than anyone expects. On average, victims of domestic violence make five attempts before they leave for good. Sometimes women feel too frightened to leave. Others imagine that their abusers will seek help or change. This rarely happens. If you are a victim of intimate partner violence, get strong— through self-defense classes and peer or family support—and move out. Leave before it's too late.

The National Coalition Against Domestic Violence offers many helpful resources online at: www.ncadv.org/protectyour self/GettingHelp_128.htmls. When investigating your options, always use a computer at a library or a friend's home so that your partner can't track your Internet searches. Also, if you have children, it's best to take them with you if you decide to move out. That's for their safety, and also to help if you end up in a custody battle.

Protecting yourself and your family from abuse by an intimate partner shows the strongest love for everyone involved.

THE COST OF COUTURE

My husband likes to dress up in women's underwear before we have sex and it's a real turnoff for me. A couple of months ago he saw distaste in my expression and he exploded. He screamed at me and hit me.

The next day to make up he came home with a new Armani outfit for me. I had a black eye and my whole face was swollen and bruised. I had to wear dark glasses and a hat for a month to cover it up when I went out. I told people I'd had a facelift if they asked what happened.

Geraldine, former teacher

WHY SHE DOESN'T LEAVE HIM:
I tried once. He said if I ever did it again he'd find me and kill me.

stopping harassment

For years I avoided self-defense courses. I knew they made you say NO a lot and I was terrified of saying NO in public— shouting NO out loud seemed so embarrassing. A colleague in my department asked me to come to her Model Mugging graduation [Model Mugging is now called "IMPACT"], and I said to her in a very lofty tone, "You know I'm really against self-defense workshops for women because they make the victims do all the work. Men are the ones who should be taught not to molest women."

I was somewhat annoyed that I had agreed to go to the graduation, but within moments I was absolutely hooked. I loved watching women on the floor kicking the shit out of the guy in the padded suit. Whatever he was doing—jumping on top of a woman while she was lying down—the woman would attack the parts of him that weren't protected. I was so thrilled by what I saw that I signed up for the course. I even took advanced Model Mugging where the assailant has a weapon, because I figured if I got attacked and the guy didn't have a weapon, I could say to myself: "Piece of cake—this is just the Intro course."

Esther Rothblum,
Women's Studies Professor

Women deserve the right to walk down the street without being harassed by men making lewd or suggestive comments. Though many women believe that the most effective strategy is to ignore harassers, self-defense instructors like **Lauren Taylor** encourage women to speak up and confront harassment to build our "self-defense muscles."

Street harassment feels like an attack, and for good reason. It could be a rape test. If you react by standing up for yourself, you're not a good candidate for victim. Setting limits with harassers may help keep you safe. You wouldn't run a marathon without getting up off the couch, then walking, then jogging, then running long distances. If you don't resist harassment, you will be out of shape should you ever have to deal with an abusive partner or a rape attempt.

The first step in self-defense is to use your voice to say NO. **Penny Sablove, a third-degree black belt Aikido instructor in San Francisco,** tells her students never to underestimate the power of the voice.

*A number of women say that one self-defense course was literally a lifesaver. Often the most valuable part of the course was learning to use their voice—yelling "get away from me, I don't know you." **The voice happens to be the most powerful thing women can use to protect ourselves.** But for women to do sound production publicly is a big stumbling block. I force myself to practice it. In some Aikido classes, I require that every time someone strikes, they make a loud yelling sound. That has helped me get over my discomfort with yelling when I need to, and it's helped other women as well.*

Susie Brodsky, director of women's training and development at Tukong Moosul, says her NOs have become so powerful through martial arts that she can't imagine ever having to resort to physical force.

I've learned to be very assertive verbally rather than back down. When I first started in martial arts, I couldn't make a sound. Now, if I were harassed, I would stand up to them and yell NO as loudly as I could and that probably would do it. I wouldn't show any signs of weakness. I wouldn't back down.

In martial arts, you yell to signal that you are ready to attack. If you are punching or kicking, you have to yell because it makes you far more powerful when you make a noise. It forces you to breathe out. Not only does it scare the person, but it also makes whatever technique you use more powerful. So, if I or anyone I love were being attacked, I'd be yelling as I tried to contain the situation.

Author Dorothy Allison's mother had plenty of practice saying NO to sexual advances at work. Dorothy compares the affable Southern NO with the fierce Northern NO, as practiced by waitresses in each location.

My mother was incapable of saying NO, except when she was working. She was a waitress, and she could say NO to sexual advances at work. There's a whole culture of how to say NO as a waitress. When she took me in to be a waitress, which I did starting at fourteen, that was the thing she taught me—how to say NO to men who make sexual advances at you.

I learned to handle it in a particular Southern working-class waitress manner, which is a lot about humor and deflection. You don't learn to break their fingers when they grab your butt—you charm these men into not asking again.

It wasn't until I was a grown up working as a waitress in New York that I saw New York waitresses and a whole other technique of saying NO. I worked this counter where this guy reached over to touch this waitress. She caught his hand, and said, "Do you want them back or do I keep them?" Wow. I would never have been able to do that. God, it was good.

Lauren Taylor has developed the following guidelines for speaking up in response to harassment or abuse:

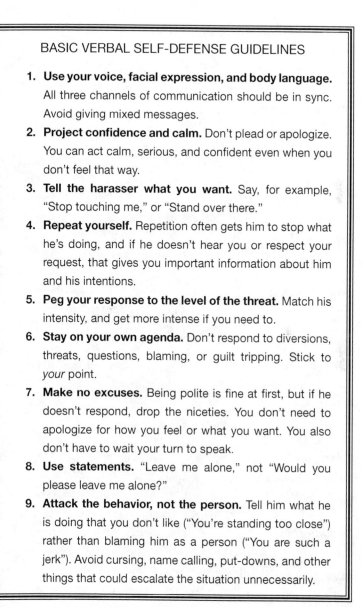

BASIC VERBAL SELF-DEFENSE GUIDELINES

1. **Use your voice, facial expression, and body language.** All three channels of communication should be in sync. Avoid giving mixed messages.

2. **Project confidence and calm.** Don't plead or apologize. You can act calm, serious, and confident even when you don't feel that way.

3. **Tell the harasser what you want.** Say, for example, "Stop touching me," or "Stand over there."

4. **Repeat yourself.** Repetition often gets him to stop what he's doing, and if he doesn't hear you or respect your request, that gives you important information about him and his intentions.

5. **Peg your response to the level of the threat.** Match his intensity, and get more intense if you need to.

6. **Stay on your own agenda.** Don't respond to diversions, threats, questions, blaming, or guilt tripping. Stick to *your* point.

7. **Make no excuses.** Being polite is fine at first, but if he doesn't respond, drop the niceties. You don't need to apologize for how you feel or what you want. You also don't have to wait your turn to speak.

8. **Use statements.** "Leave me alone," not "Would you please leave me alone?"

9. **Attack the behavior, not the person.** Tell him what he is doing that you don't like ("You're standing too close") rather than blaming him as a person ("You are such a jerk"). Avoid cursing, name calling, put-downs, and other things that could escalate the situation unnecessarily.

To teach her students to say NO more easily, Lauren has them pair up and take turns asking each other for something.

The person asked is only allowed to say "NO." The requests range from trivial to significant, and most students find it very challenging—even as an exercise—to say NO without apology. Here are some examples of the questions Lauren's students use in this exercise:

1.	Question:	*Can I use your pencil?*	Answer: NO
2.	Question:	*Can I touch your hair?*	Answer: NO
3.	Question:	*Can I borrow your sweater?*	Answer: NO
4.	Question:	*Can I have sex with you?*	Answer: NO
5.	Question:	*Can you give me a ride?*	Answer: NO
6.	Question:	*Will you watch my kids this afternoon? I have a doctor's appointment.*	Answer: NO
7.	Question:	*My cat just got hit by a car and I need a ride to the vet. Can you give me a ride?*	Answer: NO
8.	Question:	*Can I kiss you?*	Answer: NO
9.	Question:	*Can I borrow your cell phone?*	Answer: NO
10.	Question:	*Do you think I'm pretty?*	Answer: NO
11.	Question:	*Do you like me?*	Answer: NO

After the exercise, Lauren asks her students to talk about when it's easier and harder to say NO, how they feel saying NO, and what they feel compelled to add to the NO, such as "NO—sorry." Or, "NO—you know, I would never say this in real life." The exercise helps women explore their reluctance to hurt people's feelings—especially when somebody needs help. Then as homework, the women are required to say NO—without apology or explanation—to something they would ordinarily say YES to, as a way of strengthening their self-defense muscles.

Learning to make the word "NO" a complete sentence is a powerful tool in women's self-defense.

fighting for your life

> *It was about six o'clock at night when I left church. I was bundled up because it was snowing so I didn't hear him come up behind me. When I was walking past an alley, he pushed me so hard that I fell onto my knees. Something crashed into my head. I put my hands up to my head and he grabbed me and dragged me behind a dumpster in the alley. [Crying] He raped me in my rectum. Then he did it again in my mouth. I thought he was going to kill me. My only chance was to scream, and as soon as I could take a deep breath I screamed as loud as I could. He hit me in the face and then got off of me and ran.*
>
> Mary Catherine,
> peace corps trainer

Most women engage in an all-out fight for our lives if we find out that we have a potentially fatal disease, such as cancer. Yet when it comes to hurting someone else to prevent that person from assaulting us, we hesitate. The prospect of injuring another person—even in our own self-defense—can be distressing.

When she was on active duty, former **Police Chief Jan Tepper** taught self-defense to the women in her community. Initially, Jan says, her students had all kinds of issues about defending themselves: they worried about being nice, hurting people's feelings, injuring people physically. Some women had a visceral objection to fighting.

Jan tried various strategies to help women get past their reluctance to use physical force for self-protection. The only technique that proved effective was when Jan asked her students to imagine that an assailant had targeted a loved one. Without hesitation, every woman in the class said that she would use whatever techniques she had at her disposal to protect the endangered person.

Harvard Medical School Professor Judith L. Herman, MD, is the **training director** and **co-founder** of the Cambridge Health Alliance **Victims of Violence Program.** Judith has been studying the devastating effects of trauma for many decades; her program helps women recover from abuse. When her own daughter was a teenager, Judith signed the two of them up for a mother-daughter Model Mugging self-defense course. She wanted her daughter to have all the skills she needed to protect herself against violence.

So many women are inhibited in their fighting skills. The Model Mugging course was very powerful because it involved muscle learning—like learning to ride a bicycle—more than intellectual learning. It taught us how to fight under circumstances that simulated what an actual attack might be like. We learned to fight when we were being verbally abused and threatened and when we were pinned to the floor. We learned to deliver a knock-out blow.

As a mother-daughter pair, it was incredibly heartening to see my daughter competently fighting and being able to ward off an attack, and I'm sure she felt the same way about me. My daughter not only gave me courage and modeled it for me, but it was reassuring for me to think about her being able to face the world with these skills.

Some women worry that they aren't big or strong enough to defend themselves effectively, or that they will be killed if they resist assault. These common misconceptions were promulgated, even by law enforcement officers, until the 1980s when **Pauline Bart,** at the time a **professor of sociology** at the University of Illinois, Chicago, did a series of studies that showed otherwise. Pauline found that women who used physical or verbal skills to fight back against their assailants were less likely to be raped and more likely to escape uninjured. Not only were these women often smaller than their attackers, but they were also unarmed, while some of their assailants had weapons. Moreover, the women in Pauline's study who resisted but were nevertheless raped recovered psychologically much more rapidly than the raped women who had not fought back.

Although resistance works much of the time, it's not the best strategy all of the time. **Lauren Taylor** says that in a dangerous situation, only you can decide what approach to take.

Self-defense is about having choices, and different resistance strategies are effective in different situations. But if harassment, abuse, or an attack is happening, you are the only one who can assess everything about the situation—how committed he is to the attack, how likely it is that you can get help, what you're feeling capable of at the moment, and so on.

There are times when resistance isn't the best strategy, because your intuition is telling you that you need to go along with it to survive, or to wait for a moment to escape. For example, I know women who were attacked who were sure that their assailant would kill them if they resisted. In some abuse situations, compliance is needed until you can find a way out of the relationship or get help. In those cases, you are deciding to comply, not doing it because you have no other choices. I call that "strategic compliance."

Women who grew up with rough-and-tumble siblings or playmates sometimes have an easier time defending ourselves when we are attacked. Others of us can't recall the last time, if ever, we hit anyone. Before taking self-defense classes, many women don't even know where the vulnerable parts of the body are. But we need to learn to fight and, as Lauren says, keep our self-defense muscles in shape. If we are assaulted, that training may make the difference between life and death.

. . .

Even though she's earned a third-degree black belt in martial arts, **Susie Brodsky** doesn't particularly like to fight. But she wouldn't hesitate to use all the skills at her disposal to protect herself if she were threatened.

I don't like to hurt anybody and I don't like to fight. When my older brother and I fought when I was a kid, he'd punch me and I couldn't even hit him back. But now I have the ability to injure or kill if I'm seriously assaulted. As a black belt, I have deadly techniques at my disposal. I wouldn't fight unless I had to, but if my life or somebody I care about's life was in danger, I'd do whatever I needed to do to protect us.

The sequence of responses for me would be:

1. *If someone is verbally harassing me, I'd tell them to cut it out and I'd keep walking past them.*
2. *If they grabbed me, I'd do a quick release—meaning I'd use a technique that allows me to get away—and I'd yell loudly, "Stop!" Or, "Stay back!" The technique you choose to use depends on how they grab you.*
3. *If they kept coming at me, then I would punch or kick them. Kicks are very powerful. When you combine power and accuracy, that should be enough to stop an attacker.*

My Grand Master always says, "Don't fight. But if you have to fight, win." He also has taught us, "il kyuk pil sa," which, in Korean, means, "one-strike finish." So if I had to kick, I'd take the person down with one kick and be done with it.

Rita, a nurse, fought off a potential rapist before she learned self-defense skills. In retrospect, Rita feels that she could have deflected her assailant more easily if she had the knowledge she has now.

I was walking home from the subway and a man came up behind me, put his gloved hand over my mouth, and dragged me into a yard. I wasn't able to pull his hand away or bite him through the glove, but he didn't have a weapon and I fought and yelled as much as I could, and he ran away without raping me.

I realized how much different it could have been if I'd had even a little training. I knew someone was walking behind me, but I didn't cross the street, confront him, yell at him, or go to a house. Instead of trying to pull his whole hand off my mouth, I realized after one short self-defense class that I could have bent back one of his fingers instead. With even a very little training it could have been very different.

It takes time and practice to develop these skills, but as you acquire them, you'll have a much better idea what to do if you are harassed, abused, or assaulted. Meanwhile, your self-confidence will grow each time you say or enact the word "NO."

Until we create a culture in which women can live alone, hike in nature, date or socialize, drive at night, and travel the world without fear of harassment or worse, self-defense training gives you a powerful and effective set of tools to amplify your NOs.

chapter ten
_____

Doctor, NO

(saying NO to your shrink or doctor)

*I was in the hospital for two months after a terrible car acci-
dent in a state far away from where I live. I broke my back
and a lot of other bones, and I had to wear a body cast. My
doctors were great, but they almost never washed their hands
before they examined me. None of my family or friends could
be there to advocate for me. I was afraid I might make my
doctors angry if I told them I was worried about contracting
a hospital-based infection from their hands. I was too dependent on them for everything else to take that risk.*

*Sure enough, when they took off my body cast, I had
green fungus growing all over my chest and stomach and
back. It was freaky. It took about seven months and all
kinds of medications to get rid of it. Really, I'm lucky that
fungus didn't kill me.*

Tori, musician

Can you say NO to medical practitioners? Are you able to disagree with treatments your physicians propose? Could you ask
for a second opinion? Could you request that a nurse be present
during a physical examination? If a doctor comes into your hospital room to examine you, can you say, "May I ask you to wash
your hands to prevent infection?"

There is no room for error when somebody's life or mental health is on the line. Yet, thousands of mistakes are made every day by healthcare providers, and many of them are caught by a patient's family members or friends. In this chapter, I explore why we are reluctant to challenge authority in a white coat. I discuss the discomfort of speaking up when procedures or prescriptions feel wrong to us. I look at situations where we need to say, "NO. I need to think it over," or "NO, I'd like to check with my primary care doctor before I make a decision."

When you have a health problem, you don't go to a doctor seeking sex. But in surveys I conducted, nearly 10 percent of male doctors acknowledged sexually abusing their female patients. As a leading expert on the enforcement of professional ethics, I discuss the importance of saying NO to healthcare providers whose behavior is out of bounds.

calling the shots

Women do most of the interacting with the healthcare system on behalf of ourselves, our families, our elderly parents, our partners, and our children. Sometimes we're reluctant to disagree with our doctors or double-check medications before they are administered because we worry that our assertiveness might backfire—that our health providers might not be available when we need them.

Yet, according to the Institute of Medicine of the National Academy of Sciences, there are a minimum of 1.5 million preventable medical errors per year, making them the third leading cause of death in this country. Very often, prevention is a matter of checking the label on a pill bottle or an IV bag to make sure that the medicine it contains is what has been prescribed. Asking our health providers to wash their hands before they examine us is just as important. Study after study has shown that hospital personnel practice poor hand hygiene—physicians topping the list of worst offenders. Being assertive in order to get good medical care may actually make the difference between life and death.

KEEPING WATCH

When I was in the hospital during one of my rounds of chemo, I had to tell everyone not to take my blood pressure on the arm where I'd had the lymph nodes removed. There were notes in my chart, and still, I'd wake up with somebody trying to put a blood pressure cuff on my bad arm. I got so upset about it that I practically stopped sleeping. It sets me back months if that kind of mistake is made. I want to be nice to the staff, but I got so on edge that I started to worry they weren't going to take good care of me because I kept saying, "NO—not my right arm."

Miranda, curator

Marlene Beggelman, MD, CEO and **president** of **Enhanced Medical Decisions, Inc.** in Cambridge, Massachusetts, says that quality healthcare depends on patient participation. The mission of her organization is to improve healthcare by making medical information accessible and comprehensible to everyone. She encourages women to be proactive in the treatment we receive.

The Internet has democratized healthcare in the sense that information which is critical to getting good treatment is now available to everyone.

I tell women all the time that we need to do the research and speak up—asking "What about this treatment?" or saying, "I don't want that"—to make sure we are getting what we need from our doctors. Women who are afraid of saying NO to their doctors might find it easier to bring the printouts from their Internet searches about their symptoms or diseases or the proposed treatments, and just hand those printouts to their healthcare providers. These days, women who have access to the Internet can very quickly learn nearly as much as their doctors know by researching their diseases. Self-diagnosis is also a much more common phenomenon because of information on the Internet.

Doctors sometimes pretend that medical information is too complicated for lay people to understand. I don't believe that is the case. The barrier to lay people understanding medical information is the language. There is a secret code in which we physicians speak, and if you just translate that into common language, then everyone can understand it.

Often there isn't one right or wrong answer in terms of a particular treatment. An option may be good for one person, and bad for the next—depending on your personal lifestyle requirements. Back surgery might be very helpful for one person and terrible for another—depending on physical activity and other factors. It's really important not to let your healthcare provider choose for you, but to stay informed, and make the best decisions you can based on what you have learned.

My mission in life is to translate medical information into a common language so that consumers have as much information as doctors have. I created a software program to give people more targeted information based on their own personal health problems. For instance, **people can go to our website, www.doublecheckmd.com, to find out if symptoms they are having are possible side effects of a medication or group of medications they are taking.**

Of course, you can't believe everything you read on the Web. A few precautions can help you find reputable resources like Marlene's. When you are looking at medical sites, consider the following:

- Where did the information come from—is it a commercial site trying to sell something as a cure?
- Who publishes the site—is it listed on the home page or the "about us" page?

- How current is the information—when was it last updated?
- What are the credentials of the people giving medical advice?
- Is what they are saying backed up by references to medical journals?

Two credible sites you might check are www.webmd.com and www.MayoClinic.com.

In some specialties such as breast cancer treatment, women have become strong advocates for quality healthcare; because of advocacy groups, most breast cancer specialists expect patients to be assertive about their needs. At some hospitals, patient allies are available to guide the newly diagnosed through the decision-making process. Also, breast cancer survivors have proactively established informational websites and support groups to help women decipher protocols and treatment possibilities.

But often, you will be on your own. If so, it's up to you to find a doctor you like, whom you can see at appropriate intervals, whom you (or if you're lucky, your insurance) can afford to pay.

Once you have chosen a doctor you feel is respectful, you can do a number of things as a patient to ensure that you are holding up your end of the partnership. If you do these things, it will make it much easier to say NO when you disagree with what your provider is suggesting. Being honest with your doctor is the most basic requirement for getting good care.

Before every appointment, make a written list of things you need to tell your physician and questions you want answered. Put them in priority order. Try to express them succinctly. This will allow you to have your most important issues addressed.

Bring a list of all the prescription medications, vitamin-mineral supplements, over-the-counter drugs, and herbal remedies you are currently taking, along with the dosing schedule and amount. This is essential if the doctor prescribes a new medication that might interact with one you are already taking. Ask about the risks and side effects of the new medication, and any potential problems with drug interactions. Be sure to tell your physician about allergic reactions you have experienced with any medication.

It is important, and not always easy, to understand what the doctor is telling you. There are several ways to help you do this. One is to bring a pen and paper and try to write everything down. A tape recorder might be a better option. You should ask in advance if this is okay. Make sure you explain that you are trying to keep track of all the information, because some physicians think "lawsuit" when they see recording devices.

The advantage of a tape recorder is that it allows you to pay attention to the conversation without being distracted by writing notes. Also, you can review what the doctor said at a later time when you may be less stressed. Alternatively, you could bring someone with you to the appointment for support. A trusted friend or family member can listen, take notes, and ask questions. Another way to make sure you know what is expected of you as a patient is to ask the doctor to write it down or give you preprinted instructions or information.

Taking care of yourself means asking questions even if you are worried that they may be considered silly or embarrassing. If you don't understand what a word means; if you don't know why a medication or a treatment is being recommended, or what to expect from it or how much it will cost; if you don't know whether to take a medication with food or on an empty stomach; if you aren't clear about what will happen if you refuse the medication or treatment, you must ask your healthcare provider. Asking is not only smart, it's your right. Remember that you are the consumer: you know your body better than anyone, and you get to make the final decisions.

QUALITY OVER QUANTITY

I have recurrent ovarian cancer. I've been very fortunate to be treated in one of the top cancer hospitals in the country. I've been on a series of research protocols that really have prolonged my life, and I'm grateful for that.

But I've reached the point where I feel so bad all the time that I don't want to go through more chemo—especially when it's all experimental, with only a tiny chance it will help me. I'm afraid to tell my doctors I've had enough, because they've worked so hard to get me to this point.

Bernice, philanthropist

WHY SHE'S RELUCTANT TO SAY NO:
It comes down to pain. I want my doctors to give me the pain medication I need. And I don't have the energy to change doctors.

ONE WAY TO START A CONVERSATION:
"If I ever decide to stop chemo, would you still be willing to be my doctor?"

Many women assume that their doctors are impartial, and that there is only one appropriate treatment for every illness. **Breast surgeon** and **author Dr. Susan Love** points out that doctors' opinions are derived from many influences, including our own health concerns and fears.

Women sometimes don't realize that doctors have their own agenda. And it may not even be something the doctor is aware of. Surgeons have a tendency to overbiopsy and overoperate because we generally see people who are sick, it is what we're reimbursed for, and we're not sued if we do it and find out that the lesion is benign. Patients like it when we call them up and say it's benign. If anything, we do too much surgery.

Women patients often don't think about the fact that doctors have our own influences and neuroses. They think doctors are acting completely objectively. So patients will say, "What would you do if you were me?" The reality is that my decisions for myself are based on how I feel about my body, and how I feel about my mother's early death, and what kind of a risk taker I am—lots of things that have nothing to do with them. It's not necessarily the right answer for them.

When women disagree with their doctor's recommendations, I encourage them to get a second opinion. Many women worry that it will hurt their doctor's feelings, but I tell them that if the doctor's ego is so fragile that your getting a second opinion is going to crush him or her, this is not the right doctor for you. *Your doctor is working for you, and you need to keep this in mind.*

If women need ammunition that their opinion of what's needed for their medical care is correct—and their doctor is not doing the right thing—now there are lots of places on the Internet where you can get information to back you up. But all patients need to keep in mind that most things in medicine aren't black and white—they are gray. The doctors are making their best guess at the moment, but you have a vote!

My mother had a nipple discharge two years before she was diagnosed with breast cancer. Her doctor said there was nothing to worry about. Even though my mother was really concerned, she was afraid to challenge the doctor or to get a second opinion. By the time she was diagnosed the cancer was all over the place. My mother would probably still be alive today if she'd been able to say that she didn't agree with her doctor, or if she'd gotten a second opinion.

Marlene Beggelman, MD

• • •

If you feel hesitant about a treatment that your physician has proposed—and this physician is a clinician you trust—what is the best way to communicate your reluctance to proceed? I suggest that you practice what I call "informed dissent."

Step 1. Tell your doctor that you need time to consider the proposed treatment.
Don't fill the prescription or schedule an appointment for the suggested test or treatment. Instead, thank your physician for explaining your condition and recommending a way to proceed. Tell the doctor that you would like to do some research to become better informed. Say that you might need to ask more questions after you have had time to think it over.

Step 2. If you discover options that your doctor didn't discuss, if you are anxious about debilitating side effects, or you have other concerns, make another appointment to discuss these.
If you find articles that form the basis for your concerns, bring copies with you to your next appointment. Make sure the reference source (name of website or journal) is clear. Physicians are accustomed to inquiries that come from Internet research. Citing a specific reference that explains your position is sometimes easier than challenging a doctor without backup documentation.

Step 3. Get a second opinion.
Contrary to popular misconceptions, physicians these days welcome the input of colleagues. Second opinions reduce the likelihood of malpractice claims and contribute to greater patient satisfaction. Patients are more receptive to treatments when they feel they have been given a choice. Some physicians keep a list of qualified colleagues whom they recommend for second opinions. It's also possible to locate the experts in a particular field through online searches or by calling hospitals in your area to ask for the name of the leading specialists.

Step 4. If your doctor gives you the brush-off, find another provider.

If your doctor doesn't listen, doesn't answer your questions, or makes you feel bad for saying NO, it's time for a change. If your insurance company allows you to choose another provider, do so. If not, bring a friend or ally to all appointments. Sometimes the presence of another person in the examining room puts physicians on alert to the need to be more attentive to a patient's unease.

Quality healthcare depends on informing yourself about your health problems and the proposed treatments, asking for a second opinion if you have questions about treatment options, double-checking whatever medications are prescribed, and saying NO if a doctor's recommendation doesn't work for you.

bidding your shrink adieu

When I moved to the West Coast, I shopped around for a new therapist. After seventeen years on the couch, I decided to try something different, since psychoanalysis hadn't really helped me with my ambivalence.

So I called this cognitive behavior therapist some friends recommended. When I showed up for my first appointment, this shrink tells me she has a migraine coming on, so she's only gonna charge me half the usual fee. I love a bargain, so I figure, hey, great!

At the end of the session, the shrink says the migraine never materialized, so she's charging me the full fee. I couldn't believe it! But did I walk right out of there and never return? I wish! I wrote out a check for what she asked for, then I came back every week for six months because I couldn't figure out how to stop!

Merri, writer

Women are the main consumers of mental health services in the
United States. Good treatment depends on disclosing intimate
details of our lives to the clinicians we see. So whether we've
done short stints with different psychotherapists or made a lifelong commitment to a single clinician, it's no surprise that we
feel vulnerable when it's time to call it quits.

Many women find it quite distressing to tell their therapists
that the treatment isn't going anywhere, or that they've met their
goals and they're ready to move on. Some even have a hard time
saying it doesn't feel like a good fit after the first appointment.
They worry that their reluctance to sign up for a series of sessions
will be interpreted as criticism of the clinician's competence.

I've been in both chairs—the patient's and the therapist's.
Though I've logged many more hours as the clinician, I appreciate the intensity of distress that accompanies the effort to stop
treatment. To circumvent this problem, I have adopted a proactive approach with my own patients—encouraging them to
check in with themselves regularly, and to speak up if something's not working for them.

I tell prospective patients up front that therapy needs to be a
good fit just like any relationship, and that I don't want them to
waste their time and money if it doesn't feel right.

But not all therapists take the same approach. Some are quite
insistent that prospective patients sign up for a series of appointments to allow the therapists to get a "good look" at a problem.
Others try to dissuade long-term patients from leaving—using
the "I know what's best for you" pretext—when, truth be told, the
therapists are trying to avoid a loss in self-esteem or income.

What's the best way to say NO to a therapist who appears to
have an agenda that you don't share? Here's what I recommend:

**Step 1. Before the first appointment, explain that you are
shopping for a therapist who is a good fit.**
When you make your first phone call to a prospective therapist,
explain that you are meeting with several therapists in the hope

of finding the best fit. On the phone, ask about the therapist's style, expertise, rates, and availability for a consultation. If you are interested in scheduling an appointment based on how she or he answered your questions, do so, but restate your intention to meet with several possible clinicians.

Step 2. Don't commit to a second appointment without thinking it over.

Even if you think the therapist seems like a terrific match, give yourself a few days to reflect on your decision. Tell the therapist how soon you will be back in touch. You may still elect to meet with other clinicians to be certain that you are making the best choice.

If you are hesitant about your interaction with the therapist or you disliked her or his response to your concerns, check out the others on your list. If you find someone you like better, leave a phone message indicating that you've decided to work with another clinician.

Step 3. Once you begin treatment, don't commit too far in advance.

Try it out. Therapists aren't always as good as we may appear. You should have a very good idea by two or three sessions whether a psychotherapist is helpful to you. If you are prescribed a medication, it can take six to eight weeks for the medication to kick in and for you to feel its full effects. In that case, you may be too depressed or anxious to assess the usefulness of treatment until the medication is fully on board.

Step 4. Make a list of your treatment goals. Review them regularly.

Discuss these goals with your therapist at the beginning of treatment. Your goals should include the things you'd like to change, the distress you'd like to be rid of (anxiety, depression, poor self-esteem, unsatisfactory relationship, etc.), and the time frame you have in mind for working together. The therapist can tell you if your time frame is realistic. Then plan to check on your progress every three to six months.

If you find when you check in that you aren't making headway or you've already met your goals, it's time to call it quits. Having a plan that you and your therapist agree on at the outset makes it easier to speak up when you reach this point.

Be wary of shrinks who propose a series of sessions to process your decision to stop treatment. You have the right to take as many—or few—sessions as you need to stop therapy—even if you decide to do it on the spur of the moment. If you're having a hard time saying that you want to quit, or your therapist isn't listening to your NO, you can say that you're going to take

---

NO EXIT

I've been seeing this therapist for four or five years, and I've run out of things to talk about. Basically, at this point, I'm just chatting about what I do each week. So a few months ago I said that I thought I was ready to stop.

My therapist said, "Oh, I disagree. I think we've only just begun to scratch the surface." Now every session she asks what I'm running away from in wanting to stop therapy. I mean, she's the expert and maybe she's right about this.

Adele, speech therapist

WHY SHE DOESN'T JUST QUIT:
I'm trying to leave on good terms so I can go back if I need to. But I'm starting to feel irritated that her agenda is different from mine.

ONE WAY TO SAY NO:
"I feel like I'm at a good stopping place. Even though you disagree, I'd like you to support my choice to take a break."

a break to see how you feel without treatment, and that if you decide to resume, you'll be back in touch.

Your therapist may feel genuinely sad that you're planning to discontinue treatment, but that's no excuse for pressuring you to continue therapy to give him or her time to resolve the loss. In my experience, supporting patients' right to leave when they want to makes them more likely to return if a need arises.

THE PRICE OF ADMISSION

My father has Parkinson's. For the last two years, I couldn't ever reach his doctor when I needed to speak with him. Then all of a sudden, I get a call at work from this doctor saying he needs to speak with me as soon as possible. I called him thinking my father had died. Well, it turns out that the guy's daughter was applying to the college where I teach, and he wanted me to write the daughter a recommendation.

Kristine, classics professor

WHY SHE DIDN'T SAY NO:
I was over a barrel. I needed the doctor's help with my father, and I worried that it might jeopardize my father's care if I said NO.

---

bad boundaries

Every health professional in the United States is responsible for maintaining appropriate boundaries. The only personal gratification clinicians should get from our patients is the pleasure of helping or healing. Physicians must not seek gifts or special favors from patients, and we are ethically and legally prohibited from engaging in sexual relationships with patients. Sexual involvement with former patients is also not allowed if the professional relationship was terminated specifically for the purpose of initiating sexual contact. A patient's willingness to engage in a sexual relationship with her doctor does not excuse the offense.

I first became aware of boundary violations when I was a resident in psychiatry at Harvard Medical School. My supervisor was the senior clinician on the staff of the student mental health service. The first time I entered his office I was struck by the low lighting and had an eerie feeling that something was awry.

Several years later, a student sent an anonymous letter to the mental health service claiming that my ex-supervisor—her psychiatrist—had charged her $35 per session to perform fellatio on him, twice a week for four years. I informed the medical licensing board. Eventually, several other patients of his—also Harvard students—pressed similar charges. While the case was being investigated, my ex-supervisor became a fugitive from justice and has never been heard from again.

The number of physicians sued by their patients for sexual misconduct skyrocketed in the years following the Harvard case. I spearheaded the movement to stop physician abuse by collecting data on how frequently doctors were taking advantage of their patients. I surveyed physicians in five specialties—internal medicine, psychiatry, family practice, obstetrics-gynecology, and surgery—and found that nearly 10 percent of U.S. doctors freely acknowledged sexual involvement with patients. In the vast majority of cases, the physicians were men and the patients were women. My studies were used to revamp ethics codes for doctors, to educate consumers about appropriate professional boundaries, and to criminalize physician misconduct.

Sexual exploitation of patients by physicians is now a felony in many states. Physicians who are found guilty of sexual misconduct can also lose their medical licenses and be sued for malpractice. Nevertheless, some doctors consider themselves above the law, and they still engage in unprofessional conduct.

When doctors ignore the rules and make an inappropriate proposition to their patients, it's up to the patients to say NO. Some women imagine that a loving relationship might evolve if they go along with their doctors' advances. What these patients don't know is that most predatory doctors are involved with many women patients at the same time. It is psychologically devastating to women patients to become sexually or romantically involved with physicians who are abusing the power of the doctor-patient relationship to satisfy their own needs. Women who are seduced by their doctors often end up depressed—even suicidal—once they realize how deceptive their doctor-lovers have been.

HEART MONITORING

I made an appointment to see a cardiologist about my irregular heartbeats. I've been waking up with palpitations ever since my divorce. The cardiologist was extremely helpful, and he had me come back a couple of times to follow up. The last time I saw him he suggested we have lunch together. I figured, what the heck—he seems like a perfectly nice guy.

At lunch, the doctor told me that he and his wife were separating and he's been really lonely. He said he found me very attractive and wanted to know if I would see him again. Something told me this is not right, but I said I'd go to a movie with him. Then my friend told me that this was very inappropriate.

Lucinda, retailer

WHY SHE DIDN'T SAY NO:
I kind of felt sorry for him. I didn't want him to stop being my doctor, and I thought he might if I said that doctors aren't supposed to date their patients.

Boundary violations don't always involve sex. They also include situations in which a physician behaves unprofessionally in the office or even off duty. Not so long ago, I witnessed inappropriate behavior by my mother's plastic surgeon. My mother had decided to give herself a facelift for her seventieth birthday. She selected a top-notch doc who, by all reports, constructed "beautiful" faces.

Cosmetic surgeons usually require their patients to pay cash up front, long before any incisions are made. My mom paid the hefty fees in advance, and when I took her for the procedure, we were shown into an examining room to wait for the doctor.

Moments later, he appeared—with his fly unzipped and his belt undone.

As if his attire weren't bad enough, the surgeon walked over to me and said, "You must be Nanette." (Physicians usually address each other as "Dr." on the first meeting, so the familiarity was also inappropriate.) Then he planted a big wet kiss on my cheek.

I've met hundreds of physicians in my medical career, but never have I been greeted in this way by a professional I didn't know. If my mother hadn't been so determined to see it through, I would have yanked her out of that office as fast as I could.

LATE NIGHT RAMBLINGS

Our pediatrician was so helpful to me when my son was first diagnosed with diabetes. He allowed me to call him at home at night if I had questions, and I was very grateful for his availability. About a year later, he started calling me at night after he had clearly been drinking. He'd ramble on about my son, and I didn't know how to get him off the phone.

Rebecca, stay-at-home mom

WHY SHE DIDN'T CHANGE DOCS:
He's the best in the area for diabetes. He didn't smell like alcohol when we saw him, so I just prayed he'd get help for his problem.

So what is the best way to ensure that your doctor will behave professionally?

Here is what I recommend.

Step 1. Ask for a nurse or aide to be present during a physical examination.

The presence of an attendant decreases the likelihood of any inappropriate conduct. Don't feel embarrassed if you have to ask. This is standard medical practice—something all physicians should do. The medical licensing boards in many states advise physicians to take these precautions with all patients.

Step 2. Ask your doctor to explain the exam before he or she starts.

Whenever a physician plans to examine an intimate area, the purpose of the exam must be explained before he or she touches you. If something seems inappropriate about the intended exam—say, your doctor proposes a breast exam when you've come for a flu shot—speak up: "I can't see how that is relevant to my immunization."

Don't allow a doctor to proceed with any exam that feels wrong: "I don't feel comfortable continuing with the exam at this time." Get dressed and leave the office.

Step 3. If your doctor behaves in a flirtatious or overtly sexual manner, leave immediately.

Write down everything that happened. Contact the medical licensing board in your state capital (many have online websites) to investigate your options about reporting this physician.

Most important—find another doctor.

The Hippocratic Oath obligates physicians above all else to do no harm. Sadly, it is up to women patients to set limits if we ever find ourselves in a situation in which a doctor is coming on to us or acting inappropriately.

Overall, proactive patients get the best medical care. The most effective way to prevent a medical mistake is to speak up when a procedure, a prescription, or a professional's conduct doesn't seem right to you. Saying NO to your practitioner when your instinct or observation tells you that something is wrong may literally save your life, or the life of someone you love. That's a NO you can't live without.

chapter eleven

NOble intentions

(saying NO as a caregiver)

My mother-in-law had a stroke and we invited her to come live with us after she was discharged from the hospital. We felt we could manage it, with all kinds of outside help and all the resources of the county. After a while it became clear that however much it suited my cultural conscience that you don't put family out of your house—you nurse them until the end—we couldn't do it. It was too hard.

We picked out the best place, but of course she didn't want to go. It was very painful trying to explain it to her.

"Mother," I said, "You need to go. We just can't manage otherwise. Everybody loves you, and I know that you love us and don't want to do us in. Keeping you here is doing us in. We're drowning—we can't keep doing this."

**Sylvia Boorstein, author and
meditation teacher**

An estimated 44 million Americans provide unpaid care for another adult, and most of those caregivers are women. Caring for the aging or infirm is something women have always done and will continue to do, despite the toll on our own physical and mental health. We grow up expecting to assume responsibility for elderly relatives, because that is a basic family value. We look after spouses who become ill or disabled, because that is the embodiment of a loving commitment. When friends and siblings develop health problems, we step in to lighten their load.

Still, there are only twenty-four hours in a day, and to be fully engaged as a caregiver, something's gotta give. We must say NO to other responsibilities, ask friends and family to take a turn, and find other ways to replenish ourselves. Caregiving can be one of the most rewarding jobs we ever undertake—provided we set some limits.

Many years ago, I learned about the conflict between being present as a caregiver and fulfilling my other obligations when my sister Yvonne was diagnosed with cancer. I had just accepted my first faculty position at Beth Israel Hospital in Boston as she began chemotherapy in San Francisco. Yvonne was well cared for: our parents had dropped everything to be with her. But I knew deep down that Yvonne would have loved to have me closer. Daily phone calls and monthly visits just weren't the same as living nearby.

Almost every day I asked myself why I didn't give up my job and move back to California. The obstacles seemed enormous. I'd never met a doc who'd taken leave for any reason—let alone to care for a family member—so I imagined such a choice would be frowned upon. Had I known that Yvonne would live only a few months, I would have made a different decision.

In retrospect, I wish I'd been brave enough to say "NO can do" to my boss and been at her side while she was ill. Eventually, I would have found another job, but I'll never have another sister.

creating time for caregiving

Helping a beloved spouse, friend, or relative cope with chronic illness or prepare to die can be a profoundly meaningful bonding experience that deepens one's feelings of connection. Every moment can be precious. The two of you grieve together and become even more intimate. You share joys, hardships, and vulnerabilities. Very often, you develop a unique appreciation for one another that might not otherwise have been possible.

Even so, you can't be an attentive caregiver if you're always on the run. If you're like most women, you'll probably overextend until you feel totally frazzled before you're willing to acknowledge that caring for an ailing adult on top of your routine responsibilities is more than you can handle. At the point of sheer exhaustion, you begin to say NO. You reprioritize the people and activities that give your life meaning and purpose, and say NO to anyone or anything that's not at the top of the list.

Journalist and **author Jane Futcher** took an indefinite leave of absence from work to care for dying parents who lived three thousand miles away. Jane had to weigh the cost of putting part of her life on hold against the feelings she had for her parents.

My mother died of cancer in 1985 and my father died in 2003 from pneumonia. In terms of caretaking, I'm essentially an only child because my sister, who has a long history of mental illness, has been estranged from the family for more than thirty years.

The strength of the bond between me and my parents made it an easy decision to give up other responsibilities to care for them. They were in terrible trouble and needed me. I couldn't have said NO and I wouldn't have said NO.

When my father was dying, I took an open-ended leave of absence from working at a newspaper. It was very stressful, because I felt responsible for covering my beat, guilty for not being a good employee, worried that I might be fired—even though I had my employers' blessings, and the Family Leave Act allows you to take time off to care for sick relatives. But all that guilt was nothing compared to how I would have felt if I couldn't be present with my parents when they needed me. I wouldn't have traded the experience of being with them when they died for anything. It was worth every ounce of worry about being disconnected from my partner, job, friends, and community to be there.

I was fortunate that my partner's daughter was able to housesit and take care of the dogs and the plants, because you have to have resources when you leave for an indefinite period of time to care for someone who lives far away. I have sympathy for women who, through no fault of their own, can't drop everything to take care of someone they love who is ill or dying. Not everyone has the resources to do that. Or they have other people they're caring for and just can't.

Growing up in the rural South where everyone pitched in to help with the farming, educating, and caregiving gave **Faye Gary Harris,** endowed **chair** and **professor of nursing** at **Case Western Reserve University,** an appreciation of community. As an adult, when her friends and relatives became ill, Faye took them in, forgoing several endowed professorships because she was needed at home.

I think African American people traditionally have cared for each other and my family is an example of that. I grew up in rural, central Florida in a relatively poor family, but in many ways we had a wonderful extended safety net and support system, with numerous aunts and uncles, many of whom did not have children of their own. My aunts and uncles shared with us whatever they had—oranges, eggs, fruit, vegetables, and time. They also shared the same values— children were respected, revered, were to be cared for, educated, supported. My mother had sent four of her brothers and sisters to school, and one of them helped to finance our education.

I never really saw caregiving as a burden. I admit that it's hard work and I lost a lot of nights of sleep. But in many ways I found it a real privilege. I'd say for me it was more of a privilege than it was ever a burden.

I had my aunt living with me and she died in 2002 at age

ninety-two or ninety-three. And I had an uncle whose care I was supervising in a nursing home, who died at about age ninety-six. During that time my niece who was a physician was diagnosed with cancer of the appendix and she became very ill very quickly. My brother and his wife filled in, caring for my aunt and uncle, so I could take a leave and care for my niece. I stayed in the hospital with her twenty-four hours a day for about six or seven weeks until she died.

Then a church member became ill. Her daughter, who was a good friend of mine, developed breast cancer and she couldn't care for her mother. So her mother came to stay with us, because as I saw it, we had everything all set up for my aunt. I had enough space to share. I had enough food to share, so this woman stayed about two months, until her daughter was well enough to care for her.

Caregiving is hard work, but growing up on a farm, you learn the value of that. You live by certain rhythms. The sun comes up at a certain time in the morning, the rooster crows, you get up. You have to feed the chickens, the cows have to have water, whether you are tired or not. In the summertime this is what you plant, this is what you harvest. It's all driven by the seasons, just as caregiving is driven by the need. And if you miss the season, you just completely miss out.

Estelle Freedman, Stanford University's Edgar E. Robinson chair and professor of U.S. history, had to cut back on her obligations when her mother developed Alzheimer's at the same time as her partner began to lose her eyesight. Estelle said NO to many invitations and commitments in order to be available for her family.

About nine years ago, I was administering an academic program, had a book deadline, and was elected to a major heavy-duty university committee—already on overload—when two things happened in my personal life: my mother was diagnosed with Alzheimer's, and my partner was diagnosed with an incurable eye disease and began to lose her vision. Fairly soon afterwards, the level of my responsibilities really got out of hand.

There were several years that were so stressful because of prior commitments that I had to say to myself, "You have to say NO to everything now, and you have to extricate yourself from commitments. Every time you're asked to do something, you need to weigh it heavily against the fact that you need both family time and recuperation time." So in the last five years or so, I've gotten extremely good and comfortable about saying I can't do things. What I found is that by creating that boundary about not taking on a lot of extra things, I learned how to exercise choices, only taking on things I really care about.

Though most women anticipate someday caring for sick or disabled friends or family, relatively few of us have the resources—time, energy, finances—to take on the responsibility without saying NO to other activities. We're lucky if the person needing care is someone we love, because that makes everything easier. Still, it's difficult to decide what to give up, and stressful to disappoint people who are unhappy when we aren't available.

Very often, competing commitments—raising children, your job, your own health problems, caring for multiple ailing friends or family simultaneously—make it impossible to devote yourself fully to the medical, practical, emotional, or financial needs of any one person. When this is the case, all you can do is your best. When you can say NO to unnecessary activities, you do. If you could do more, you would. At a minimum, even simple acts of kindness can alleviate an ailing person's pain.

As a caregiver, your goal is to provide as much comfort as possible to the person who is suffering. It helps to check in regularly—both with yourself and the person needing care—to avoid later regrets.

Helpful check-in questions to ask the patient:
- *Can I do anything to ease your discomfort or make things better for you?*

- *Is there something you don't understand that I could try to explain or find the answer to?*
- *Is there anything you want to talk about?*

And questions to ask yourself:
- *Am I providing the best possible care that my resources allow?*
- *Do I need to set limits with others so that I can be more available to the patient?*
- *Do I need to set limits with the patient to take care of myself?*
- *Am I asking for and getting the help I need (using all the resources available in my community and from family and friends)?*

Shouldering the responsibilities of bathing, dressing, changing, feeding, and medicating sick or disabled family or friends can be severely stressful. Many of us have never seen our parents naked, let alone washed and dressed them or wiped their behinds before. Such sudden intimacy can make the strongest of souls feel shy and embarrassed and sometimes downright uncomfortable. That's okay. This is an unscripted role for most of us; we have to rely on our intuition and the support and encouragement of close friends and family. Don't be self-critical if you decide there are some aspects of the care you cannot do yourself.

Be sure to reserve down time for yourself in your weekly schedule. Give yourself at least thirty minutes of quiet time each day—with no interactions and no interruptions. Limit well-intended calls from other family members to specific times; don't use all your breaks to give updates.

If you feel frustrated or overwhelmed, take a twenty-minute walk or a hot bath. Write in your journal. At least once a week reward yourself with something you enjoy doing, like going to yoga class, reading a book, watching your favorite TV show, or going shopping. To avoid burnout, eat decently, exercise regularly, and get enough sleep.

Discussing your experiences with professionals or other caregivers gives you an opportunity to let off steam and to bolster your day-to-day coping strategies. In addition to the many other responsibilities of caring for someone who is ill, there is the emotional work of grieving the loss of the person you knew before the illness. Counseling services and support groups offer a way to deal with feelings of sadness, frustration, and isolation. Caregiver support groups can also help you figure out solutions to medical, legal, financial, or insurance issues that you may be struggling with. They can hook you up with outside resources like transportation, home-delivered meals, and respite care. Saying "NO, I can't do ___ (fill in the blank)" is easier if you have figured out some other way to get it done.

Support groups are available in most communities and online. Two places to check are www.caregiver.org and www .eldercare.gov.

saying NO to the person you're caring for

In caring for the elderly, ill, or dying, most of us hope to avoid saying NO. We're likely to feel anxious or guilty if our needs conflict with theirs, and it's stressful to set limits that disappoint. Sometimes we can't visit as often as they want us to, or our style of caregiving conflicts with their expectations. Or we're asked to do something that isn't in their best interests. Or we are forced to say NO to preserve our own sanity when caring for those who are inconsiderate or inappropriate.

Saying NO to a request that may very well be someone's last can be extremely challenging. Do we say YES to avoid later guilt? Do we imagine—if we acquiesce—we will finally have the relationship we've always longed for? Do we believe that accommodating the ailing person's every wish will win us the love and respect we think we deserve?

In most cases, we are likely to feel better and make healthier choices if we tend to our own needs as effectively as we care for those of the ailing relative or friend. And maintaining firm boundaries is even more important if we're in the unfortunate position of caring for someone who is inconsiderate or hurtful.

Our job as caregivers is not to make our friends or family members happy, but to provide them with the best care our resources allow as long as our limits are respected. If, prior to becoming ill, the person you're caring for was constantly complaining about your availability and attentiveness, don't expect him or her to acknowledge or appreciate your caregiving—regardless of how much effort you put into it.

Joanell, a successful **business woman,** has said NO at least a thousand times to her drug-addicted brother. Yet every time he approaches death's door, it pushes her caregiving buttons. Whenever Joanell interacts with him, she tries to have clear but compassionate boundaries.

My brother and I were both adopted into a gutter-class family. We had an alcoholic mother who was very abusive. She wouldn't come home for days at a time. By the time I was twelve, when my brother started doing drugs—he's three years older than me—there was no parental guidance around. I took care of the house, I took care of him, I took care of my mother when she'd come home wasted.

My brother's friends raised a ruckus in our house—raping me, abusing me, smoking, drinking, eating all the food, what have you. They'd steal from us, whether it was my baptism cross or whatever. We were extremely poor, but they took whatever they could to sell for drugs. My brother just let them do whatever they wanted.

There were years and years of my brother's drug use and my co-dependency. Then, in January of 2005, I got a call from the Mayo Clinic saying that my brother wasn't going to make it through the night. I hadn't spoken to him in over six months. The last time I'd talked to him I refused to give him financial help, even though I felt really guilty because I have a hugely successful business. But I'd done a lot of therapy and I knew that was the right decision.

Somehow he miraculously pulled through after the Mayo Clinic did an experimental procedure on him and glued his liver back together. At that point the doctors said he could live anywhere from a day to a year, but one more drink would kill him.

Four days later I talked to my brother on the phone and I said, "You know, I'm really sick of this. Do you want to live or do you want to die?" The thought of him living his last year on the street—cold and hungry—was really hard for me. I mean, here he is this homeless drug addict and I'm incredibly successful with a multimillion-dollar business that I've built myself, without help from anyone.

Well, I decided to give him one more chance. I invited him to stay at my home to get better—after I thought I was really good at saying NO. After two and a half or three months of me supporting him—organic food, acupuncture, yoga, trying to give him the life-style that I would live if I was sick—he invited friends over, broke boundaries, disrespected rules, and started using heroin again. So I kicked him out.

That week was one of the most difficult weeks I've ever had. Him calling me crying in the middle of the night: "It's raining, I'm cold, I'm hungry, I have nowhere to sleep, and I got beat up. My shoes have holes in them. Can I sleep downstairs in your guest room?"

And I would say, "NO. NO you can't." I'd hang up and cry for hours.

In the morning, I'd have to wake up and go to work and be cool and get my game on. But what was really clear to me in the epiphany that I had at that time was that as much of a nurturer and a caretaker that I am, I cannot help everybody. It felt like a huge weight off my shoulders to say NO to him, as sad and difficult as it was.

• • •

Supermodel, TV host, and **author Emme** faced many unexpected challenges when her husband Phil was severely depressed. She found herself saying NO in a way that she never could have anticipated.

When Phil was depressed, there were two or three days in a two-and-a-half year period when he was very ill and I was about to lose my mind. I hadn't showered, I hadn't shaved, I hadn't done anything for myself. Phil had to be babysat: if he said he wanted to go for a walk, I would have to go with him. I had to be his mother and his wife.

So I gathered up his sleeping clothes, pants, and shoes, and I put Phil literally into the car—poor man, I swear it was horrible because he was feeling so shitty, it was so fucking bad—but I said, "That's it. You're getting in the car and going to your mother's house. I am about to lose my mind. I cannot be with you right now because I do not want to say anything wrong."

After I dropped him off at his parent's home, Phil ran away. He left me a message saying, "You don't have to worry about me anymore."

We drove around looking for him. When he returned to their home, I said, "Now you get in that house and you stay in there!" It was like the ultimate NO, saying "I cannot handle you anymore" to someone who is my husband, my very dear friend, and someone that I love. But when somebody is that ill and that dependent, you have to be aware of what you are able to do and not do.

I've told Phil, now that he's well, that we've got to find a facility if this happens again—and there is a 40 percent chance of recurrence—that he's going in until he gets well, and then he's going to come back out when everything's fine, because our family can't deal with this again.

• • •

When the responsibility of caring for her mother-in-law at home became overwhelming, **Sylvia Boorstein,** a **co-founder** of **Spirit Rock Meditation Center,** moved her into a nursing facility.

The place we chose was good, and we visited regularly. It turned out to be the right decision to move her. We made the compassionate choice.

A friend of mine once said when you do a thing like that it's a no-karma event—you don't create any karma. It has no karmic fallout because the mind is clear. And no intention other than compassion, really for everybody, including yourself.

Not infrequently, we choose to back off when saying NO would be painfully disappointing to an ailing loved one, even though the consequences may be intolerable for us.

Real estate developer Carol Kerley faced complicated decisions in caring for her brother Joey, who had cerebral palsy. When Carol and Joey disagreed about firing his drug-addicted attendant, she deferred to Joey's wishes.

When Joey became bed-bound, we hired attendants to care for him. One attendant turned out to be a drug addict. He wrecked Joey's life-equipped van, driving it without permission. He used Joey's pain pills and was sometimes so drugged out that he didn't get Joey out of bed. I desperately wanted to fire him, but Joey said the attendant was his only friend.

It was one of the most difficult situations I've ever faced. I had to figure out my priorities, and it basically boiled down to deciding that Joey's happiness was what really mattered. I ended up making huge sacrifices to preserve Joey's relationship with the attendant. I agreed to keep the attendant as long as he went into treatment. I sent him to rehab and footed the bill myself.

Carol couldn't have tolerated the guilt of firing or incarcerating Joey's only friend. She got the attendant cleaned up and kept him on the payroll.

Louise, an attorney, is reluctant to say NO to her life partner Meredith who is being treated for ovarian cancer.

Meredith's mother, grandmother, and aunt died of ovarian cancer. So when we heard about the possibility of having a genetic test for breast and ovarian cancer, Mer decided to do it. She tested positive. A month later, her younger sister had a breast lump removed, and it turned out to be malignant.

Mer is only thirty-six, and she's always wanted kids. But we just didn't feel safe going ahead with inseminations now that we had all this information. Mer decided to have her ovaries out and a double mastectomy. I supported her decision because I don't want her to get cancer like all the other women in her family. Well, when we got the path report back, it was the worst possible news—she had ovarian cancer.

It's been so awful. Mer's now in her fourth round of chemotherapy. All she talks about is adopting kids. When she has the energy, she trolls the adoption sites on the Internet. Mer wants us to complete the paperwork so we can move ahead with adopting a baby. For me, bringing a child into our lives is just about the last thing I'm interested in at this moment, but I would never say NO, because I don't want my lack of enthusiasm to be misinterpreted as not being hopeful that Mer will beat the cancer.

Louise would rather proceed with an adoption and deal with the prospect of ending up a single mother herself than throw Mer into even more anxiety about her health and future by asking to delay the decision.

Everyone feels anxious about setting limits with a person who is suffering. It helps to explore your reluctance, and here is what I suggest:

Step 1. Figure out what you're most afraid of losing.
Are you worried that the ailing relative or friend will stop loving you, or love you less, if you can't accommodate every request? Are you afraid of his or her anger? Do you believe that your needs should always be secondary to those of anyone you are caring for who is sick or disabled?

Reviewing your worries helps you decide whether you can handle the NO on your own, or if you need support. Check it out with someone you trust. Ask this person if she or he thinks if it's reasonable to try to manage your feelings about setting limits, and/or the patient's reaction to your NO, without professional assistance. If you decide to seek counseling, make sure you select an experienced professional who is familiar with the stresses of caregiving. You will want a therapist or counselor who can offer practical day-to-day suggestions.

Step 2. If you weren't worried about disappointing your ailing relative or friend, what decision would you make?
Rate how important this preference is to you on a scale of 10 = essential to 0 = worthless. If the score is 6 or higher, it's time to look for an appropriate moment to speak up.

Step 3. Be realistic.
You can't accommodate every wish or need when a loved one is healthy, so don't expect that of yourself when she or he is ill.

Step 4. Remind yourself that your goal in setting limits with your ailing friend or family member is to preserve your own physical and mental health so that you can provide the best possible care.
Disappointing an ailing loved one is always painful, but if your relationship is solid, explaining why you need to say NO helps the person understand your dilemma, even if she or he hoped you'd come to a different decision.

Psychologically healthy people are, by definition, flexible: they cope, they adapt, they move on. They realize that burning the candle at both ends is rarely in anyone's interest, and that disappointments are part of life—even at the end.

On the other hand, dysfunctional relatives who are sick or disabled may respond to your limits with the same guilt-inducing or hurtful behaviors they've used in the past when their wishes were thwarted. Being in pain and feeling powerless rarely make people more pleasant than they were before their illness. Relatives who are not well are unlikely to morph into the loving family members you've always hoped for even if you bend over backwards to avoid saying NO.

Having compassion for everyone—including yourself—is the ultimate goal of caregiving. Saying NO to an elderly, sick, or disabled person under your care can be enormously stressful, but you can't stay healthy without clear boundaries.

Whether you have a positive or a difficult relationship with the person you're caring for, you can't provide quality care if you're spread too thin. Sometimes you have to say NO to give yourself psychological space or to take a breather. On other occasions, you're bone-tired and simply need time to sleep. Or, you realize that being the primary caregiver takes more out of you than you can handle, and you need to pass the responsibility on to other providers or family members.

Caregivers often neglect their own health when they are ill. But you can't care for others if you don't take care of yourself. On some level you know that whatever you do to keep yourself sane and strong will help everyone around you. That can go a long way in fortifying you to say NO when you need to.

The idea of respite care is to give the caregiver a break for the sake of her own physical and mental health. Both governmental and nonprofit groups provide respite care. If you need short-term time off, you may be able to find a group near you that could help, at www.respitelocator.org/index.htm.

saying NO to unavailable bros

Although most of us couldn't tolerate the guilt of abandoning relatives in their hour of need, we—the caregivers—can always use more support. Adding elder care to our other responsibilities is a recipe for exhaustion and burnout if we don't get help.

How about our siblings—can they take a shift?

More often than not, sisters—even sisters-in-law—take turns caring for elderly parents. Sisters feel obligated to help out and irresponsible if we can't. Being on call during a family health crisis feels like the right thing to do; it gives us a positive sense of who we are.

But what about brothers? When I asked women caregivers about their brothers helping out, boy, did I get an earful!

Even though more American men than ever are pitching in to care for elderly relatives, by and large, women—the sisters, wives, and daughters—still do more than our share.

Ronnie, a special events coordinator says that saying NO to her brother is as much of a job as caring for their elderly mother.

Not so long ago my mother became confined to a wheelchair. She was having a hard time taking care of herself—she couldn't clean her house or prepare meals or handle her paperwork very well. She was eating cold cereal for most meals. At one time she had $250,000 in the bank, but she gave most of it to my thirty-seven-year-old brother, Jeff, who has depended on her for support for about the last ten years. He can't keep a job, and he has pretty much drained her resources.

I put her name on a list for assisted living, and when they had an opening for a low income person, I suggested that she move. I explained that they would do her laundry and cleaning and feed her three meals a day, which is what she needed. At first she said NO, because if she spent her money on assisted living she wouldn't be able to give any money to Jeff. But two case managers and her doctor convinced her she needed to move because she couldn't live independently any longer.

I used my own money to pay off all her credit card debt—that Jeff charged up—and said I'd handle her bills. Jeff then started coming to me to ask for rent money. I gave it to him twice and told him it was the last time. I also explained the situation to the attendant at the assisted living facility who said my mother had tried to borrow the rent money from her.

Jeff is a breath away from being homeless. He blames everybody else for his problems. He never takes responsibility. I'm in the position of having to say NO to giving him money, because that is the only way I can take care of my mother.

Psychotherapist and **social worker Diane Goldstein,** who often hears complaints about unavailable brothers from the women she treats in her clinical practice, describes the brother-sister dynamic in her own family.

After my mom died of Alzheimer's, my dad, who is a doctor in Chicago, lived alone in our family home until he was ninety-two. Basically, my two sisters and I kept tabs on him; my brother has always been totally checked out. When we have family conferences, my brother's wife does his part. She's Japanese and comes from a culture where people expect to take care of family.

When it was time to move Dad out of the house, we all went to Chicago to deal with the fifty years of stuff that had accumulated. After a day or so, my brother just opted out. He went into his bedroom—the one he grew up in—and didn't come out. My sisters and sister-in-law and I did all the work.

Dad's now ninety-seven, and we four women coordinate his care. When I ask why my brother won't be more helpful, he becomes obstreperous. He says he can't deal because he has too many negative memories from growing up. Well, we all do, but we work on them and take care of business anyway.

Yo, bro! How about a little less hindrance and a little more help? If your brother has taken a pass during a family health crisis, you may be inclined to let it go, because the last thing you need at a time like this is another project. But do you really want to shoulder a disproportionate share of the responsibility? Isn't it about time to even out the playing field and divvy up the chores?

Here's my advice. Don't give up on your brother. Don't let him opt out. Start with a gentle nudge, and be prepared to push. If you are persistent, your brother may learn to be more considerate.

This is what I recommend to bring a brother back into the fold:

Step 1. Set up a time for you to speak privately with your brother.

Invite him to a quiet meal when neither of you is pressed for time. Explain that you'd like to discuss the best way of caring for your ailing parent(s) or relative(s).

PRODIGAL SON

I adore my parents. I've had two really difficult years since my mom had a stroke. I live in North Carolina, and my parents live in Arizona, near my brothers. I've made it a priority to spend one week out of every six helping Dad take care of Mom. But my brothers—what can I say? They do nothing to help out and they're right there! Not only that, but they live on handouts from Mom and Dad. Of course when one of them does make an appearance, you'd think the Lord himself had just walked through the door—Mom and Dad are that grateful.

Catherine, minister

WHY SHE PUTS UP WITH IT:
I only have a certain amount of energy, and I don't want to spend it fighting with my brothers.

Catherine, in "Prodigal Son," ultimately had lunch with each brother separately during one of her trips to Arizona. She began by explaining that their father was overwhelmed with the responsibility of caring for their mother. She conveyed a sense of confidence that each brother cared about helping out.

Step 2. Focus only on current or upcoming issues, instead of who's done what in the past.

Avoid pointing out how generous you have been and how unavailable your brother is. Outline what is needed and make assignments. The more task—and time-specific the better.

Catherine made a list of their mother's needs, and she gave a copy to each brother. She discussed dividing up the responsibilities among the three of them. Once the brothers agreed to help out, Catherine became the care coordinator—contacting each brother with a weekly list of chores to choose from.

Step 3. Be prepared to serve as on-the-spot shrink. Expect resistance.

Explain that you'd like to figure out the best way to care for the family member. Listen to the reasons your brother says he can't help out. Express sympathy for genuine hardships. Don't get defensive if he says you're being co-dependent or overinvolved.

Step 4. If your brother agrees to specific responsibilities, talk at regular intervals about how it's going for both of you.

Don't become his parent. He may not do things as well as you do, but you have to let that go.

Perhaps your brother will agree to take turns being on call for the family member. Set up a schedule for checking on the person who is ill, and try to back off when it's your brother's responsibility to keep in touch. Every two months, meet over lunch to strategize about caring for the family member and taking care of yourselves.

Step 5. If your brother believes that caregiving is not his responsibility, try to figure out what he is willing to do.
Can he manage the finances for the ill family member, schedule appointments, pick up supplies, research medical treatment options, pay for in-home help or respite care, or make sure all the legal papers are in order?

MISSING LINK

OK, so there are only two of us—my brother Chris and I—and our mom is pretty sick. Periodically she needs to be hospitalized—she has congestive heart failure—when things get out of hand. I'm the family caregiver on call for two reasons: (1) I'm a doc; and (2) Chris either doesn't get it or can't be bothered. Though he and I are both busy professionals who work long hours, and we both have kids—whenever Mom gets sick, I'm the one who drops everything and drives two hours to help out.

When I go on vacation, I ask Chris to be available if Mom has an emergency. Actually, it pisses me off that I even have to ask, but that pretty much sums up his level of involvement. Last winter I took my kids to Brazil for two weeks. I checked my messages at home every day and one day there was a message from Chris—"Hi, it's me. Call me about Mom"—his voice sounding totally flat, not giving me a clue about anything.

Of course the guy never calls me ordinarily, so I figure something bad had happened. When I reached him, Chris said: "Mom's in the hospital. She has pneumonia. She's on antibiotics and she'll be out in a few days." I asked if he'd gone to the hospital, and he said it wasn't necessary.

I called the airline and we went home immediately, all the way from Brazil.

Ruth, pathologist

WHY SHE PUTS UP WITH IT:
What can I do? The guy needs a compassion transplant.

Let your brother know that you will continue to solicit his help as long as there is a need.

In "Missing Link," Ruth decided to ask her brother Chris to visit their mother in the hospital. Ruth was surprised that Chris blamed his unavailability on his spouse. "Jane feels that I don't spend enough time with our kids, so she'd really be irked if I were with Mom when I could be at home."

Quickly, Ruth changed gears, offering this advice: "Why not take the kids with you to see Mom? I know hospital visits aren't particularly fun for anyone, but illness is part of life. And some of the things Mom needs can be handled by phone from your

---

OPTING OUT

When my younger brother Maurice was dying of AIDS, he started having panic attacks. He was afraid to be alone. My mom and my sister and I took turns being with him at my parents' home, but my older brother Louis said he couldn't take time off work. That was of course ridiculous, because he worked for himself.

Francoise, translator

WHY SHE PUT UP WITH IT:
I think Louis just couldn't deal with his feelings about Maurice's death.

---

office, so you wouldn't be taking time away from home—only your work."

In "Opting Out," many years after their brother's death, Francoise spoke with her surviving brother Louis about his absence during Maurice's illness. Louis regrets his unavailability, and he feels bad about letting everyone down. He realizes that his sisters and mother made their peace with Maurice's death, but he can't let go of his guilt. "I almost wish you'd forced me to be involved," Louis said.

Of course these recommendations apply to any sibling—male or female—who is a no show during a family health crisis. But to brothers who, riding on the coat tails of twentieth century gender role expectations, consider caregiving "for the girls"—it's time to say, "NO DICE, dudes!"

planning ahead

Suppose, in the abstract, you and your spouse have different expectations about caregiving. Now would be a good time to explore these perspectives. It's never too early to begin discussing the ideal caregiving scenario.

If your spouse—who at this moment is young, vibrant, and healthy—were to become chronically or terminally ill, how would he or she envision your role as a caregiver? During minor illnesses, does he or she expect to be doted on, or prefer to be left alone? Is it okay to fluff up the pillows, provide meals in bed, buy a few magazines, rent a couple of DVDs, and head out to your other responsibilities? Or will your spouse feel slighted if you don't cancel other obligations, sit by his or her bedside, always within arm's reach?

How about your preferred style as a caregiver? Do you like to hover? Do you need to stay busy? Are you better at supervising than providing care? Do you keep an eye on your own physical and mental health as you're caring for others?

How easy is it for you to say NO to low-priority obligations or invitations? Are you in charge of your life or are your commitments in charge of you?

Just as saving for retirement, keeping your will up to date, and considering long-term health insurance options helps you plan for the future, engaging loved ones in a dialogue about caregiving expectations offers the opportunity to work out some of the wrinkles in advance—and, perhaps, to avoid later disappointments. Conversations about prospective caregiving deepen connections and bring people closer.

my mother's NOse

While I was writing this chapter, my mother developed a serious health problem. She had a severe sinus infection that abscessed behind her eye, compromising her vision. The proposed surgery was potentially life-threatening, but avoiding surgery was equally risky. I consulted many physicians and coordinated her care.

During the first week of her illness, I tried to continue my normal work. I was soon running myself ragged—skipping meals and scrimping on sleep to squeeze in the added responsibilities. Eventually, I had to cut my patient schedule by half, because caring for Mom consumed more time than I had allocated. My patients were disappointed that I was less available, and I felt guilty about letting them down. It was painful to listen to their frustration about my limited schedule. Though I understand why patients feel anxious when a family health problem forces me to cancel, I had to remind myself—sometimes hourly—that Mom was my first priority. In this situation, I simply couldn't accommodate everyone who needed me.

At the start of the second week, I made a personal commitment to jog thirty minutes each morning, eat at least two decent meals per day, and sleep at least seven hours each night. Exercising was a terrific stress reliever during the ordeal.

In the days between her appointments for second and third opinions, Mom left a message each morning at my office, describing her condition. I knew that this was her way of handling her anxiety, but unfortunately, the update contained—there is no delicate way to describe this—a report on the color, size, shape, and consistency of the discharge from her nose.

Even though I've dealt with all sorts of bodily fluids in my medical career, I've never had an iron stomach. Envisioning this goop coming out of Mom's nose made me queasy. I worried that if I asked her not to describe it, she'd think I was unconcerned about the infection or unsympathetic to her fears. I didn't want to upset her—especially when she might be at death's door. Finally, I came up with a strategy: I told her I appreciated the reports, but instead of the vivid details, I'd like her to rate her overall condition on a 10-point rating scale, between 1 = feeling the best she's ever felt, and 10 = the worst she's ever felt. I explained how this numerical score made it easier for me to figure out when she needed emergency treatment, since severe infections always made her feel gravely ill.

Mom continued to call every day and thankfully deleted the description of her nasal discharge. I learned to be less timid about setting limits with my schedule, my patients, and Mom. I took care of myself by carving out time for exercise, food, and sleep. And whenever I felt distressed about having to say NO, I reviewed my priorities and reminded myself that I was doing the best I could. I was determined to avoid feeling guilty about my caregiving, and I successfully accomplished that by being very clear about what I could and could not do.

chapter twelve

---

heavens NO!

(saying NO to the dead and dying)

I had this client at the hair salon who took an incredible liking to me. She was an older woman, slowly losing her sight, and she would talk to me in a way that just made me melt and feel like doing anything for her—and I did.

She had lung cancer, and she asked if I'd do her hair after she passed. I said, "Sure I will, sweetheart," hoping her family wouldn't remember this promise when the time came. Next thing I know her daughter's calling to say her mom died and she wanted me to do her hair. I was like, "What? Her hair—oh, absolutely!" How could I say NO?

So I get to the mortuary, and they take me to this dimly-lit room, remarkably similar to a romantic setting, but ice cold. They pull the body out. I was tweaked when I touched her hair. It felt like broom hair. She looked like Riddler in Batman. But I did her hair, and by the time I was done, I was running out of that mortuary, girl. I couldn't eat for like a week.

**Regina Louise, hair stylist
and author**

Before a family member died, did you make a promise that you're having a hard time keeping? Have you already agreed to help your parents or spouse or friends move on if their suffering becomes intolerable? If you don't live up to a deathbed commitment, can you reconcile that with your conscience?

There are many things our family and friends would like us to promise, and it's especially difficult to say NO when people are dying. At times like these, we may say YES to whatever is asked without considering the possible consequences. Later, despite our best intentions, we feel guilty when we fall short.

In this final chapter, I examine the challenges of saying NO to end-of-life requests from the people we love, and even some we don't.

deathbed promises

My grandfather died of lung cancer. He smoked for fifty years. He and I were really close, and he was the inspiration for my whole career. One of the last things he said to me was, "Greta, promise me you'll stop smoking." I looked him in the eye and said I would. That promise lasted about two weeks.

Greta, CEO

Let's say before she died, you promised your mother that you would invite your brother to share the Christmas holidays each year. But you never told her that your brother was abusing methamphetamine. During your brother's first holiday visit, your money and jewelry disappear. He behaves inappropriately in front of your children. If you stop inviting him, will your mother—wherever she is—understand?

What about a vow to remain faithful to a partner? Suppose you promised your dying spouse that you would never love anyone but him or her. Then several years later, you find yourself in a new relationship. To be faithful to your pledge of loyalty, must you hold yourself back from fully experiencing this romance?

Does the new love tarnish or diminish what you felt for your deceased spouse?

Your father requests a nonreligious funeral and your sister won't attend unless a clergyperson is presiding. Do you insist on respecting your father's wishes or do you ignore his preferences to placate your sister? Or, do you try to keep everyone happy by having two services—one secular and the other religious?

Suppose your grandfather founded a successful business that your father passed on to you and your brother on the condition that the two of you keep it intact. You'd like your son to take it over, but your brother objects. The two of you are unable to come to an agreement about administering the company, so you decide to divide it and sell your part. Will your father forgive you for preserving your relationship with your brother at the expense of the family business?

Most of us are raised to believe that keeping a promise is good and breaking a promise is bad. Keeping deathbed promises seems even more compelling since they are the last wishes expressed by our loved ones. But there are many reasons why we might not be able to fulfill a commitment. Perhaps it just isn't possible on a practical level. Or, the consequences would be harmful to us or someone else. In some cases, we may feel morally obligated to do something different. And we may even believe that our dearly departed would have made a different choice if he or she understood the current circumstances.

Since we can't explain our inability to keep the commitment to the person to whom we made it, he or she can't relieve us of our guilt for failing to do what was asked. If our departed loved one was caring, considerate, and psychologically healthy when he or she was alive, most likely this person would want what is best for us now. But often it's the people who were difficult to please in life that we're most anxious about disappointing after they are gone.

• • •

Reverend Nell Rose Smith, a minister at the **Chapel of Awareness Spiritual Church** in San Diego, believes in reincarnation. Her calling is to help people communicate with relatives, lovers, and friends who have passed over. Nell Rose says she has never encountered a spirit who expressed recrimination or judgment toward someone who was still living. She finds only compassion and understanding on the other side. Nell Rose offers these words of comfort to those who feel distressed about breaking a deathbed promise:

The guilt or feeling of responsibility toward those who are on the other side resides entirely within the living. In our understanding of it, no matter what a person's spiritual, religious, or cultural beliefs are, everyone everywhere is learning some aspect of how to give and receive love. And since there simply is no one right way to do that, getting all caught up in belief systems is not of value.

Many people come to me and say, "I made this promise to my mother ten years ago and I didn't keep it. I've just been wracked with guilt about this ever since because it was so important to her. I feel like I've betrayed my mother. Can you talk to my mother and tell me what she says about this?"

I talk to dead people all the time. I have probably talked to, or touched into, between eight and ten thousand dead people in the last twenty-two years. They are always honest with some compassion. They move me to tears more times than I can count with the love and the respect that they have for the person that they're dealing with.

stairway to serenity

If you find chatting with the dead a bit of a stretch, there are other ways to avoid feeling guilty for failing to keep an end-of-life promise. The best is to build flexibility into the original agreement. Don't agree to anything on the spot if there is time to talk it over and think about it. After you have carefully considered your willingness to do whatever you are asked, only say YES if you feel fairly certain you can follow through. Be sure to make room within your promise for unanticipated circumstances that might prevent you from carrying out the person's wishes.

Before you commit, consider the following steps:

Step 1. Ask yourself, is the request reasonable?

Parents sometimes feel that they stand a better chance of resting in peace if they can reunite their adult children who have parted ways. If your dying parent asks you to reach out to a troublesome sibling—and you would say NO in any other circumstance—you may be conflicted about saying YES. Most likely you have good reasons for maintaining your distance, and it's important to remind yourself of them.

For instance, if you agree to invite your drug-addicted brother to your home to appease your dying mother, you'd probably feel alarmed the moment you say, "Of course I will, Mom." You didn't invite him while she was healthy, and you wouldn't include him if it weren't your mother's final wish. You might have given yourself more latitude if you'd said, "We haven't been that close lately, Mom, but I'll do my best to make it happen since it's important to you." Because you promised you'd do it, you extend the invitation. Then if it doesn't work out, at least you tried.

Promises that have the least likelihood of being kept are those with no time limits. As much as you might hope to keep a lifelong commitment, unpredictable circumstances may make it impossible to honor your word. If you are asked to help or take care of someone or pay for something, you're more likely to be successful in your follow through when you stipulate a time frame.

An example of this more flexible and realistic promise is:

I will do my best until they're back on their feet/ until they're on their own/ in the coming year/ as long as I can.

Step 2. Ask yourself, is the request appropriate?

Are you the right person for the task or assignment? If you agree to the request, are you setting yourself up for conflict with other family members?

Let's say your terminally ill stepfather asks you to be the executor of his estate. He elected to bypass his three biological children because they fought for years over an inheritance from their grandmother. You are reluctant to put yourself in the middle of a feud with your stepsiblings. Instead of accepting the responsibility to be the executor, perhaps you can suggest that your stepfather call a family meeting to figure out which child might best be suited to settle his estate. If the children can't come to an agreement, an independent executor could be hired to administer his estate and the cost could be deducted from each child's inheritance.

Step 3. Ask yourself, is the request doable?

Do you have sufficient funds to accommodate the request? Has caring for other people limited your availability to take on more obligations? Are you up to the task health-wise?

For example, your dying father would like you to use your inheritance to take time off to travel. You've been experiencing health problems that don't have an immediate solution. You'd rather use the money to see a specialist and, hopefully, get the treatment you need. You don't want to worry your dad when he's got his own issues to deal with, so you ask if he's willing to be flexible: "Thanks, Dad. I would love to use my inheritance to travel. But if I need it for something more important, may I have your blessing to make that choice?"

None of us has a crystal ball. We can't possibly foresee all the obstacles that might prevent us from fulfilling a promise. Nor can we anticipate the ways that a shift in circumstances might influence our choices. If you haven't followed through on a promise in the way you intended—and, in your opinion, you don't have a good reason not to—redoubling your efforts may reduce your guilt. But if circumstances outside your control have altered your ability to keep the agreement, acknowledge that you are choosing to break your promise. Remind yourself that you did the best you could with the resources you have.

Alternatively, you may decide to adhere to the spirit of the commitment while saying NO to the specifics.

Let's say that your dying friend, who has no written will, makes you promise to use her money to build a basketball court in a particular neighborhood. But there is no suitable site on which a court could be built. You decide to contribute the money to a nearby YMCA to upgrade its sports facilities, on the stipulation that the Y offers a certain number of free memberships to neighborhood children. This seems to honor your friend's intentions as much as possible.

final exits

> *My father wanted me to help him commit suicide after my mother died. I said NO. He pleaded with me and I said NOPE. I was his primary caregiver. He'd had a series of strokes, and I knew he wouldn't live very much longer. But I told him it was against everything I believe in and I would never do that. That's one time when I was very clear about a NO.*
>
> **Bettina Aptheker, professor of**
> **women's studies, U.C. Santa Cruz**

Requests to end a life can be serious or casual. Perhaps your boyfriend, who is currently in great health, has just returned from a visit to the nursing home where his grandmother lives. Over dinner, he says, "Look. I don't want to end up like grandma. If I get Alzheimer's, as soon as I can't remember who you are, put a pillow over my face."

Or perhaps you have a close friend who has cancer that has spread to her lungs. The only way she can control her pain is to take medication that is severely sedating. On several occasions, your friend has inquired if you'd be willing to help her overdose if she decides she's ready to move on.

Sometimes it is easier to decide whether you can accommodate this type of request from someone else if you consider your own end-of-life wishes. Let's say that you don't believe in suicide unless a person has an end-stage terminal illness. If you were that person, would you want the option of ending your own suffering? If the answer is YES, could you see yourself implementing the final request of someone you love who is too ill to execute his or her own exit plan? Or do you feel that this would constitute the taking of a life—an act that you oppose for religious or moral reasons?

Suppose you said you would turn off the life support, or turn up the morphine drip, when a family member became comatose or suffered from end-stage disease. When the time came, you couldn't bring yourself to do it. Maybe you weren't ready to say goodbye. Or you just couldn't bring yourself to end a life. Or you were afraid of being arrested. Do you carry the guilt of failing to keep this commitment for the rest of your life?

If you believe that you could not carry out the wishes of a loved one who wants you to facilitate his or her departure, convey this clearly so that there is no misunderstanding. A considerate response might be, "I'm sorry, but I don't think I would be able to do what you're asking. But I will do everything I can to help you manage your pain and make you as comfortable as possible."

Since it's impossible to anticipate all the factors that will influence your feelings when the time comes, try to find out exactly what your loved one has in mind. Then add a caveat to any agreement: "I'll do my best to respect your wishes. However, I need to know that you'll forgive me if I can't do what you are asking. Maybe the situation will be more complicated than we imagine. Or I might be unable to let you go when you're ready to leave." By stating this matter-of-factly, you reduce your chances of feeling guilty if you can't follow through on your promise.

If you've pledged to assist someone who appears to have many years left before dying, make sure you reevaluate your willingness to follow through on the agreement at regular intervals. I suggest a review at least every five years to take into account anything you can't anticipate at the moment.

FINAL EPISODE

A friend of mine's mom is dying next Thursday. She's going to overdose before things get worse. Her biggest fear is that she'll fall and break her neck and end up a quadriplegic. She has multiple myeloma, and her spine is crumbling. It's excruciatingly painful, and she's decided to leave while she's still able to do it.

Why next Thursday? She's hooked on *Desperate Housewives.* We think she might be waiting until the season ends.

The mom is going to take between thirty and sixty Seconal tablets and wash them down with a bottle of vintage brandy. She's a former alcoholic, so she knows her liquor. Her family won't be there when she does it.

Madeline, rancher

WHY HER FAMILY DOESN'T SAY NO:
The mom is completely rational. It's her life and her choice. Her family understands that she doesn't want to go on when the suffering is unbearable.

---

holding on and letting go

Throughout our lives, we strive to stay connected to the people who matter to us and to say NO to those who treat us poorly.

After family members or loved ones pass away, we continue the same dynamic—only now, for most of us, the conversations with these individuals take place only in our heads. We feel comforted as we replay the tapes of the people we cared about—welcoming these poignant recollections as a way of mitigating our grief. Likewise, as best we can, we say NO to reliving the painful interactions we had with individuals who abused or injured us when they were alive.

To sustain loving connections, some women try to preserve the scent of the dearly departed by holding on to their clothing. Others keep the deceased's belongings just as they were before the passing. Many of us find it comforting to reread correspondence from lost loved ones, or to page through photo albums and reminisce. And we feel a bone-chilling pain when these images begin to fade.

To counteract this loss, some of us hold on to more than just the memories or personal effects of loved ones who have passed: we also keep their remains nearby. With cemeteries seeming so cold and far away, we'd rather create a special place for them at home.

When my beloved dog Sophie died, I couldn't bear to consign her ashes to a pet cemetery. I bought a tiny cedar box to hold her remains. The box sits on my bookshelf, with her collar and photo on top. Another woman I know whose son died of cancer keeps her child's ashes in a teddy bear. She cuddles the bear whenever she wants to be close to him. And a colleague of mine has placed some of her husband's ashes in a pendant she wears around her neck. "This way," she says, "he's always next to my heart."

Dr. Marny Hall, a couples therapist and author, tries to conjure up her beloved brother Richard during an annual Thanksgiving ritual.

I was very close to my brother Richard, who died of AIDS. When he was first diagnosed—he was about sixty at the time—Richard tried to stay healthy by working out. One day he came home from the gym and told me about a gorgeous young guy he'd seen with the most beautiful legs.

A few months later, my partner Susan and I invited both our brothers to dinner. When Susan's brother Glen walked in, Richard was shocked—Glen was the guy Richard had admired at the gym. But Glen wasn't interested in Richard, much to Richard's dismay.

I was very attached to Richard and I didn't want to part with his ashes when he died. Susan felt the same way about Glen, who also died of AIDS. So we put them together in a bookcase, hoping that Glen might be more tolerant of Richard's affection in the after-life, and figuring that Richard would be thrilled to be next to Glen's long shank bones in perpetuity.

Every Thanksgiving, we put Richard and Glen in our back-packs and take them out to dinner. We reserve a table for four, set Richard and Glen in their respective chairs, and explain to bemused waiters that we need extra drinks for our brothers— wine for Richard and whiskey for Glen. Then we clink glasses, reminisce, and try to imagine what their lives would be like if they were still with us.

Some women converse with their lost loved ones on a regular basis as a way of keeping the connection alive. **Journalist** and **author Jane Futcher's** father died several years ago. Each night, in her prayers, she thanks him for taking good care of her when she was growing up, and for watching over her still.

When my father died, I inherited his Ford Taurus. Not so long ago, we were driving it on the freeway and an enormous bear appeared right in front of us. There was no way to avoid hitting it. Sadly, the bear was killed and the Taurus was totaled. It's amazing that we're still alive. I felt like my father protected me with his car.

I also inherited the shotgun that he'd been given in college. Because I live in the country, I learned how to shoot. I've shot at least four rattlesnakes that tangled with my dogs. I don't like killing anything, but I love my dogs and I don't want them to be hurt. The shotgun is another way that my father is protecting me.

If we're lucky, after a family member dies, we're left with mostly good memories and the painful ones dissolve. **Psychotherapist,** producer, and **author JoAnn Loulan** describes how this transpired when her mother passed.

I really loved my mom. She died when I was twenty-six of breast cancer that had metastasized to her bones. She was a wonderful mom: she was hilarious and understanding and a great storyteller and a social activist. She worked for Planned Parenthood, and she helped other women with breast cancer learn to cope with their illness.

But there were also things about her that drove me absolutely nuts—like, she was a rabid Republican to her dying breath. She always said she'd vote for Nixon if he ever ran again.

After she died, the negative feelings I had about her just melted away within a matter of months. To me she became Saint Billie— Billie was her name. Thirty years later, I still think about her all the time, and really, I only think about the good stuff. I feel sad that she never got to meet my son or see my niece grow up. My mom would have loved all the wonderful things they have done. I also think about how helpful she would have been to me at difficult times in my life. I really wish she were still here.

Parents who were hostile or critical in life often hang around after death as brain chatter, telling us what we're doing wrong. Their directives can serve as useful reminders of the people we don't want to become, but we sometimes need them to pipe down. JoAnn Loulan still finds it necessary to keep her deceased father's negativity in check, many years after his death.

My father was mean and hypercritical and volatile, not to mention a full-blown alcoholic. He died unexpectedly of a heart attack when I was thirty-two. Even now I hear his voice in my head, being critical of something I'm doing, and I have to keep saying NO to it.

If memories of the deceased are mixed—or worse—our well-being may depend on coming to peace with the hurts and disappointments that haunt us long after people who were unkind or abusive have died. In these cases, letting go can take time, as we review the events that happened, gain insight into why these individuals behaved as they did, and gradually release the suffering caused by their mistreatment. When this work is done, saying NO to the memories allows us to move on with our lives.

a final note

For women, the never-ending effort to strike a balance between caring for others and tending to ourselves lies at the heart of almost every NO. We must continually sort out our priorities so that we can say NO without jeopardizing our relationships with the people who are important to us.

I would like to thank the talented and thoughtful women who shared their struggles and triumphs in saying NO for this book. The scenarios they recounted capture the complexity of our efforts to enforce boundaries with compassion in a world that values simple assertiveness. These women care about being nice even as they say NO. Many take the time to explain the reasons for their NOs and to offer helpful suggestions or alternatives when they decide to refuse a request. And all enjoy being generous when they have something meaningful to give.

I hope that this book has given you a new perspective on the ways that women's empathy, thoughtfulness, generosity and compassion contribute to our reluctance to say NO, and how the fear of loss can compromise our ability to set self-protective limits. I hope you will use the steps I have provided to help diminish your fears.

Now that you have strategies to establish sensible priorities without feeling selfish, and a process for setting limits while staying connected, when you say, "My answer is NO," you can feel good about it. Remember, every time you say NO, you're saying YES to something that is more important to you. And it's always easier to say NO if you believe in your own worth. Understanding that you deserve to be treated respectfully gives you an advantage in setting limits, in establishing healthy relationships, and in creating a life you choose.

I hope that this book has provided the tools you need to carve your own unique NOs—with just the right mixture of decisiveness and flexibility to suit your responsibilities—and to appreciate the opportunities that saying NO can bring.

acknowledgments

This book is a collaborative effort that would not have been possible without the participation of many people who helped bring it to fruition.

I would like to extend special thanks to Joan E. Biren and Jane Futcher for brilliant editing and conceptual suggestions. This book benefited enormously from the creative input and feedback of Diane Goldstein, Marny Hall, Karen Johnson, Susan M.A. Kennedy, Janice Larkin, JoAnn Loulan, Esther Rothblum, Penny Sablove, Robin Sumrall, Lauren R. Taylor, and Jan Tepper, and from my terrific conversations with Nancy Snyderman. I would also like to extend my appreciation to Peter Bartlett, Helen Carroll, Brooke Chiller, Ronny Crawford, Sally Goldin, Silvana Lopez, Regina Louise, Nigel O'Rourke, Andrew Paulson, Teri Ralston, Sylvia Rhue, and Jennifer Jewell Thomas.

I am especially grateful to my agent, James Levine, who has been an ardent champion of this book from the beginning; to both James Levine and Lindsay Edgecombe for invaluable feedback and incisive commentary. I am thrilled and honored to be working with Leslie Meredith, senior editor and vice president at Simon & Schuster's Free Press. I would also like to thank Dominick Anfuso, vice president and editorial director at the Free Press, for understanding how important this topic is to women; and Carisa Hays, vice president and director of publicity, and Jill Siegel, assistant director of publicity, for their enthusiastic support.

Last but not least, I'd like to thank my family members

for their loving encouragement: Dee Mosbacher for analyzing every concept and overseeing every word; my father-in-law, Robert Mosbacher, my aunt-in-law, Barbara Mosbacher, and my cousin-in-law, Clint Smullyan, for connecting me with prospective interviewees; and my mother, Nan Gartrell, for having the foresight to name me "Nanette" so that I could one day write a book about the struggle to say NO under the nom de plume "no-NO Nanette."

Index

Abandonment, fear of, 18, 20, 47
Abuse, saying NO when you have
    been a victim of 10,14,18,47–49
Affirmative NOs, 117–121
Allison, Dorothy, 53, 80, 164–165,
    188
Aloneness, fear of, in saying NO,
    29, 32
Anger, "clean" vs. "mean," 179
Antidepressant and antianxiety
    medication, 40, 41
Aptheker, Professor Bettina, 7,
    22–23, 244
Assault. See Sexual harassment and
    assault
Assertiveness, 2, 5, 43. See also Say-
    ing NO
Assertiveness training, 182

Barry, Nancy, 160–161
Bart, Professor Pauline, 192–193
Beggelman, Dr. Marlene, 198–199,
    203
"Beyond 12" Family Services, 153
Biren, Joan E., 168
Boorstein, Sylvia, 57, 167, 214, 225
Borderline personality disorder
    (BPD), saying NO to people
    with, 15, 18, 20

Breaking up, saying NO when,
    29–30, 36, 50–52
Breast cancer, saying NO when ill,
    156–158, 200, 203
Brodsky, Susie, 175, 187–188, 194
Brush-off NOs, 3
Bush, former First Lady Barbara,
    127, 155

Caller ID as a way of setting limits,
    70
Cambridge Health Alliance Victims
    of Violence Program, 192
Cammermeyer, Colonel Margarethe,
    131, 141–143, 147
Caregiver, saying NO as, 214–237
    check-in questions, 219–220
    creating personal time, 215–221
    Family Leave Act, 216
    help from siblings, 229–235
    time management, 215–221
Caregiver support, 221
Center for the Advancement of
    Women, 109–110
Co-dependency, 4, 42, 222
Co-workers, saying NO at work,
    81–84
Community, saying NO in the,
    149–174

Community *(cont.)*
  choosing your causes, 153–159,
    170–171
  preventing burnout, 162–167
  women's ways of financing,
    160–162
  women's ways of fundraising,
    159–160
Compassion, 1, 3, 5, 149, 228, 251.
  See also Saying NO
Compassionate NOs, 3, 100–101,
  167–170
Conlin, Kelli, 106
Connection, need for, 1, 3, 8, 30, 37,
  39, 52, 215
Considerate NOs, 111–112
Counseling, learning how to say NO
  in, 18, 20, 33, 36, 44, 48–50, 227
Cross-cultural communication,
  112–114
Culturally appropriate NOs, 112–114

Dating situations, saying NO in, 31–37
Davis, Gray Governor, 138, 139
Dead and dying, saying NO to the,
  238–250
  deathbed promises, 239–244
  end-of-life wishes, 244–246
  memories of deceased, 247–250
Demeaning comments, setting limits
  on, 178–180, 183–184
Depression and anxiety, 20, 40–41,
  224
Divorce, preserving your self-esteem
  during, 41, 45, 46
Doctors, setting limits with, 196–205
  boundary violations, 197, 209–212
  ensuring quality healthcare, 200, 203
  hand hygiene, insisting on, 196, 197
  Internet research, 198–200, 203, 204
  second opinions, 203, 204
  tape-recording visits, 201
  therapists, 205–209
Domestic violence, saying NO to,
  178–185

Doublecheckmd.com, 199
Dukes, Betty, 114–115
Dunea, Melanie, 57–58
Dysfunctional and difficult parents,
  saying NO to, 7, 9–14

Eldercare.gov, 221
Emme, 57, 224
Empathy, 1, 3, 149, 251. See also Say-
  ing NO
Employees, saying NO at work, 81–84
Employers, saying NO at work,
  88–92, 96–97
Empowerment groups, 94, 95, 168–
  170, 173–174
Enhanced Medical Decisions, Inc.,
  198
Eye Movement Desensitization and
  Reprocessing (EMDR), 48–50

Fade-out NOs, 122, 124–125
Family Leave Act, 216
Fearless NOs, 101–102
Fears
  of abandonment, 18, 20, 47
  of aloneness, 29, 32
  dealing with, 24, 26
  of rejection, 30, 36
  for safety, 82
  of singlehood, 29, 33
Feinstein, Senator Diane, 137–138
Financial ramifications of saying
  NO, 41–43
Financing, women's ways of, 160–
  162
Fisher, Mary, 128, 129–130, 147,
  156–157
Freedman, Professor Estelle, 118–120,
  218–219
Freelance Radicals, 168–170
Friends, saying NO to, 53–79
  best pals, 56–67
  needy friends, 55, 73–74, 78–79
  passive aggressive friends, 55,
    77–78

self-centered friends, 54, 68–69
stale rituals, 54, 67–68
Fundraising, women's ways of,
159–160
Futcher, Jane, 216–217, 248–249

Gandia, Margarita, 65
Gender discrimination, 114–115
Generosity, 2, 3, 149, 251. See also
Saying NO
Goldin, Frances, 120–121
Goldstein, Diane, 230
Gomez, Jewelle, 58, 163
Government service. See Public service, saying NO in
Grupp, Beth, 110–111, 159–160
Guilt, 7, 21, 216, 221, 223, 229, 241,
245
Guilt-free NOs, 4

Hall, Dr. Marny, 51, 247–248
Hanks, Tammy, 153
Harris, Professor Faye Gary, 217
Health advocacy and informed dissent, 204
Health problems, saying NO when
you have, 156–157
Herman, Dr. Judith L., 192
Holidays, saying NO during the, 7, 8,
16, 19, 27–28, 67–68
Holmgren, President Jan, 111–112
Honesty, 37–39
Hughes, Reverend Jennifer, 23, 159

"I" statements, 94, 184
Illness, saying NO during, 156–157,
196–213
IMPACT—women's self-defense, 186
Impersonal NOs, 107–109
Inequity and injustice, saying NO to,
114–115
Institute of Medicine of the National
Academy of Sciences, 197

Jaeger, Marilyn, 48, 60, 149

Job interviews, setting limits during,
96–97

Kennedy, Susan P., 128–129, 137–139
Kerley, Carol, 23, 225–226
Knockout NOs, 5

Lagomasino, Maria Elena, 107–108
Law enforcement, women in, 100–
101, 134–137, 145–146
Limit setting, 13, 16–17, 19, 25, 34–
35, 37–38, 79. See also Saying NO
Loaning money, 73–74
Loeb, Lisa, 116–117
Loss, dealing with, 3, 24, 26, 38,
44–45
Loulan, JoAnn, 249–250
Love, Dr. Susan, 157–158, 202–203
Loving partnerships, saying NO in,
37–41

Martial arts training, 175, 177,
187–188
MayoClinic.com, 200
McKechnie, Donna, 116, 164
Medical Internet sites, 198–200, 203,
204
Mentoring, 137, 139–140
Mills College, 111
Model Mugging, 186, 192
Money, loaning to friends, 73–74
Morfitt, Marti, 105–106, 112–113

NARAL Pro-choice, 106–107
Narcissistic parents, saying NO to,
15–18
Nasty NOs, 122, 124–125
National Academy of Sciences, Institute of Medicine of, 197
National Coalition Against Domestic
Violence, 185
National Domestic Violence Hotline,
183
Newman, Reverend Dr. Susan, 98,
165–166

Nice NOs, 122, 123–124
Noonan, Peggy, 103–105
Nursing home, deciding when it's
    time for placement in, 225

O'Brien, Judy, 117–118
O'Connor, Supreme Court Justice
    Sandra Day, 130–131
Officer training school, 130
O'Toole, Commissioner Kathleen,
    100–101, 134–135
Ovarian cancer, See Health prob-
    lems, saying NO when you have
Oversharing, 99

Parents, saying NO to, 7–28
    borderline parents, 15, 18, 20
    dysfunctional and difficult parents,
        7, 9–15
    healthy parents, 20–28
    narcissistic parents, 15–18
Partners. See Relationships, saying
    NO in
Passive Aggressive, saying NO to
    people who are, 55, 77–78
Pastoral care, saying NO in,
    165–166
Personality disorders, saying NO to
    people with, 15–20
    borderline (BPD), 15, 18, 20
    narcissistic, 15–18
Physical abuse, 30, 31
    saying NO after, 47–50
Pitzer College, 108–109, 155
Politics, saying NO in, 137–139
Pope, Chef Monica, 152
Promises, deathbed, 239–244
Psychotherapy, 18, 20, 36, 44, 48–50,
    227
Public service, saying NO in, 127–148
    moral dilemmas, 141–146
    public scrutiny and, 136–137
    pushing the limits, 128–131
    refusing to pull rank, 131–133
    saying NO in politics, 137–139

Rand, Yvonne, 167
Rape, saying NO to prevent, 175,
    176, 191, 193, 222
Ready-made responses, developing,
    4, 13–14
Rejection, fear of, 30, 36
Relationships, saying NO in, 29–52
    after abuse, 47–50
    breaking up, 29–30, 36, 50–52
    dating situations, 31–37
    loving partnerships, 37–41
    sexual harassment and assault,
        178–185
Respite care, 228
Role models for setting limits, 102
Role-playing, 2
Rose, Colonel Patricia, 21, 130,
    132–133
Rothblum, Professor Esther, 126,
    151–152, 177, 186

Sablove, Penny, 187
Safety, fears for, 82
Saying NO
    as caregiver. See Caregiver, saying
        NO as
    in community. See Community,
        saying NO in the
    to dead and dying. See Dead and
        dying, saying NO to
    to doctors. See Doctors, saying
        NO to
    to friends. See Friends, saying NO
        to
    introduction to, 1–6
    to parents. See Parents, saying NO
        to
    in public service. See Public ser-
        vice, saying NO in
    in relationships. See Relationships,
        saying NO in
    to sexual harassment and assault.
        See Sexual harassment and as-
        sault

at work. See Work, saying NO at
Second opinions in healthcare, 203, 204
Self-defense training, 94, 175–177, 180–182, 186–188, 191–194, 222
Self-esteem, 31, 33–34, 43, 52
Self-preservation, 31
Self-preserving NOs, 109–110
Self-talk, loss-preparation, 44–45
Sensitivity, 1, 2, 85
Separation anxiety, 36
Sexual abuse, saying NO after, 48–49
Sexual harassment and assault, 83, 94
  at home, 178–185
  in military, 143
  saying NO to, 175–195
  self-defense training, 94, 176, 177, 180–182, 186–188, 191–194
  standard precautions, 177
  verbal self-defense guidelines, 189
Shapiro, Dr. Francine, 49
Showbiz NOs, 115–117
Siblings,saying NO to, 16–17, 229–235
Singlehood, fear of, 29, 33
Smith, Reverend Nell Rose, 241
Snyderman, Dr. Nancy, 2, 122
Spirit Rock Meditation Center, 57, 167, 225
Stanford University, 118, 119, 218
Steel, Danielle, 29, 37, 47, 53, 59, 88
Stephenson, Vivian, 22, 154
Stritch, Elaine, 158
Supermom NOs, 103–107
Supreme Court of the United States, 130–131

Taylor, Lauren R., 178, 180, 186–189, 193
Tepper, Chief Jan, 96, 133–134, 136–137, 145–146, 191
Teresa, Mother, 174
Therapists, saying NO to, 205–209
Thoughtfulness, 1, 85, 251
Thoughtless NOs, 3

Traverse, Carol, 98, 101–102
Trombley, President Laura, 108–109, 155–156

Unsafe sex, saying NO to, 34

Valuing NOs, 110–111
Verbal abuse, putting a stop to, 178–179
Victims of Violence Program, Cambridge Health Alliance, 192

Wattleton, Faye, 109, 113–114
Webmd.com, 200
Weinberg, Rabbi Sheila, 167–168
Wishy-washy NOs, 122, 124–125
Women's support groups, 93–94
Women's World Banking (WWB), 160–162
Woodford, Director Jeanne, 99, 155
Work, saying NO at, 80–126
  affirmative NOs, 117–121
  as co-worker, 85–87
  compassionate NOs, 100–101
  considerate NOs, 111–112
  culturally appropriate NOs, 112–114
  as employee, 81–84
  as employer, 88–92, 969–97
  fearless NOs, 101–102
  impersonal NOs, 107–109
  job interviews, 96–97
  nice and nasty NOs, 122–126
  NO to inequity or injustice, 114–115
  self-preserving NOs, 109–110
  showbiz NOs, 115–117
  supermom NOs, 103–107
  valuing NOs, 110–111
Wright, Colonel Ann, 143–144

"You" statements, 94

Zimbalist, Stephanie, 75, 115–116

about the author

Nanette Gartrell, M.D., an associate clinical professor of psychiatry at the Center of Excellence in Women's Health for the University of California, San Francisco, was previously a faculty member at Harvard Medical School. She is a clinician and researcher whose groundbreaking investigations have been published in professional journals and cited in the media. Dr. Gartrell has appeared on network televsion, including *Good Morning America*, *NBC Weekend*, and *Fox News*; on NPR's "On Point;" and in documentaries produced for PBS, Showtime, and French and German public television. Her articles appeared in *The New York Times Magazine*, the *San Francisco Chronicle Magazine* and *The Christian Science Monitor*. Dr. Gartrell has a private practice, and she volunteers her psychiatric services to chronically mentally ill homeless people. She lives in San Francisco with her spouse and a Maltese dog.

9 781416 546955